Cranfield on Corporate Sustainability

CRANFIELD
ON CORPORATE SUSTAINABILITY

Greenleaf
PUBLISHING

© 2012 Greenleaf Publishing Limited

Published by Greenleaf Publishing Limited
Aizlewood's Mill
Nursery Street
Sheffield S3 8GG
UK
www.greenleaf-publishing.com

Cover by LaliAbril.com

Printed in the UK on environmentally friendly, acid-free paper
from managed forests by CPI Group (UK) Ltd, Croydon

British Library Cataloguing in Publication Data:
  A catalogue record for this book is available from the British Library.

  ISBN-13: 978-1-906093-75-4 [paperback]

~

Cranfield on Corporate Sustainability is dedicated to the memory of Nigel Doughty (1957–2012) whose sudden death in February 2012 robbed the world of a powerful champion for responsible business and sustainable development.

Nigel was one of Cranfield University's most distinguished and successful alumni. He was a dedicated supporter of the Cranfield School of Management and the wider University. He funded the establishment of the Doughty Centre for Corporate Responsibility, served on the School's International Advisory Board and had just become President of the independent Cranfield Trust, through which many alumni of Cranfield and other leading business schools volunteer their management expertise to charities.

Shortly before his death, Nigel had written the foreword to this book. He was enthusiastic about the book as a practical way to engage many more of the School's faculty beyond the Doughty Centre itself in integrating sustainability thinking into their research and teaching.

~

Contents

Figures, tables, boxes and case studies

Figures

Tables

Boxes

Case studies

Foreword

Nigel Doughty (1957–2012)

As a businessman and a financier of businesses, I am interested in long-term value-enhancement. As a father and as an active citizen, I want to see sustainable development: that is, development that meets the needs of the present generation, without compromising the ability of future generations to meet their needs. Achieving all this is *the* management challenge of the 21st century. We have to find different ways to build bigger, better and more sustainable businesses.

Companies must develop the tools to respond to these challenges if they want to retain their licence to operate and build the foundations for sustainable growth.

I believe that the corporate sustainability arena is where we will see some of the key innovations that can help bring about this change.

Businesses have become increasingly accountable to a broader base of stakeholders that has elevated the importance of a range of environmental, social and governance issues (ESG). All of these areas now have a material impact on the financial and reputational risks to which companies and their investors are exposed. At Doughty Hanson, the private equity firm I co-founded 26 years ago, we have been an early advocate of ESG engagement. I see the tangible results that we are generating from active management of these issues across our portfolio and I am also conscious of the increasing importance that investors attach to a responsible approach to company management.

I want the Management School that gave me my formal business education to be at the forefront of the debates about how corporate sustainability can improve the way we manage our businesses. That is why I am an active member of the international advisory council of the Cranfield School of Management, and why in 2006 I endowed the Doughty Centre for Corporate Responsibility at Cranfield.

Cranfield on Corporate Sustainability is the latest project from the Centre, and is part of the efforts of the School of Management as a whole to embed responsible management within the heart of the School's research, teaching and practice—and in its own operations as a responsible organisation. The book is part of Cranfield's commitment to the UN Principles of Responsible Management Education and its involvement in organisations such as the European Academy of Business in Society and in initiatives such as the Pears Foundation Business School Partnership.

Cranfield School of Management is the first to recognise that it has only started on the journey towards embedding sustainability and responsibility, but is committed to continuous improvement. The School and I hope that this collection of essays will encourage further debate both within Cranfield and our alumni community, and with a much wider audience in business, business schools and civil society about just how to improve the practice of responsible management and of corporate sustainability.

This foreword was authored by Nigel Doughty a few weeks before his untimely death in February 2012.

Acronyms and abbreviations

B2B	business to business
B2C	business-to-consumer
B4B	business to 4 billion
BOP	base of the pyramid
BRIC	Brazil, Russia, India and China
CE	concurrent engineering
CEO	chief executive officer
CR	corporate responsibility
CS	corporate sustainability
CSR	corporate social responsibility
Defra	(UK) Department for Environment, Food and Rural Affairs
EABIS	The Academy of Business in Society
ECR	Efficient Consumer Response
EFMD	European Foundation for Management Development
EIU	Economist Intelligence Unit
ESG	environmental, social and governance
ETI	Ethical Trading Initiative
FMCG	fast-moving consumer goods
GDA	Guide Daily Allowance
GRI	Global Reporting Initiative
ICT	information communications technology
ICTI	International Council of Toy Industries
IIRC	International Integrated Reporting Committee
IPEA	Institute of Public and Environmental Affairs, China
IR	integrated reporting

JMSC   joint management–stakeholder committee
KPIs   key performance indicators
MSC   Marine Stewardship Council
NED   non-executive director
NPD   new product development
PBDE   polybrominated diphenyl ethers
PLC   product life-cycle
PRI   Principles of Responsible Investment (UN)
PRME   Principles of Responsible Management Education (UN)
PSS   product–service systems
RCA   responsible competitive advantage
RoHS   Restriction of Hazardous Substances
SAB   stakeholder advisory board
SCOR   Supply Chain Operations Reference
SEC   (USA) Securities and Exchange Commission
SER   social and environmental reporting
SNPD   sustainable new product development
UAE   unanticipated effects
UNGC   UN Global Compact
USLP   Unilever Sustainable Living Plan
VPI   Value Producing Item

Introduction
The business of business
is sustainable business

Frank Horwitz
Director, Cranfield School of Management

Business schools have a special contribution, indeed responsibility, to develop responsible and independent-thinking future leaders and managers. The Cranfield School of Management's binding ideology is one of transforming the practice of management and living its core value of developing leaders who put knowledge into practice. These principles form the basis of this book and its theme of developing responsible and ethical leaders for the next-generation enterprises. The next-generation organisation needs leaders who are passionate, purposeful and responsible—leaders whose primary aim is to make a difference in the lives of people and create sustainable value premised on sound ethical values.[1]

The recent credit and sub-prime crisis and various corporate scandals have reinforced a vigorous and ongoing debate about the role of business schools, and specifically about what they 'teach' or don't teach about ethics, good corporate governance and sustainable development. The contemporary debate about excessive performance bonus payments highlights vexatious issues about whether business school education reinforces or even encourages organisational behaviour inimical to how future managers should best lead people to achieve imperatives of both sustainable high performance and ethical behaviour.

As many an experienced senior executive will attest, the 'soft issues' are often the most difficult and complex—the hardest for executives. Unlike the 'hard' quantitative subjects such as finance and accounting, there are no formulaic answers; there are often potential conflicts of interest and stakeholders with common but also differing interests; there are ethical dilemmas; and there are questions as to what constitutes good corporate governance. Indeed even these so-called 'hard' subjects if thoughtfully and contextually taught will infuse a questioning of ethical dilemmas in these disciplines as encouraged by the UN Principles of Responsible Management Education (PRME).

What does all this mean for today's business school student? Our students will graduate into a work milieu that is increasingly complex, diverse, technologically inter-connected and socially networked and where economic power shifts see emerging market economies assuming significant prominence in the global political economy. This offers exciting challenges but also the need for new mind-sets for the next generation of business leaders. Corporate responsibility and the tough ethical and governance choices managers have to grapple with, where there are no simple, easy answers, reflect the need for business education to embrace the stakeholder model. Our next generation of business and organisational leaders needs to be confident and aware of, and able to negotiate their way around, multiple perspectives and conflicting and common interests of stakeholders such as employees and managers, shareholders, trade unions, customers, suppliers and civil society organisations that have an interest in the behaviour and decisions of an organisation. Business schools need to create understanding and sensitivity to this new and changing world of work. Today, the challenge for business schools and business itself is to implement effectively a new maxim: 'the business of business is *sustainable* business'.

There continues to be confusion among business, media, civil society and academics about what is meant by terms such as 'corporate (social) responsibility' (C[S]R). While the term corporate social responsibility is widely used, it is often understood by journalists and others to refer only to a business's involvement in the community such as employee volunteering and corporate philanthropy, whereas we understand that what is important is not what companies do with a small percentage of their profits, but how they make all their profits; how business does its business; how it behaves to employees, customers and suppliers; the impacts it has on the environment and society, as well as on the communities in which it operates.[2]

We are focusing, therefore, on corporate sustainability as:

> a business approach that creates long-term value to society at large, as well as to shareholders, by embracing the opportunities and managing the risks associated with economic, environmental and social developments; and builds this into corporate purpose and strategy with transparency and accountability to stakeholders.[3]

The term 'ESG' (environmental, social and governance) issues has been popularised by Goldman Sachs—especially for the investment community.[4] A commitment to embed corporate sustainability can be understood as a commitment to improve ESG performance. Typical ESG issues would include topics such as energy efficiency, use of renewable energy, waste reduction, recycling, tackling climate change, promoting equality and diversity, creating a great place to work, and health and well-being.

Some see this as a moral issue or even one of planetary survival.[5] Many more business people simply regard this as good business—hence references in CEO speeches and CR reports to 'just good business' or 'how we do business around here'. For example, Raymond Ackerman, founder and Chairman of Pick n Pay, one of the largest and most successful retailers in Africa, argues that 'doing good is good for business'.[6] Such companies are moving from a focus on risk minimisation to opportunity optimisation. Professor Michael Porter of Harvard Business School and Mark Kramer, co-founder with Porter of the FSG social impact consulting firm, talk of 'shared value', arguing that shared value is not 'about "sharing" the value already created by firms—a redistribution approach. Instead, it is about expanding the total pool of economic and social value.'[7]

The overall challenge for leadership development is to develop the core know-how, acumen and 'active citizenship' needed for responsible strategic and operationally sound decisions in next-generation organisations. In doing this we have to ask:

What will the effective business school graduate of the next generation look like, and what does 'graduateness' for the next-generation organisation mean? Our work suggests the following:

- Developing business know-how or acumen—a fundamental and integrated knowledge of the core business processes, including strategic, people management, financial and technological resource capabilities

- Learning about ethical, principled leadership and responsible managerial practice; knowing how to move from knowledge to action and how to make key strategic and operational choices

- Understanding both the internal and external context of business including stakeholder, not only shareholder value; how to manage with diversity, multicultural and transnational teamwork; conflict management; and systems thinking in grasping the complexity of leadership in a dramatically changing global geopolitical landscape

- Ability to move beyond change management to leading transformational change, understanding good corporate governance and ethical practice

- Learning how to build new organisational cultures and effective managerial teams, and learning to simultaneously collaborate and compete, and developing the judgement to know which to do when

- Developing problem-solving capability and the ability to align people, processes and performance capabilities

These are some of the leadership development challenges. They are key issues that management education and development must engage and grapple with. The next-generation enterprise needs leaders who are passionate, purposeful and responsible—not just visionaries but missionaries. It is the missionaries who make things happen. Can we develop leaders who will make a difference in addressing the imperatives of the next generation? We believe we must. Our ambition is that this book, and parallel faculty research that we are supporting, will further stimulate a process of shared learning with Cranfield's stakeholders.

So what is the purpose of this book? *Cranfield on Corporate Sustainability* is designed to:

- Stimulate debate among people in organisations and future leaders about what sustainable development means for business and, therefore, what Cranfield, as a leading global business school, should research, teach and advise on. We are using the content of this book in our MBA, MSc and executive programmes

- Develop an extended conversation with stakeholders, about corporate sustainability and responsibility, in order to identify what is needed for transforming and embedding policy and managerial practice within businesses; and in so doing transforming mind-sets, behaviours and skills

- Signal the multiplicity of valid yet differing viewpoints on the topic, reinforcing the philosophy that views can and should be challenged in, one hopes, a dialectic way

- Increase our sustainability brainprint—see Box I.1.

Box I.1 **Cranfield School of Management brainprint**

The positive impact the School of Management has through doing research which makes a difference, teaching and management practice to help others to improve sustainability.

Over the next decade, we will teach more than 70,000 students (projected figures of MBA, MSc, doctoral students and participants on open and executive programmes). We will reach more corporate clients in Research Clubs, Knowledge Transfer Partnerships and consulting. Additionally, we will reach many more people as a result of faculty contributing as visiting faculty elsewhere and our impact on visiting faculty coming to Cranfield; and through our engagement in professional bodies and management-discipline-related academic networks; and in business school and management education organisations such as the European Foundation for Management Development, the Association of Business Schools, the Academy of Management and through initiatives we subscribe to such as the UN Principles of Responsible Management Education (PRME) and The Academy of Business in Society (EABIS).

This book involves a collaboration of more than 30 Cranfield faculty and associates. I would like to thank all the authors, editors and reviewers, particularly members of Cranfield's Doughty Centre for Corporate Responsibility, Professor David Grayson, Nadine Exter, David Ferguson and Melody McLaren, who coordinated the development of the book.

The book is dedicated to the memory of Nigel Doughty, one of the Cranfield School of Management's most distinguished alumni. Nigel was a committed and thoughtful supporter of the School and particularly of our efforts to embed corporate sustainability and responsibility. This particular project was made possible by matched funding for part of Nigel Doughty's charitable donation to Cranfield from the UK's Higher Education Funding Council.

1
Overview of embedding corporate sustainability

David Grayson
Professor of Corporate Responsibility

An influential survey of Chief Executive Officers conducted by Accenture for the UN Global Compact (UNGC) in 2010 found that 96% of CEOs from around the world believe that sustainability should be fully embedded into the strategy and operations of a company.[8]

The survey was specifically among CEOs of companies that have signed up to the Global Compact. In a sense, therefore, one might ask, what were the other 4% doing as CEOs of Compact companies! While clearly not representative of business as a whole, the Accenture survey (to be repeated in 2013) is indicative of greater recognition among business leaders (and not just those who are regular attendees at the annual Davos World Economic Forum) that managing a company's environmental, social and economic impacts is now business critical.

The reasons for this are now well rehearsed:[9] a global population already over 7 billion with expectations of 9–9.5 billion by mid-century; an increasing middle class, with predictions of 100–150 million[10] more people joining the world's middle class *every* year between now and 2030, with increasing demands for *stuff*. This will require 50% more energy, 50% more food and 30% more water supply by 2030—all to be generated while the world tackles the challenge of climate change.[11]

Hardly surprising, therefore, that other recent surveys reinforce the conclusions of the Accenture study. Just over 60% of companies surveyed by KPMG in 2011, for example, said that they currently have a working strategy for corporate sustainability—up from just over half polled in a similar survey in 2008; and nearly 50% of all executives surveyed believed that implementing sustainability programmes will contribute to the bottom line, either by cost reduction or increased profitability.[12]

Even the Accenture study, however, found a performance gap between what CEOs themselves said was necessary to embed sustainability and what they thought their own companies were yet doing.[13] Allowing for some CEO rose-tinted spectacles, there remains a major challenge to convert intent into reality.

At the Doughty Centre, we have been refining a model for **embedding sustainability**, which emerged from the Academy of Business in Society (EABIS) Colloquium hosted at Cranfield in 2008. It was first proposed by then Cranfield doctoral student, David Ferguson, based on his PhD thesis looking at embedding in EDF Energy. Our model encompasses all the elements cited in the Accenture/UNGC survey: board oversight; embedded in strategy and operations of subsidiaries; embedded in global supply chains; participation in collaborations and multi-stakeholder partnerships; and engagement with stakeholders such as investors.[14] However, we also explicitly incorporate the importance of leadership ('top-down') and employee engagement ('bottom-up'). We also include more operational enablers such as knowledge management and training for sustainability; engaging more stakeholders than just investors (important though it is to explain better to investors how sustainable development changes the strategy of business); and the role of the specialist corporate responsibility (CR)/ sustainability function (see Fig. 1.1).

Figure 1.1 **Embedding sustainability**

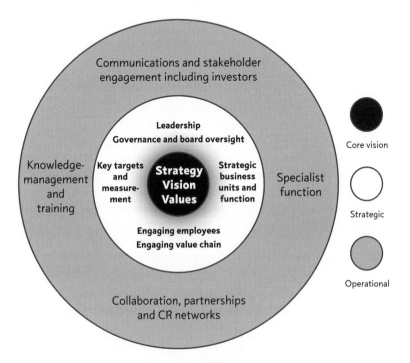

Internally, we call this the 'bull's-eye' model after the popular game of darts where, ultimately, the winner has to score a bull's-eye—the centre circle of the dartboard. The core of embedding is that sustainability is integrated into business purpose and strategy. Research from the consultants Deloitte in 2011 found that over a fifth of *Fortune* Global 500 companies already have a clear, society-focused purpose underpinning their activities.[15] Procter & Gamble, for example, amended their global mission and strategy in 2007 to say that their purpose is: 'We provide branded products and services of superior quality and value that improve the lives of the world's consumers, now and for generations to come.' P&G's values now include: 'We incorporate sustainability into our products, packaging and operations.'

Top leadership has to believe in and 'walk the talk' on sustainability. Staff and other stakeholders need to hear their leaders explain regularly what it means for the business, why it is important, and how it is integrated. More importantly, they have to lead by example. As Sir Andrew Witty, CEO of GlaxoSmithKline said when lecturing at Cranfield in January 2012:

> How do you, as an individual leader in your space, make a difference? What's important? How are you going to set those expectations for the people who are around you? How are you going to set the language of your organisation? How do you set your incentive schemes? How are you thoughtful about sending substantive signals through your organisation that you are serious about running an organisation which is aligned with, not disconnected from, society?[16]

Embedding sustainability requires effective board oversight—the 'governance of responsibility'. Some companies have a dedicated board committee or have extended the remit of an existing committee. Some have a lead non-executive director (NED) in charge. Some have a mixed committee of executives and non-executives.

It is also important that the approach to corporate sustainability matches the organisation's strategic approach to doing business—to be real and relevant, sustainability should mirror the culture of the organisation as the strategy defines it in its objectives, approach, targets and measurements. Typically, companies have some over-arching sustainability commitment, such as Plan A at Marks & Spencer (see Chapter 11, Case study 11.2) and Zero waste to landfill at Xerox and Herman Miller. Companies need a process for getting each part of the business, each business function, to understand its significant social, environmental and economic impacts, and to embed sustainability within its operating plans.

Following the middle circle of the diagram around to the bottom, in addition to 'top-down' leadership and governance, companies with embedded sustainability seek to engage employees 'bottom-up', and engage their value chains from initial sourcing and suppliers through to customers and consumers.

The outer circle identifies operational enablers such as knowledge management[17] and training (both formal education and experiential learning); stakeholder engagement, measurement and reporting, and communications; making use of the coalitions and collaborations that the business is involved in; and having a specialist function that increasingly is not seen as direct deliverer but as fulfilling 'seven Cs': Coordinator, Communicator, Coach, Consultant, Codifier, Connector and Conscience.

On the following pages, this embedding model is illustrated with the example of the fast-moving consumer goods (FMCG) company Unilever.

Case study 1.1 **Embedding sustainability in Unilever**

Unilever is one of the companies at the forefront of embedding sustainability in the heart of business. This is not a new development. Indeed the founders of Unilever in the 19th century instinctively recognised that economic value can only be created if the needs of different stakeholders (consumers, customers, civil society, etc.) can be better met. William Lever's insight was that the business would prosper if consumers actually benefited in their lives, and that the business would prosper if the workforce also prospered—there was a mutuality of interest.[18] The company's earliest vision was to 'Make cleanliness commonplace, to lessen work for women, to foster health and contribute to personal attractiveness, that life may be more rewarding to people who use our products.'[19]

More recently, in the 1990s, Unilever was one of the first major companies to mature from corporate community involvement to a broader understanding of corporate social responsibility (CSR). Unilever's CSR came from making explicit what was already being done as normal business practice in the management of the business. In the early days they concentrated on de-mystifying the jargon and encouraging the businesses around the world to have the confidence to explain what they were actually doing and how. This is important because it gave managers the confidence to get involved *and* created the solid foundation from which to set out on the sustainability journey.

One of the executives credited with developing the intellectual basis for Unilever's subsequent sustainability commitments was Dr Iain Anderson, who worked for the company from 1965 to 1998, ending as a member of the executive committee after stints as chairman and chief executive of Unilever companies in agri-business, speciality chemicals and food. Guided by Anderson and others, the company developed strategies on fish, water and agriculture during the mid-1990s. This— combined with significant external pressures—led Unilever to co-found the Marine Stewardship Council (MSC) in 1995 with the non-governmental organisation (NGO) WWF. Another long-serving senior Unilever executive André van Heemstra explained:

> The Marine Stewardship Council goes back to the days that I was CEO of our frozen foods and ice cream company in Germany, Langnese-Iglo. It was 1995, the year of Brent Spar. At the same time Greenpeace had chosen fish depletion as a spear-point project. They did their homework, and rather than bothering with the complexity of fishermen and politicians they decided to tackle the issue downstream, at the processor level. Then following the leverage principle, they found out that Unilever was the leading fish processor in Europe, and that Germany was the largest fish processing country within the Unilever family. The next thing I knew was facing a sophisticated Greenpeace campaign. With the help of a superb English external adviser by the name of Simon Bryceson we took the initiative and started a public dialogue in Germany on fish depletion. This brought momentum, and at a certain point Simon came to see me together with Mike Sutton of the WWF. Mike came with the vision of the analogy from the Forestry Stewardship Council for fish, and it took him only 30 minutes to get me on board. I took the plane to Rotterdam the next day to convince Antony Burgmans, my then time frozen foods boss. And that is how the MSC was born.[20]

→

Around the same time Unilever established its Sustainable Agriculture Programme. In 2006, the then CEO Niall Fitzgerald and the then Corporate Responsibility director Mandy Cormack outlined what they had learnt in their respective roles about embedding responsibility in *The Role of Business in Society: An Agenda for Action*.[21] More recently, in 2008, the company committed to buying 100% sustainable palm oil by 2015. These and related developments are seen as essential foundations without which Unilever's subsequent commitments would not have been feasible. In retrospect, they were, however, important but essentially still separate from much of the mainstream business and the development of future strategy.

Embedded within overall business purpose and strategy

In November 2010, Unilever launched its Sustainable Living Plan (USLP).[22] This ten-year sustainability programme is central to the delivery of Unilever's overall corporate strategy. The corporate strategy is set out in a document called 'The Compass' which commits the company to 'double in size while reducing its environmental footprint.' This makes Unilever one of the first FMCG companies to set itself the objective of decoupling growth from environmental impact. Indeed, Paul Polman, Unilever's CEO since 1 January 2009, has said: 'Sustainability is our business model.'[23] The USLP makes a series of specific commitments to reducing the company's environmental footprint while increasing the social benefit arising from its activities.[24]

According to *Marketing Week* in 2011, 'Like M&S, Unilever has set out to entirely reform the impact of its business on the planet and its people. While there is an aspect of social conscience behind the decision, there are also significant economic benefits.'[25]

A powerful example is delivered by Unilever's hand-washing campaign across Asia and Africa. Studies have demonstrated that washing hands with soap is one of the most effective and inexpensive ways to prevent diarrhoeal diseases. This simple habit could help cut deaths from diarrhoea by almost half and deaths from acute respiratory infections by a quarter. In India, Unilever's Lifebuoy soap hygiene education, Swasthya Chetna (Health Awakening), has touched the lives of more than 120 million people in rural areas. It has also delivered commercial

→

benefits for the brand, driving up the sales of soap in districts where the campaign ran.

Leadership

Paul Polman has taken the lead on Unilever's sustainability commitment. Those familiar with the company suggest that as a Dutch national, Polman is instinctively comfortable with sustainability. His task has been made easier because of the hard work done by his predecessor, Patrick Cescau, to simplify the corporate structure and create 'one Unilever'. 'One Unilever' was a fundamental simplification project. In fact its formal title was 'Simplification'. Certainly, Polman himself declared on becoming CEO that Cescau had put the wiring in place and that his job was to drive more electricity down the wires!

According to *Forbes* magazine:

> In driving the plan, Polman has led from the front. He responds to emails from his senior executives, often even on Sundays. He follows an open door policy, encouraging employees to reach out to him and he communicates directly with all its global employees through email and videoconferences.[26]

Unilever insiders credit Polman with creating 'space' and giving 'permission' for more radical and ambitious targets on sustainability. Indeed, *Marketing Week* argues that, 'Sustainability, it's now clear, is the yardstick by which Paul Polman's tenure as chief executive of Unilever will be measured.'[27] He has, however, made sure that the USLP is owned by senior management generally and by the Board, with key executives carrying the accountability for different goals within the plan. Polman reviews progress on the plan with his executive team every quarter.

Governance and Board oversight

Unilever has a Board committee made up of non-executive directors—the Corporate Responsibility and Reputation Committee—which is charged with ensuring that business is conducted responsibly and that Unilever's reputation is protected and enhanced. It ensures that the Code of Business Principles and Unilever's Supplier Code remain fit

→

for purpose and are properly applied. The Committee meets quarterly. It comprises three independent non-executive directors: the British parliamentarian and former cabinet minister Sir Malcolm Rifkind MP chairs, and the other members are Hixonia Nyasulu and Louise Fresco. A member of the Executive attends the meetings of the committee. This committee played an influential role in the development of the Sustainable Living Plan including refining some of the specific targets and commitments.

In addition, one of the roles of the Board's Audit Committee is to review Unilever's overall approach to risk management and control, and its processes, outcomes and disclosure. The Committee considers the application of the Code of Business Principles as part of its remit to review risk management.

There is also an executive Corporate Code Committee, chaired by Unilever's chief legal officer and group secretary, which oversees the implementation of the Code of Business Principles and Unilever's Supplier Code.

This formal board and executive governance oversight of sustainability is supported by a number of experts' groups and stakeholder advisory panels, including an external group of 'independently minded experts who guide and critique the development of our strategy'. They are: Ma Jun, water specialist and Founder Director of the Institute of Public and Environmental Affairs (IPEA), China; Malini Mehra, Founder and CEO of the Centre for Social Markets, India; Jonathon Porritt, Founder Director of Forum for the Future, UK; and Helio Mattar, President of the Akatu Institute for Conscious Consumption, Brazil. Polman tries to have dinner with this group whenever they meet.

Key targets, measures, accountabilities and reporting framework

At the heart of Unilever's sustainability strategy is a BHAG—Big Hairy Audacious Goal—to decouple growth from environmental impacts. It is an implicit challenge to the arguments of the environmentalist Tim Jackson.[28]

A number of more detailed targets support the BHAG. The first is to help more than one billion people improve their health and well-being by improving their hygiene habits and bringing safe drinking water to 500 million people; and doubling the proportion of the food brands' portfolio that meets the highest nutritional standards.

The second is to halve the environmental impact of Unilever products: halving the greenhouse gas impact of Unilever products across the entire value chain, halving the water associated with the consumer use of its products, and halving the waste associated with the disposal of those products.

And the third is to source 100% of agricultural raw materials sustainably, linking more than 500,000 smallholder farmers and small-scale distributors into the Unilever supply chain.[29] Underpinning these three broad goals are around 60 time-bound sustainability targets across the value chain, from the sourcing of raw materials through to consumers' use of Unilever products.

In order to get to these targets, Unilever spent three years establishing robust base-line performance figures for greenhouse gases, water and waste. This involved analysing 1,600 representative products in 14 key markets, which represented 70% of Unilever revenues, using life-cycle analysis. It was a formidable exercise. 'The people involved are still recovering in sanatoria,' jokes Gavin Neath, then Unilever's Senior Vice President for Sustainability. One of his predecessors, Mandy Cormack, adds that this work built on the performance measurement (particularly on environmental impacts) that was developed in the 1990s.

Different members of the executive have accountability for each of these goals, and the company has committed to publishing regular progress reports on implementation. In order to do this there are now detailed USLP scorecards reviewed on a quarterly basis. The quarterly reviews are an integral part of the perceived toughening up and speeding up of performance reviews and accountability that Polman is driving through the business—and arguably these also have a management education function.

Unilever has also pioneered country impact studies, examining the totality of their impacts on the country under review. The first, with Oxfam, focused on Unilever's operations in Indonesia; the second, with INSEAD, looked at Unilever in South Africa; and the third, with a top Vietnamese think-tank, examined Unilever in Vietnam.[30]

→

Embedding in divisions and business functions

If sustainability is to be truly embedded in a company, it cannot just be a series of 'initiatives', a 'bolt-on' to operations. It needs to be built in to business purpose and strategy and this then has to be translated into each part of the business. Unilever is a brand-dominated company. André van Heemstra argues that, 'one of the extraordinary Unilever insights has been to build CR into our brands, as brands lie at the heart of our DNA. In this respect you will not be surprised that our acquisition of Ben & Jerry's in my view gave a notable positive stimulus to Unilever thinking in this area.'

Sustainability had to be made relevant to brand operations. Long before the conception of the USLP, Neath and his colleagues introduced a process called 'Brand Imprint'—a 'simple, intuitively obvious tool to encourage, almost coerce the brands to think more broadly' about their environmental and social impacts, and how to reduce negative impacts and increase positive impacts. Effectively, the tool forced brand managers to look beyond their traditional consumer lens and to add a broader stakeholder lens. The process has typically taken 3–4 months per brand.

> The Brand Imprint process brings together decision-makers from all along the value chain. This includes R&D, marketing, sourcing and production. The process is led by the brand's global VP, and facilitated by the sustainability team. Its aim is to identify, understand and respond to social, environmental and economic issues that may be material to the future of their brand. Often these different functional leaders have not been in the same room together before, and very few will have thought about their brand in terms of 'sustainable consumption'.[31]

Through the Brand Imprint process the group is tasked with systematically investigating the direct and indirect environmental, economic and social impacts of products, as well as the external influences (consumers, market forces, opinion formers) that might impact on the brand's future growth. This provides a structured process for each of the brand teams to undertake a 360° scan of the social, economic and environmental impact that its brand has on the world.

→

Rather than Unilever's sustainability experts presenting evidence and arguments to illuminate each segment of this assessment, they introduce the framework and then pass the ownership of each of the six areas of research and analysis on to a senior functional leader.

One of the first brands to go through this Imprint process was Lipton Tea. Lipton was chosen because of perceived civil society interest in how tea was sourced,[32] and as Unilever buys 12% of the world's annual tea production, the company is a significant player in the industry. The tea Imprint process culminated in a workshop held on a tea plantation in Kenya, facilitated by a manager who had served in Ben & Jerry's—the iconic Vermont ice cream manufacturer acquired by Unilever in 2000—who was steeped in the business imperative for sustainability. As a result of the Brand Imprint, the decision was taken to select a third-party certification scheme to build consumer confidence in both the environmental sustainability and the social equity of Unilever's tea supply chain.

In May 2007, Unilever signed an agreement with the NGO Rainforest Alliance and set a target for all Lipton Yellow Label and PG Tips tea sold globally to be fully Rainforest Alliance Certified by 2015. Implicit in the initiative was a conscious aim to move the whole industry.

Positive experience with tea got the Brand Imprint process off to a good start. A further boost came from one of Unilever's principal customers: Walmart. Following Hurricane Katrina in the USA in 2005, Walmart's then CEO Lee Scott had something of a Damascene conversion on sustainability and committed to turning Walmart green in a seminal speech broadcast to all of Walmart's facilities in November 2005. One of the key levers he used to implement the commitment was Walmart's long-established VPI programme. When the programme was created in 1976, VPI stood for Volume Producing Item, but Scott shifted the emphasis and changed the name to Value Producing Item. In addition, sustainability emerged as an important attribute for a product to possess if suppliers were going to put forth an item for VPI consideration. Each senior Walmart executive has to champion a VPI and after committing Walmart to sustainability, Scott chose the Unilever detergent brand All as his VPI. In fact, at that point, All was a struggling brand. In desperation, Unilever had converted the product into

→

a concentrate. The timing was fortuitous since Scott used All Small & Mighty as an exemplar of everything he was trying to achieve—less packaging, fewer chemicals, etc. Indeed, he was filmed on national television walking down a Wal-Mart store aisle, explaining to an interviewer what Walmart's sustainability commitment meant, and grabbing a packet of the All concentrate to illustrate his point. By 2008, Walmart was selling liquid detergents only in concentrate form. (See also Chapter 7, Case study 7.3, on Surf Small & Mighty.)

All Unilever's largest brands (those with turnover of more than $1 billion) have gone through the Brand Imprint process. The process has automatically triggered insights about product and packaging innovation. External adviser Jonathon Porritt argues that the Brand Imprint process laid the foundations for the USLP and demonstrates how long a journey a company has to commit to, in order to ensure sustainability is embedded. The USLP has taken sustainability into further parts of the business. It is a central part of the business case for the USLP that it will drive innovation. In the developing world, for example, water is precious, so Unilever has introduced an easy-rinsing detergent that saves billions of litres of water. Further dimensions for embedding are the operating companies across the world and ensuring that global commitments can be translated into local implementation. (Case study 6.2 in Chapter 6 looks in more detail at Unilever's approach to sustainability in new product development and some of the challenges faced.)

Engaging employees

Embedding involves not just getting the leadership on board but also the mass of employees. The Environmental Impact team, Sustainability Champions' Network and Sustainable Packaging Steering team are three current examples of how teams of employees come together to work on specific issues. These groups work to assess Unilever's footprint, formulate strategy, agree policy, work with category and brand teams to set specific goals and support the teams in implementing them. They also seek advice from external experts. Unilever has been regularly and closely tracking employee engagement for several years with extensive surveying. André van Heemstra believes that the commitment to be a responsible business has had a positive impact on

→

levels of employee engagement—showing how often (although not always), companies are going with the grain of employee sentiment in promoting sustainability, and that the sustainability agenda can be highly motivating and energising. These regular, internal Global People Surveys have identified three key drivers of employee motivation: perceived quality of the leadership; how one feels in one's job (working conditions, adequate equipment to perform the job expected, relations with direct superiors, peers and reports, etc.); and responsible behaviour of the company. Indeed employee engagement has been another part of the business case for the USLP. The launch of the USLP has encouraged more employees to want to become involved with sustainability. One of the most recent has been the HQ Finance team.

Inside Unilever it is recognised, however, that understanding of what sustainability means for individual employees and individual businesses within the company remains mixed. Some brands, functions and geographies have grasped the relevance early on. Others have yet fully to understand. Making sustainability everybody's business is seen as critical to the next phase of embedding.

Energising the value chain

Unilever's extensive research has shown that most of the environmental impacts of its products occur not when they are made or distributed to retailers but earlier and later in the value chain.[33]

When it comes to greenhouse gases, for example, almost 70% of the life-cycle impacts are tied up in the way consumers use Unilever products—hence the company's efforts to influence suppliers and consumers. Unilever has co-founded an organisation, the Supplier Ethical Data Exchange (www.sedexglobal.com), which is now 'the largest collaborative platform for sharing ethical supply chain data'. The notion is that participating companies can share each other's sustainability-related suppliers' data in different regions, saving both buying organisations and suppliers time and hassle. Like other business-to-consumer (B2C) companies leading on sustainability, Unilever is now seeking to engage consumers, for example, to use less water and energy in showering and laundry, but readily admits that this is proving difficult.

→

Knowledge management and training

Unilever is now applying the same management discipline and science to sustainability that it applies to every other aspect of the business. Staff are supported with sustainability training and tools. The company makes extensive use of advisory bodies and outside experts. The Global Health Partnerships Group, for example, connects Unilever brands and expertise with global health organisations. Its role is to develop and implement sustainable nutrition and hygiene solutions, with the objective of creating value for society and for the business. The Sustainable Agriculture Steering Group comprises Unilever staff from around the world responsible for managing the Sustainable Agriculture Initiative. Its objective is to promote sustainable supply chains, focusing on long-term, sustainable access to Unilever's key crops. Jonathon Porritt, who has also been a key adviser to Marks & Spencer in the development of their Plan A, has played a critical role with Unilever. Gavin Neath acknowledges that Unilever has also learnt a lot from Marks & Spencer, and he is now sitting on an international taskforce for Marks & Spencer to advise on what would make them the world's most sustainable major retailer by 2015.

Early in the new millennium, Unilever in Brazil embarked on a unique project around the central idea of offering academic scholarships to outstanding high school graduates from the favelas (shanty towns) who normally couldn't expect to come anywhere near a university. During the latter years of their study the scholarship students work for part of their time in the company, with a dual objective: to gain practical experience and to increase the chance of continuing their careers with Unilever and, in doing so, to become singular connectors between the company and the favela communities. Some of these people are now indeed part of the Unilever Brazil management team and the project has become an integral part of the recruitment process. Besides this, Unilever Brazil embarked on a project where each manager of the company had to live on the budget of someone at just below middle-class income for a week. Both initiatives have continued to re-connect the business to the lower-income classes and have led to market shares within these income groups being sustained above the national averages.

→

Communications and stakeholder engagement

Unilever was an early sustainability reporter, producing its first social report in 2001. It is now active in promoting the USLP. One stakeholder group many believe has yet to be won over generally is institutional investors. In Accenture's 2010 CEO survey for the UNGC, engaging investors is seen by 71% of CEOs as being important for embedding sustainability (up from 51% in 2007)—but still regarded as the least important of six core requirements. Only 48% of the CEOs say their own company is yet doing this. This perhaps reflects a continuing perception that mainstream investors are not yet interested in sustainability. Polman, however, is being more proactive. Controversially, he has abandoned quarterly reporting to the market, endorsed McKinsey global managing partner Dominic Barton's call for 'long-term capitalism', and opined on the purpose of business:

> I do not work for the shareholder, to be honest; I work for the consumer, the customer. I discovered a long time ago that if I focus on . . . the long term to improve the lives of consumers and customers all over the world, the business results will come.[34]

Polman is clear, however, that companies must deliver financial results if their sustainability efforts are to be credible, and points to an improvement in Unilever's share price over the past three years.

Collaborations and coalitions

Unilever has long understood that sustainable development will require companies to collaborate with other companies, even sometimes direct competitors, as well as with academia, civil society, governments and international institutions. Unilever was one of the founder members of Business in the Community in the UK (www.bitc.org.uk) and an early member of the World Business Council for Sustainable Development (www.wbscd.org). As well as these generic coalitions, Unilever has been active in helping to create or lead more specialist collaborations such as the Sustainable Food Lab (www.sustainablefoodlab.org) and the Roundtable on Sustainable Palm Oil (www.rspo.org). It is also active in the Consumer Goods Forum (www.theconsumergoodsforum.com), which has significant sustainability and health and safety pillars.

→

Specialist sustainability function

The sustainability commitment is supported by a small team at corporate headquarters in London. From 2010 to 2012, this was led by Gavin Neath as Senior Vice President for Corporate Sustainability. In March 2012, Neath was succeeded by Gail Klintworth who has over 25 years' experience in Unilever, including spells as CEO of Unilever South Africa and most recently as Executive Vice President of the global Savoury Category. Klintworth has the new title of 'Chief Sustainability Officer'. Like Neath before her, she will sit on the Unilever Sustainable Living Plan Steering Team and support the Board Corporate Responsibility and Reputation Committee and the Unilever Sustainable Development Group. Klintworth, like Neath, reports to Keith Weed, Chief Marketing and Communication Officer, who is a member of the executive committee reporting to Polman.

Specialist teams within Unilever support the work on sustainability such as the Safety and Environmental Assurance Centre, the Global Health Partnerships Group and the Sustainable Agriculture Steering Group. These teams also obtain external input, for example through the Sustainable Agriculture Advisory Board.

Like Marks & Spencer, the Co-op and a select band of other well-established organisations, Unilever has the opportunity to build on a long tradition of social responsibility and to use that heritage to enhance and speed up what still remains, a long-term journey towards sustainability.

Subsequent chapters of this book explore in more detail some of the individual facets of embedding sustainability.

Patrick Reinmoeller explores some of the challenges of embedding sustainability within strategy. Donna Ladkin suggests some new dimensions for corporately responsible leaders. Andrew Kakabadse and I share some initial ideas from ongoing research into the role of boards in ensuring effective governance and oversight of corporate commitments to sustainability. Mike and Pippa Bourne and David Ferguson examine how commitments are operationalised in performance management. Keith Goffin asks how companies can systematically incorporate sustainability considerations into the innovation process. Lynette Ryals and eight of her marketing faculty colleagues examine the issues involved in embedding sustainability within marketing, and then how to implement this. Mike Bernon and supply-chain colleagues look at how companies are engaging their supply chains. David Ferguson and Martin Clark discuss how to engage employees. Sharon Jackson highlights some of the practical challenges in helping people inside companies to make sense of concepts such as sustainability and work out what they mean for them. Ruth Bender examines the rapidly evolving field of how companies measure and report on their environmental, social and economic impacts.

In this book, we do not address most of the operational enablers of the outer ring of our 'bull's-eye' embedding-sustainability model: the use of knowledge management and training; how companies make the most of their networks and the coalitions they belong to, and how they build collaborations to assist sustainable development; and the way in which specialist sustainability functions can facilitate improved performance. However, the Doughty Centre has produced material on each of these operational enablers, details of which can be found on our website: www.doughtycentre.info.

Stages of maturity

In practice, companies are at different stages of corporate sustainability maturity, and even within the same company there may be different stages of maturity, as to what degree of responsibility they take for different sustainability impacts.[35]

Some companies are in denial that they have any responsibility for their social, environmental and economic impacts. Some choose simply to comply with legal requirements, which for companies doing business internationally may lead to inconsistencies in their approach in different parts of the world. Some companies take a more proactive approach by seeking to mitigate risks. Some have moved beyond this in order also to find business opportunities. Arguably, for a company to take a more proactive responsibility for sustainable development—as a for-profit business—is possible only if the company can find commercially attractive opportunities on a regular, systemic basis from its commitment to sustainability. The various academic and practitioner models of stages of maturity posit a final stage where some companies are willing to share technologies and expertise, and to work in transformational partnerships with others, in order to respond to the scale of global challenges that humankind now faces (see Fig. 1.2).

Figure 1.2 **Five stages of corporate responsibility maturity**

Stage 1	▶	**Denier**
Stage 2	▶	**Complier**
Stage 3	▶	**Risk mitigator**
Stage 4	▶	**Opportunity maximiser**
Stage 5	▶	**Champion or Civil corporation**

At the earlier stages, much will depend on the perspective of the leaders of the business, and a change of CEO, a merger or acquisition, or significant external shock, may trigger evolution—forwards or backwards. At higher stages of maturity, when sustainability has become part of 'the way we do business around here', backwards evolution is harder to envisage. By this time, the company has moved from unconscious incompetence through conscious incompetence and conscious competence and is heading for unconscious competence.[36] Sustainability thinking has become ingrained in organisational culture and behaviours. However, this does imply that the company retains the capacity to, and does regularly, scan the horizon to spot the new technologies and disruptive innovations that are going to occur with increasing frequency as markets and societies wake up to the 'great disruption'[37] that we are now in.

Conclusion

Companies that want to thrive in this new world will be looking not only in their own sector but across industries and across markets, for emerging good practice in embedding sustainability; and as groups such as the World Economic Forum and Boston Consulting Group have identified,[38] more of this innovation is likely to come from companies headquartered in the Brazil, Russia, India and China (BRIC) and other fast-growing economies, so the search for leadership examples will increasingly need to be truly global.

2

Embedding corporate sustainability as a knowledge-creation journey

Patrick Reinmoeller
Professor of Strategic Management

Companies worldwide seek competitive advantage, striving to be preferred over their competition by their key customers and stakeholders. To increase this preference many firms focus on improving the efficiency of their processes, boosting quality and reliability, and most often seek to reduce costs so that they can offer a better deal than the competitors. Frequently, competitors will compete on price in the hope of gaining a position of cost leader, which leads to an emphasis on creating the lowest cost structure in their industry.[39] As there can be only one cost leader, such a race is bound to be disappointing to many. At the same time, the more rivals there are who compete on cost, the less enjoyable the position of even the cost leaders will become, as margins—and therefore profitability, quality and investment—will be affected. Hence, in many cases competitive advantage is only achievable not by focusing on costs but instead by increasing perceived customer preference through, for example, design, variety, loyalty, brand creation and availability. Finding and implementing the right positioning to achieve competitive advantage is fundamental to business strategy—yet in recent years the fight for competitiveness, and commercial success, has come under increasing scrutiny when achieving said advantage is perceived as being not particularly responsible with respect to broader economic, environmental and societal needs.

Mounting research shows that societies worldwide favour companies that enjoy competitive advantages in responsible ways.[40] Increasing employment, taxes, technological know-how, helping to prevent labour unrest and avoiding environmental disasters that destroy local communities are some of the motives behind why local communities and customers have woken up to the consequences of industrial activities.[41] While it is true that some local communities may still relax their demands for some social and environmental responsibilities in order to attract economic activity and create jobs in the short term, yet the recent changes in how economic activity has come to be seen in a broader societal context gives much credence to the assumption that such pockets of tolerated irresponsibility will eventually become too costly to sustain.[42] Similarly, theories and empirical evidence may still be subject to intense debate[43] and some companies may still search for the lowest possible constraints, that is, the pockets of irresponsibility. However, in the long term, companies worldwide need to consider their contract with society about how to formulate and implement strategies that seize the opportunities provided by sustainable and responsible behaviour.[44] Hence, this chapter focuses on how companies can avoid irresponsible advantage, which provides competitiveness without responsibility, and responsible non-advantage: that is, much responsibility but a lack of competitiveness to stay viable. More importantly, this chapter seeks to outline how to prepare for developing responsible competitive advantage (RCA), that is, achieving high competitiveness with high responsibility through compliance *and* co-creation of new ways to increase sustainability (see the upper right quadrant of Fig. 2.1).

Figure 2.1 **Dialectics of competitive advantage and corporate social responsibility**

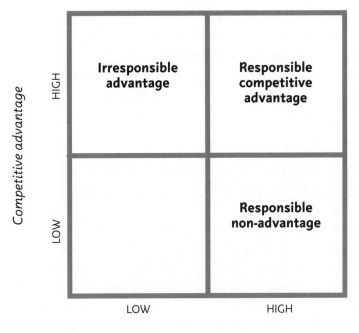

Corporate social responsibility

Developing a strategy for RCA, explicitly or implicitly, is necessary but not in itself sufficient. Many a leading firm espouses sustainability strategies, yet—as with BP, Shell and Coca-Cola—the very same firms are tainted by scandals because the implementation of the same strategies remains flawed.[45] For turning a responsible advantage successfully into corporate sustainability (CS), embedding is key. However, what does embedding CS really mean? What does it mean to be a CS leader, and what does it take to become a socially and environmentally responsible corporation?

We examine a generic process for increasing the quantity and quality of relationships between responsible actions within organisations—their embeddedness—as an important antecedent for CS. How corporations develop and implement strategy,[46] can be enriched by a process of embedding CS, which can be applied across sectors and companies. Embedding CS can be applied to develop blueprints and implementation of sustainability initiatives in headquarters and organisational networks. Therefore, in this chapter we first outline the generic process, illustrated with examples from practice; then we describe the steps to embed sustainability into organisational practice so that the generic process can be translated into practice.

The generic process: corporate sustainability strategy as a knowledge-creation journey

The journey of how companies relate to CS differs for each firm in each industry but basic similarities remain; knowledge development has been identified as a fundamental component of strategic change within a company.[47] The knowledge-creation journey here has two different phases that do not follow a particular order and can quite easily occur in parallel; these phases can be labelled as:

- Compliance

- Co-creation

Compliance focuses on putting into business practice what societies explicitly demand, the legal or non-legal standards that companies find in different contexts. Companies have to comply with legal requirements, regulations, and civic society institutions. They need to put these standards into action impeccably. The challenge is the rapid and flawless implementation of what local laws, regulations and customs clearly require (often referred to as the 'licence to operate'). Firms failing to manage this well will often find themselves embroiled in the scandals we read about so frequently. While implementing explicit standards seems straightforward, motivating and monitoring all organisational members in their execution of what is legal—and excluding practices that are not—can be challenging. For example:

- The unexpectedly high costs of implementing Sarbanes-Oxley are well documented[48]

- Some sales employees may see that what is considered corruption and bribery in one country may seem malleable and more acceptable in other countries depending on time, place and occasion[49]

- Some employees in research and development may be tempted to experiment in ways that are not legal in some countries because the promise of breakthroughs for mankind is overwhelming for them, for example, stem cell research or animal testing[50]

- Today, according to the international regulations that seek to prevent future atrocities through terrorism, airlines and airports need to comply with requests for information and have access to private material of their passengers that previously were seen as confidential between company and customer. The challenge of implementing this has been repeatedly shown by inquisitive journalists smuggling pseudo-explosives inside airports and planes, evading the security measures that were neither sufficient nor followed[51]

Compliance is particularly important when companies internationalise and enter a regional context that does not have in place the law or regulatory institutions on which they rely at home. Different legal systems, the presence of different laws, the absence of laws, or their enforcement (e.g. intellectual property rights) may thwart a company's foray into a promising market.[52]

Case study 2.1 **Siemens (I): kicking bad habits is hard**

Failure to comply

Europe's largest engineering firm was rocked to the core by the largest bribery scandal in Germany. Prosecutors found €1.3 billions-worth of suspected payments by hundreds of managers to officials around the world designed to win contracts. Bribery is not a unique phenomenon in the business world.

Unlawful bribery practices to secure contracts at Siemens had become a useful technique. Each year units at Siemens set aside millions of dollars for the payments of bribes to government officials to win government contracts. The most common method of bribery was indirect and involved hiring an outside consultant to help 'win' a contract. Siemens paid a fee to the consultant, often a local resident with important social contacts, who in turn delivered the cash to the ultimate recipient. When in 1999, Germany joined the international convention banning foreign bribery, a pact signed by most of the world's industrial nations, such bribes were no longer deductible business expenses and Siemens had to change its practice.

Seven years after the legislative change, German authorities decided to raid several offices of Siemens. As Siemens is listed on the New York Stock Exchange, US authorities also became involved and started an investigation. Siemens was alleged to have made bribery payments between 1999 and 2007 in order to secure contracts.

Notwithstanding the legal changes and the illegality of its practices, Siemens had over seven years not been able to drive compliance through and kick illicit corporate habits.[53]

Co-creation requires tapping into the values and views of organisations and people around the world so that corporations can gain advantages over competitors by pioneering new products, services and practices and seizing leadership in their industry.[54] Co-creation can also serve as a mechanism for adding social and environmental values within the company's offering.[55] Sector-based institutional co-creation offers companies the opportunity to create higher levels of responsibility more collectively through unilateral adherence to industry standards and can, or should, allow the company to have a voice in the development of such standards and their regulation.

Case study 2.2 Hasbro and rivals: raising standards together

Getting together as competitors to start cooperating may seem anathema to rivalry in many industries, especially when the industries rely on offshore manufacturing to reduce the cost of labour. Often derided as paper tigers, voluntary self-regulation efforts in industries sometimes fall short of what may be ideal; however, they represent initiatives that are initiated by the companies and can lead to effective implementation.

The International Council of Toy Industries (ICTI) is a case in point. Its members such as Hasbro or Zapf Creation show how competing firms within an industry collectively seek to improve factory working conditions. While the members retain their independence and may conduct their own audits, participation in the ICTI's CARE programme requires cooperation with regular audits by an approved audit company.

Ensuring that a collective standard of professional auditing provides a basis for objectively assessing higher standards and avoiding scandals due to malpractice is part of the *raison d'être* of ICTI. Defining these standards, processes and methods has been the collective undertaking of the industry's companies, which in a concerted effort have found a way to create a basis for more responsible manufacturing of what should make people happy—toys.

Hasbro, for example, a company founded in 1923, sells more than 1,500 brands in a total of 123 countries and owns only two of more than 100 factories involved in manufacturing its products. Hasbro had resolved to increase clarity and transparency to raise the levels of responsibility. Like many manufacturers that no longer own or operate the factories manufacturing for them, Hasbro understood that a unilateral approach was not promising. Aiming at avoiding inconsistent codes of conduct, Hasbro began to partner with other companies to improve and establish higher standards in the industry in 1995. From these early efforts, ICTI and a single code of business practices emerged. Today, ICTI and Hasbro are again seeking to create, with other companies in the industry, an even higher level of transparency. As a first step Hasbro has begun to publish the names and addresses of its major suppliers and partners online, which represent about 80% of Hasbro Far East production volume in China, in order to inspire another round of co-creation.[56]

Unilateral actions to co-create, for example with customers or suppliers, can also work well. Pioneering company standards can be very cost-effective and time-efficient for the company to implement. Companies then have the opportunity to distinguish themselves by achieving higher standards around CS and responsibility elements within the protocol, such as employment conditions, carbon footprint or supplier contracts. Discovering and developing higher standards requires finding, refining and justifying ideas and new methods, that is, firms have to create knowledge if they want to become leaders in CS. Creating knowledge is the process of turning what is implicit and hidden into codified evidence, as a sound basis for action.[57] However, in some industries the process of defining the responsible behaviour of corporations can require a long and significant consultation process with stakeholders. Consider how companies involved in nanotechnologies, together with other relevant parties (e.g. legislators), face challenges to craft standards and binding norms, because it is not yet completely known and understood how to handle nanotechnology responsibly without immediately stifling the investment promise of this potent technology.[58]

Embedding sustainability into organisational practice

Because many groups have an interest or stake in a company and its activities, companies face multiple and sometimes conflicting demands regarding their sustainability performance:

- Most shareholders and some employees may be more interested in higher short-term returns on invested capital and their labour

- A local community may want environmentally friendly technologies and employment

- Some customers may want to maximise product/service safety in use, whereas others will emphasise greater affordability

These few examples illustrate the great variation that can exist, with demands varying in specificity. Some of the requirements are very explicit; some may even be codified in the laws of countries or states. Other requirements may not be explicit at all and make it hard for a company to identify what needs to be embedded to deliver on that demand. In some cases, the difficulties inherent in articulating the more emotional and less quantifiable aspects of CS can explain why some aspects of sustainability remain tacit. This has important consequences for compliance and co-creation.

Step 1: Doing what needs to be done: compliance as process

In practice, complying in most cases means meeting the requirements as stipulated by the law, rules or standards. When efforts to be compliant result in success, this is often because a set of clear activities was developed specifically for that purpose. If this can be understood and described as a process, compliance can then become easier to implement and be implemented in a consistent manner. However, the demands and expectations placed on corporations trying to be sustainable are usually more implicit or tacit than normal compliance programmes and are therefore harder to comply with. They require discovery, learning and refinement. It can, in practice, be challenging to:

- Identify the rules

- Translate these rules into actionable routines

- Effect change in the existing routines in the company to deliver the outcomes

Identifying rules is particularly challenging in environments that undergo accelerated change and are therefore often expanding and creating new rules. The case of countries in political and social transition illustrates the point. After the collapse of the Soviet Union, many former Eastern European countries started the transition towards a more market-oriented economic system. During the transition, many new rules were crafted; often the old rules and new rules competed for compliance, with the rule-book changing in quite unpredictable ways. Complying in such an environment is extremely challenging. Complying in Cuba today, for example, also poses similar challenges to firms (those that are already operating in Cuba and those preparing to enter). The possibility of a change in leadership, and subsequent changes in societal, economic and political systems, makes it difficult to prepare for compliance as it is unknown how the future Cuban society will articulate its understanding of what a sustainable business is. Furthermore, identifying explicit rules generally may be less difficult than identifying the actual rules that matter in society, that is, not all social rules need to be complied with versus legal and regulatory rules that do. We suggest scanning business environments to identify existing rules and regulations (to see if these fit with your organisation's values and standards) should precede the usual new market entry steps such as new product development and analysis of market-share potential.

There are four key steps for successful identification of rules:

1. Clarify what the organisation stands for (We?)

2. Scan the environment and select carefully (What?)

3. Use and develop specific expertise (Who?)

4. Create realms of autonomy (How much?)

Case study 2.3 **Google and China: understanding the rules**

'Don't do evil': Google's entry into the Chinese market in 2006 was as spectacular as its decision to retreat to Hong Kong in 2010. As a symbol of the advent of the liberties of the Internet society in China, albeit self-censored, Google's entry was significant. Executives declared in 2006 'We're in it for the long haul'. In fact there was history behind this entry: in China, Google's search engine had already been in use for years. Hosted outside China, Google had provided access to its services but suffered severe slowdowns and obstacles for its users in China, including days of complete inaccessibility in 2002. Meanwhile, China's market was growing rapidly and so were competitors such as Baidu. Google found that it had to play by the rules, which were not yet entirely clear, and signed a licence to become a Chinese website in December 2005.

We? Adhering to its corporate credo, Google sought to do good by organising information for one of the most populous countries in the world, China. Entering this large and quickly growing market made much business sense.

What? The diffusion of computing, Internet access and the ensuing explosion of demand for search services made the Chinese market look attractive. Scanning the legal segment of the environment revealed rules and regulations that foreign firms also had to abide by, including censorship of political and pornographic content.

Who? In 2006 Google appointed Kai-Fu Lee, at the time a 44-year-old computer scientist, as the new head of operations for Google in China. Lee grew up in Taiwan, was educated in the USA (Columbia and Carnegie Mellon universities) and is fluent in English and Mandarin.

After working for Apple in California, Microsoft in China and setting up Microsoft Research Asia, the company's R&D lab in Beijing, Lee personalised the expertise needed to comply with rules and find the implicit 'dos and don'ts'. After Lee opened the Beijing office, Google introduced a Chinese version of its search engine. In line with China's censorship laws, the new Chinese version would not display any websites disapproved of by the Chinese government, including websites promoting free speech in China or mentioning the 1989 Tiananmen Square massacre.

How much? Google made decisions about how much autonomy to retain and which compromises to tolerate. It would not offer email or blogging services inside China, since that could force it to censor blog postings or hand over dissidents' personal information to the secret police. It would offer two search engines in Chinese. Chinese surfers could still access the old, unfiltered google.com, which would be slowed down and occasionally blocked entirely by the firewall. The new google.cn would deliver censored results, quickly and reliably. Without asking for permission, Google's co-founder Sergey Brin and his team decided to put a disclaimer at the top of the search results on google.cn explaining that information had been removed in accordance with Chinese law—in fact revealing the degree of censorship to its users. As the government would not provide lists of sites to block, Google programmed a computer located in China to access one website beyond the borders after another. Progressing site by site the computer could then record which sites were blocked by the firewall; Google thus mapped the implicit rules of the Internet.

About two years after Kai-Fu Lee had left Google in 2009, seeing its market share eroded by fierce local rivals such as Baidu, numerous attacks by sophisticated hackers located in China and progressive tightening of China's restriction on free speech on the Internet, Google decided to reassert its position on free speech and announced it would no longer censor. Acknowledging that its decision to leave for Hong Kong could have severe consequences, Google found playing by the emergent rules of competition in China challenging and incompatible with its view of itself.[59]

Translating articulated rules into routines that are relevant to organisational members is the most important challenge when embedding strategy—and CS is no different. Companies need to expend considerable effort in translating the rules of compliance into the context of stakeholders and working routines, for example, of their employees, to enable acceptance, relevance and embedding. If the relevance of responsible behaviour is not translated in ways that make it possible for individual employees to see that it matters to them personally, they may not become involved and motivated to implement it.[60] Difficult tasks, such as aligning employees with organisational resources and goals, require skills to create a supportive climate, to empathise with employees' views and to provide effective training,[61] which are needed for translating the new rules in ways that enable employees to rule out making other choices, even in difficult economic times. Consider how safety has become an important part of how oil companies conduct their business; however, highly 'routinised' safety processes on their own may turn precautionary measures into mere rituals that are ignored or not seen as important. The customary exclusion of outliers, such as the possibility of worst possible outcomes actually occurring, leads to an inherent underestimation of risk,[62] which became pervasive in, for example, parts of the financial industry. This also exists in other industries; a classic case is the pharmaceutical industry, which has in the past received much bad press for 'kickback' sales techniques that try to influence doctors and the way they prescribe medications.[63]

Another example is the question of bribery, or facilitation payments or gifts. Where 'giving gifts' ends and 'buying favours' starts is certainly culturally shaded, yet legislations seek to draw lines. Translating these lines into the work objectives of all organisational employees is a task for businesses. Without doing so, companies risk behaving irresponsibly and being exposed as doing so. If this translation is not clearly communicated, it can remain subjective and is filled in by employees as their context suggests is appropriate.

There are four key steps for successful translation:

1. Employees need to care about the issue (Why?)

2. The issue needs topicality (Why now/here?)

3. Provide options to solve the immediate problem (Which opportunities?)

4. Make it tangible (How?)

Case study 2.4 **Siemens (II): how to kick bad habits**

Siemens was alleged to have made bribery payments between 1999 and 2007 in order to secure contracts. These allegations in key markets such as Germany and the USA threatened to damage Siemens' reputation, built over 160 years, and its performance. For seven years it had not been successful in ensuring that employees abided by the law. In order to translate successfully what needed to be done, the board made dealing with the scandal a priority. It led to the departure of a successful CEO who had not acted to bring employees in line with the law.

Why? These top-level changes clearly signalled that the transgressions were no bagatelles but cutting into the core of Siemens' legitimacy and viability as a company.

Why now/here? The raids by authorities in several offices clearly signalled the urgency with which change needed to happen. The news media further exacerbated the scandal and overrode all other issues with one topic associated with Siemens—bribery.

Which opportunities? In order to show that thorough investigation and radical change was the only way out, Siemens' board appointed Peter Löscher, the first outsider to head the company, sought international and independent advice, and hired an American law firm, which conducted an internal investigation and worked with federal investigators. Siemens officials made it very clear that the goal was to fully understand what had been going on for so long and to follow all leads. After 4,238 bribe payments for a total of €1.1 billion between March 2001 and September 2007 had been discovered, appropriate behaviour was made tangible.

→

How? Following the revelations of the extent of the malpractice, several managers were arrested and the fines imposed by the US and German authorities amounted to €600 million and €596 million respectively. Löscher introduced state-of-the-art measures to root out corruption (e.g. banning external advisers, introducing new compliance system), restructured at a cost of €800 million (e.g. replacing 100 top managers, linking compliance to incentives) and provided the aspiration to get the best *and* clean business: that is, reconciling profitable and ethical behaviour.[64]

Changing organisational routines is easy—on paper. Formal structures and procedures can be corrupted by ways of doing things that do not die out easily, like old habits. Employees entrenched in doing things as they have always been done may find it very difficult to change.[65] Falling back into old habits happens; rigid organisations that let this happen put their reputations at risk.[66] Like all organisational change initiatives, as in the case of Siemens above, making employees aware of the things that need to change, and then actually changing and controlling for effectiveness, is arguably the most difficult task of managers. Urgency helps to focus attention, as the academic Kotter emphasises.[67] Consider how in the case of Foxconn the sense of urgency caused by the emergence of information about sweatshop conditions and related suicides not only caused a scandal[68] but led to a series of decisions that changed the way the company was managed. Successful organisational change requires initiative, leadership and an understanding of the key systemic elements within the company[69] from top management and other key organisational members. Together they have to find answers to the following questions:

1. The change needs to be clarified: which routines are to be abandoned? What are the new routines?

2. The coordinates need to be explicit: when and where will the new routines become the standard?

3. Additional incentives beyond getting it right have to be explained: what are the rewards?

Case study 2.5 Siemens (III): making good behaviour explicit

After the clean-up, admitting to misconduct and clarifying which habits needed to change, Siemens developed a set of Business Conduct Guidelines as part of a new Siemens Compliance Programme to outline new routines. Published in 2009, the Guidelines make explicit the corporate behaviour to become the standard code of behaviour for Siemens employees worldwide with immediate effect. The new Compliance Programme includes other regulations that complement the Guidelines and are also valid company-wide. Among these are Anti-Public-Corruption Guidelines, Code of Ethics for Financial Matters, Corporate Donations, Payment and Bank Account Centralisation, Business Consulting Agreements, and Supplier@Siemens, which addresses the relationship between Siemens and suppliers.

Peter Löscher, CEO of Siemens, explains that the Business Conduct Guidelines

> set out how we meet our ethical and legal responsibility as a company and give expression to our corporate values of being 'responsible—excellent—innovative'. These Business Conduct Guidelines have been adapted in line with new legal requirements and are based on international treaties on human rights, anti-corruption and sustainability. They are intended to strengthen awareness of the law and moral standards as an integral part of our entrepreneurial actions. The key message is that only clean business is Siemens business. I call on all employees to live and breathe the Business Conduct Guidelines.[70]

While the Guidelines were being disseminated throughout the company and put into effect, the ongoing investigations led to indictments documenting extreme levels of deception and corruption and to high-profile trials in which eight individuals were charged in civil and criminal cases, including the former CEO and CFO of Siemens in Argentina and

→

former senior executives of Siemens Business Services. US prosecutors, in 'outstanding and extraordinary' cooperation with current Siemens corporate officials, enforced the Corrupt Practices Act to reward those who refused to pay bribes and to root out those 'who do stoop to those levels'.[71]

Identifying, translating and changing behaviour to comply more fully with rules and regulations is fundamental to CS. After establishing the fit of a company's core values with the context of the country and society the organisation is operating in, complying with the identified rules is imperative for receiving and maintaining a licence to operate. Being only legally compliant, however, does not equate to being responsible or engaging in CS in the more comprehensive definition of the term.

Step 2: Co-creating performance innovations: discovering new insight by going beyond legal compliance

Being legal demonstrates compliance with the law and results in competitive parity with other players in the same institutional context. Hence, compliance itself does not offer much competitive differentiation as it provides a minimum *legal* licence to operate that all companies need to adhere to. (However, as it is, not all companies manage 100% compliance with laws.) Pursuing responsible competitive advantage means going beyond the often minimal requirements stipulated by the law, often preparing for future legislation or even setting standards of what future minimum legislation should be. This pursuit can often create new insights for the company because what the front line, or best-practice understanding, of responsibility is can advance unique positioning. In other words, corporate responsibility and sustainability, in the context of exceeding minimum legal requirements, can be turned into a source of innovation by raising the standards.

Innovation in itself is normally challenging, for example when creating new products/services, but understanding how to develop and push the boundaries of CS for innovation creation can be even more difficult. However, because of their commitment to sustainability, pioneering companies such as Sony and GEC (through their Ecomagination programme) are building opportunities for innovation directly into their product ranges. By exploring how their product ranges need to be more sustainable and of a higher standard than 'just legally compliant' (e.g. through initiating dialogue with stakeholder networks, including potential customers and suppliers), they have uncovered or discovered new performance or processes that are more sustainable, innovative and beneficial for the business. Finding unknown beneficiaries of new corporate practice and developing new sustainability-related frontiers based on exploration and discovery can generate new insights. By taking that step to go beyond just compliance, they are uncovering and understanding the unintended consequences of their business, articulating these as opportunities and integrating the findings into an accelerated process of innovation development. These companies are co-creating innovation through their approach to CS in being more than just legally compliant.

Co-creation: discovering unanticipated effects (UAEs)

Co-creation first explores how UAEs can lead product and process innovation. While exploring external and internal environments to better understand their responsibilities, corporations often tap into what is, besides technological change, the most important source of innovation: the discovery of little-known or emergent customer needs and UAEs. Stumbling across needs can lead to company action that elevates its perceived responsibility. Consider how firms learn about the needs of employees regarding flexible working hours or kindergartens. Discovering how valuable small allowances in flexibility can be for employees helps companies to cost-effectively increase distinctiveness, improve the workplace and raise the quality of job applicants. The amount of publicity generated for Google by employing great chefs to provide excellent free food for all employees illustrates how setting new standards for better workplaces in response to unanticipated needs works effectively. Similarly, careful attention to unintended consequences can further help to raise the levels of sustainability. Considering the consequences of a company's supply chain's effects on the environment, even if far offshore, and thereby extending the responsibility a company takes, can lead to advantages in the marketplace and help to avoid backlashes due to local protests or global scandals. In sum, UAEs are a rich source of insight into not only how to be more responsible and sustainable, but also how to enhance a company's competitiveness; these insights can take the company from a potentially irresponsible advantage position towards a responsible advantage position (as described in Fig. 2.1). Understanding UAEs is an important first step in understanding the consequences and benefits of a product/service for different stakeholder groups.

Consider, for example, the manufacturing of toys. At first glance it provides employment in manufacturing (often in developing countries), generates revenues (and taxes), produces local employment through retail outlets and provides a broadly positive utility (e.g. fun) to the users. What, though, are the unintended consequences? Have we explored these in our assessment? Could, for example, the user perhaps be accidentally endangered? Consider the unintended consequences of US companies—such as Mattel's Fisher-Price—moving their manufacturing to China, and the US regulators subsequently needing to improve industry sector codes of conduct and toy manufacturing laws for US companies producing abroad.[72] What are the consequences of this outsourcing on the US job market, and on the Chinese employee base, employment and environment? There are clearly positive aspects around sustainability, such as education and human interaction, but what might be the negative issues? Actively considering the UAEs of new products and services can raise legitimate business concerns; some are even clear red flags that someone in the company should have already sensed.

When considering the UAEs, supply-chain or main production processes, such considerations may include:

- The handling levels of hazardous and toxic materials

- Materials that may significantly add to climate change

- Processes that may involve the exploitation of indigenous people, local labour, forced labour and children

- Activities or products that reduce biodiversity opportunities or contribute to the depletion of potentially irreplaceable natural resources

- The risk of bribery, corruption and undemocratic political influences

At a macro-economic level, UAEs of large corporations outsourcing manufacturing to developing countries may create or influence unhealthy competition for labour, with effects on local indigenous industries, and have potential knock-on effects in creating imbalanced social migration trends. In other words, analysing the value chain for UAEs of corporations' activities can reveal many opportunities in which a company can raise its CS standards and identify the business issues that need to be embedded and managed within the company's strategic and operational activities.

Various tools have been developed to understand these UAEs. The concept of 'cradle to cradle' and the tools of life-cycle analysis and environmental accounting have recently gained more credibility with businesses; these tools primarily look at the environmental impacts of products alongside increasing environmental regulatory mechanisms.[73] Although tools to measure and analyse social impact do not appear to be as developed as tools to measure environmental impacts, social impact does feature within the realms of government and civil society organisations. This is alongside aspects explored earlier, such as employee safety, consumer safety and local community welfare, which fit under 'social impact' as a UAE theme. Development agencies include these important sustainability themes that businesses should consider within their assessments of social impacts.[74]

These social issues include:

- **Demographic change**, for example, size and composition of resident population

- **Influx of temporary workforce** or new recreational users (disrupts the cohesion of a small, stable community)

- **Economic change**, for example, new patterns of employment/income, real estate speculation (marginalises long-term, older residents)

- **Environmental change**, for example, alterations to land use, natural habitat

- **Changes to hydrological regime** (causing loss of subsistence or livelihood in resource-dependent community)

- **Institutional change**, for example, in the structure of local government or traditional leadership, zoning by-laws or land tenure (reduced access or loss of control leads to disempowerment or impoverishment of the established population)

Different stakeholder groups have long been identified in academic theory and business practice as a fundamental aspect of the company's issue management capability,[75] with their relevance for embedding strategic change within the company being a recognised source of value.

Articulation: making new sustainability responsibilities explicit

When UAEs are captured, articulating these insights must follow. Lack of articulation obstructs understanding and communication of what and how responsibility can be given new meaning. Articulating opportunities arising from UAEs is clearly a first step to testing and selecting the most important ways to become more responsible quickly.

'Selecting' requires setting priorities for what matters more. Here corporations' core values play an important role. If 'providing employment to local people' or 'keeping family ownership' are core values then the company's priorities will differ markedly from companies with values, such as with our toy manufacturer example, that state 'providing the best, valued entertainment for kids' or 'being the first choice for encouraging creative talent and personal development'.

'Articulation' of issues into meaningful languages for business and their various different functions (which have their own language and business-focus perspectives) is a challenge. Strategically it is important that, in embedding CS, different mechanisms should be prepared and used for integration. These include:

- External stakeholder engagement (issue identification and prioritisation)

- Internal stakeholder engagement (issue definition and prioritisation)

- Analysis of the issues against the company culture and capabilities

- Preparatory corporate communication and open employee engagement

Broadly, these tools enable the integration of CS and business responsibility, both strategically and operationally. In practice, leading companies are developing, as a genuine strategic concern, their capabilities in these areas as they seek a deeper and more lasting embedding of CS and responsibility within the company. There are challenges when CS-related issues undergo different forms of sense-making and filtration mechanisms[76] and the very act of this sense-making can create different terms for CS (destroying a common language). A key aspect of the articulation stage is to overcome this barrier of a confused, disparate language for CS.[77] In this context, corporate communication is an essential mechanism for helping to institutionalise key CS issues,[78] and a clear communications strategy can inject a much-needed sense of urgency to enable any significant changes.[79] This is particularly true at the strategic enterprise-wide level, while at the same time enabling the flexibility for local CS relevance with respect to more localised context, culture and regulation (a balance to achieve that is particularly relevant for multinational enterprises).[80]

These 'articulation' approaches and processes of managing strategic top-down co-creation and bottom-up strategic solutions into meaningful local language around the company, while maintaining common company-wide commonality and conformity, is a key strategic management issue. It is also an issue that is essential for the integration stage and embedding CS; this enables approaching the 'tipping-point' where strategic rhetoric and senior management endorsement is embedded into corporate actions and mind-set.

Integration stage: applying the new sustainability initiatives

By Step 5, the implementation programme will have recognised the legal compliance aspects (Step 1), which are more clearly understood in terms of the business benefits and impacts. The programme will have proactively identified and set in place compliance with new and forthcoming legal requirements (Step 2). Discovering UAEs can help develop innovative ways to increase CS (Step 3). The articulation will also have occurred (Step 4) around the opportunities and institutional compliances—the co-creation developments with other stakeholders—around key strategic themes, with an emphasis on their complementary nature. Matching this communication with the commitment, the 'talk' with the 'walk', is strategically important for enabling the embedding efforts, to ensure they are received well, implemented efficiently and effectively, and provide a measurably longer-lasting benefit and advantage for the company.

Companies will now be in a better position to integrate and apply new programmes, processes and policies. As well as undertaking top-down traditional roll-outs, space for initiatives on company-wide themes (climate change, waste management, water management) should be included in the strategic plan and medium-term planning process. These can be integrated into business unit and team-level specific initiatives (community programmes, marketing initiatives, custom eco-efficiency and employee-development programmes). This creates a portfolio of project and programme initiatives that need to be enabled and resourced, having first secured a strategic prioritisation and a common understanding in the company of how CS is relevant to the company. Managing such a portfolio of sustainability initiatives and assessing the importance of each initiative against the time needed to lead to fruition helps to ensure that CS is neither a low-hanging fruit to be harvested soon but once only nor a Utopia to be realised in the too-distant future. Creating a balance between important and instrumental initiatives that mature over different periods ensures that the portfolio as a whole ensures the enhancement of CS.

Integration finally is the fundamental operation that moves the company from irresponsible advantage to responsible advantage (see Fig. 2.1).

Case study 2.6 Complying and co-creating responsibility at OFG

OFG is one of the leading European financial groups that went beyond legal compliance (Step 1). Including aspects of responsibility for the first time in the bank's history by engaging in corporate social activities that reflected its responsibility, OFG became active in generating resources for a social purpose. While such activities were common even among its competitors, OFG had hitherto not engaged in any similar initiative. The desire to become active was primarily driven by benchmarking exercises and the need to raise employee engagement and it was seen as positive to become a force for what could be considered a good cause.

➜

Ensuring that the new programme would comply with shareholder expectations and the law (Step 2), the bank proactively identified three overlapping themes (children, education and emerging markets) and set in place a centralised governance structure that ensured compliance with regulations at home and in other markets. Focusing on the overlap area of the themes, the definition of the initiative was a key step in developing CS.

Discovering UAEs helped to develop an innovative way to increase CS (Step 3). The decision to do good by providing education for children in emerging markets led first to a geographic focus on emerging markets where the company had a commercial representation. Seeking to develop ways to generate resources mostly through donations by employees, which OFG then matched, was successful. However, giving money to OFG's large non-profit partner to build schools or equip them with furniture, materials and books was perceived as a safe but rather indirect way. Through interactions with employees, OFG found that many sought to become more directly involved by donating work and time. Seizing on this emergent opportunity for more engagement, based on UAEs, OFG allowed employees sabbaticals to support the initiative and the time donated by employees would then be matched by the bank. Another unanticipated consequence of OFG's central initiative to engage all employees led to the discovery that the new initiative stood in competition with many local, successful initiatives aimed at mainly helping local people. The new initiative helped to make explicit all the different initiatives that were unfolding on the local level. Through interaction with local stakeholders, OFG was able to develop the new initiative as an umbrella to the local initiatives and thus avoid head-on competition, and generate synergies between new and old initiatives.

In OFG's case the articulation (Step 4) of the corporate initiative came first before a dialogue with local stakeholders could be commenced. This led to misunderstandings and some resistance from local stakeholders, which in turn offered an opportunity to gain new insights. Only after managing a cooperative redefinition of the corporate initiative did OFG succeed in mobilising employees around the world. One key aspect of the redefinition was the articulation and dissemination of the corporate initiative; presenting it as an umbrella for all prior existing

programmes, acceptance and support was ensured, even though donations or time dedicated in a company might go to local initiatives.

In order to keep the corporate initiative alive, the responsible unit
within the CSR department develops waves of events and campaigns
that keep the educational needs of children in emerging markets alive
in the minds of employees. These campaigns seek to sustain interest for the initiative at the highest possible levels. While events and
campaigns aim to capture attention and raise interest, it needs to be
acknowledged that CR is not the only initiative the CSR department
needs to support. In other words, Step 5 is largely about how to create
synergies between unrelated events.

Conclusions: key considerations for strategy

The focus of this chapter has been on the preparatory aspects of
embedding CS and business responsibility. Without the strategic management of knowledge creation in the preparatory stages, implementation will be fraught with difficulties and will face challenges familiar
from mainstream initiatives for strategic change management, with
some potentially facing a 50–70% failure rate.[81] Getting the preparatory aspects of embedding CS right makes implementation easier, so
much so that it can turn into a strategic asset that adds value and
expands capability.

The pioneers and leaders in CS and strategic issues management
are making some more noticeable value gains by embedding CS issues
into their strategic management and operational management activities. Doing so helps to move from positions of irresponsible competitiveness and poor performance because of responsible non-advantage
activities towards responsible competitive advantage.

3
Philosopher, poet, trickster
New role models for corporately responsible leaders

Donna Ladkin
Professor of Leadership and Ethics

Tony Juniper (Friends of the Earth) was quoted in an Economist Intelligence Unit report in 2008 saying that 'senior management or chief executive buy-in to the agenda is absolutely crucial' for organisations to really adopt and embed responsible ways of being.[82] Senior leadership is critical, but anecdotal evidence suggests that many companies lack clear leadership on sustainability. Instead of rehearsing traditional views about the kind of leadership needed, this chapter offers alternative ways of understanding the leadership task. Rather than invoking the more usual leader archetypes of 'hero', 'warrior' or 'knight in shining armour', here 'philosopher', 'poet' and 'trickster' archetypes are introduced for the kind of traction they might offer leaders attempting to mobilise their organisations towards greater levels of sustainability. These archetypes provide a number of possibilities not offered by more traditional accounts:

In order to resolve issues concerned with the very nature of what it is to be a 'responsible organisation' itself, leaders must adopt the **philosopher's** skill of asking questions concerning identity. Just what is a corporately sustainable organisation? What would my organisation look like if it were operating from principles of corporate sustainability (CS)?

Second, this chapter suggests that the **poet** archetype might be invoked in leaders hoping to connect at an emotional level with followers they would hope to influence. Leading organisations towards greater levels of sustainable management is not a value held by everyone in the organisation. Skills used by poets—the ability to connect with people's hearts as well as their heads while evoking visceral as well as logical understanding—might be useful to leaders trying to encourage followers to embrace a 'sustainable' vision for their organisations.

Finally, I propose that leading in a way that encourages and nourishes corporately sustainable organisational cultures is fundamentally a disruptive endeavour, akin to the actions of the **trickster**. Mythologically, 'trickster' archetypes work at the boundaries of communities, often negotiating between the realm of the gods and that of earthbound creatures. They use surprise, humour and the unexpected—to 'wake people up' to different realities and interpretations. Similarly, this chapter contends that trickster-type disruption can alert organisations to the generative possibilities of operating in sustainable ways, even as it destroys old mind-sets and habits.

In other words, leading for CS requires the balancing of paradoxical capabilities—connecting with others even as the leader challenges them to reconsider their ways of viewing reality. More importantly, it requires the leader to define the very purposes the corporately sustainable organisation sets out to achieve—and to facilitate the operationalisation of those purposes within their particular context. Before examining these capacities and the archetypes that might inform them, let's look more closely at the features of CS itself to consider why it might require such abilities.

Features of the corporate responsibility domain

In suggesting ways in which leading for CS might be accomplished, let us start by identifying key aspects of this terrain. Three characteristics of leading for corporate sustainability are immediately apparent:

First, the very definition of corporate responsibility itself is not agreed on. There are as many different interpretations and aims of CS as there are organisations trying to enact it in their context. This means the first step for any leader trying to create a 'sustainable organisation' involves deciding what that means for the organisation in its specific context. Furthermore, the initial goals set will need to be revisited as the organisation and the context within which it operates evolve. This requires leaders to literally define and redefine what they mean by CS as they go along.

Second, enacting CS often requires the engagement of organisational members' values and their buy-in to the organisation's responsibility agenda. Not everyone may necessarily agree with the need for or the interpretation of corporately sustainable behaviour. If it is seen as surplus to the core demands of their job, organisational members' involvement may be realised in no more than lip-service. Engaging followers is always a key leadership task; within the arena of CS, that challenge is made even more difficult by the contested relevance of the very notion itself and the fact that so much ambiguity can surround its meaning.

Finally, even once organisational members are engaged, shifting habits and practices can be a daunting task. The difficulties of moving from awareness of a problem to acting on it in a constructive way have long been noted. Behaviours often change only as a result of significant disruption or crises. Leaders wanting to shift their organisations into more sustainable patterns of behaviour need to find ways of generating disruption, even while they seek to contain the day-to-day operations of the organisation that make it a viable entity.

These aspects make leading with the purpose of achieving CS very challenging. The very goals aimed for need to be clearly defined as they will necessarily be contested and may be of marginal interest to organisational members. Furthermore, getting people to shift deep-seated behavioural habits may threaten the organisation's existing ways of maintaining its day-to-day operations. Succeeding within this arena requires additional capabilities to those more traditionally found as part of the leader toolkit. Let us consider what philosophers, poets and tricksters might offer leaders attempting to negotiate this terrain effectively.

Philosopher

> To teach how to live with uncertainty, yet without being paralysed by hesitation, is perhaps the chief thing that philosophy . . . can do (Bertrand Russell).[83]

Although philosophers and philosophies differ wildly in their approaches and views, the underlying skill that underpins philosophical work is the ability to question deeply about the nature of things and to reflect on their significance. The philosopher thrives on questioning, analysing and negotiating meaning worlds. What better skills to bring to an area that is hard to define and agree on? Additionally, the philosopher rarely settles for a 'once and for all' truth, and learns to be comfortable with allowing his or her understanding to be continually updated and developed.

The leadership scholar Keith Grint has already noted the importance the philosophical arts have for leaders operating more generally.[84] Grint suggests that the art of asking questions about 'who we are' as an organisation is an important function of the leader role. This ability is critical within the arena of CS, where there are no preset answers or agreed rules for what CS actually is. In order for this sense-making to be viable, it must be coherent; it must be driven by the reality of the organisation as it is as well as the environment in which it operates. When there are large disconnections between the goals an organisation holds and the very nature of its business, at the very least this will be met by scepticism on the part of customers and other external stakeholders. Witness, for instance, the sceptical way in which oil companies' attempts to be more corporately sustainable have been met by stakeholders.[85]

Following from this, one of the most important skills involved in leading for CS is to define what acting responsibly for a given organisation actually *means*, and how such meanings can be translated into organisational practices. Even the idea of balancing a firm's triple bottom line has to be operationalised in some way.[86] Each organisation needs to decide for itself the particular trade-offs between financial, ecological and social priorities it is willing to make. Organisational leaders are frequently called on to resolve clashes arising from the inevitable tensions caused by trying to balance financial, ecological and social targets.

The philosopher poses the questions 'Who are we?' and 'What does it mean for us to be acting in a corporately sustainable way?' The next step for the leader is to show their followers the answers to those questions. Doing so effectively might be aided through using the skills of the poet.

Poet

> I credit poetry, both for being itself, and for making possible a fluid and restorative relationship between the mind's centre and its circumference (Seamus Heaney).[87]

Heaney's quote speaks to a fundamental function of poetry and poets—their ability to connect. Poets juxtapose seemingly incongruent ideas in order to make new ways of thinking possible. Through their acute perception they notice details and nuances that enable us to connect with difference—whether that difference is embodied by other people or other perspectives. One of the features of poetic ways of working that enables this to happen is that it utilises non-linear forms. Poetry engages metaphor and simile to sidestep what is 'real' and makes us aware of what is 'possible'. For instance, consider this poem by Wendell Barry:

> The dust motes float
> and swerve in the sunbeam,
> as lively as worlds,
> and I remember my brother
> when we were boys:
> 'We may be living on an atom
> in somebody's wallpaper.'
> ('Dust', 2005)[88]

In a mere seven lines our attention moves from the mundane reality of dust motes to a complete and surprising change in perspective. Suddenly, our accepted reality is called into question, and other possibilities for interpreting experience arise. Poetry accomplishes this shift easily, without exhortation or direct influence. Instead, through common imagery (who has not at some point in their lives watched dust motes suddenly visible because of slanting sunlight?) our fixed position alters, our minds are open to new understandings.

Such a shift is also accomplished through an atmospheric quality. The understanding that is reached carries with it an embodied, kinaesthetic dimension that is not easily explained but is nonetheless powerful in its effect.

How could such sensibilities be used in the context of leading for CS? A key challenge for organisational leaders in this arena is to connect with the meanings and values of those they are trying to influence and lead. This may not always be best accomplished through direct logical arguments. Values are deeply held aspects of individuals' identities, not prone to being swayed by objective accounts. They do not often shift just by leaders admonishing them to do so. Leaders may have greater success by adopting more poetic means.

I am not suggesting that leaders wanting to influence their organisations should go around reciting Keats to their followers (although that may not be a bad idea!). Instead, I am suggesting that leaders may benefit from considering 'poetic approaches' to influencing others. Poetic approaches 'wake people up' to really 'see' what might be going on. For instance, McVea and Freeman tell the following story of Walmart's attempt to become more socially responsible.[89] During an away-day event, while charting 'stakeholder maps' photographs of the children working in sweatshops to produce Walmart's famously cheap clothing were introduced. The leader of the event encouraged the top team to place these photographs of the children in the centre of their maps, and then see how that encouraged them to think about their priorities. This intervention was a 'poetic' one, I would suggest, in its use of non-linear logic in bringing people's attention to the impact of the company's strategy on other human beings. It did it without 'telling', but instead by 'showing'.

By showing rather than telling, poetic interventions connect people's affective ways of knowing with their intellectual ways of knowing. I think this is what Heaney is getting at in the quote that opened this section when he refers to poetry's ability to restore the relationship between the mind's centre and its circumference. Poetry fosters a connection between something that may be deeply held knowledge with what is going on at a more obvious level of reality. In making this connection clear, the poet addresses the question of 'why' an organisation might strive to operate in more sustainable ways.

The example from Walmart above also demonstrates something of the final archetype I would like to introduce: the trickster.

Trickster

> Trickster is at one and the same time creator and destroyer, giver and negator, he who dupes others and who is always duped himself ... He knows neither good nor evil yet he is responsible for both. He possesses no values, moral or social ... yet through his actions all values come into being' (Paul Radin).[90]

The trickster is known as the 'Great Awakener' in Native American mythological traditions. This archetype creates disruption and chaos, even as it offers the possibility of creativity. Similarly, leading for CS is at its heart a disruptive pursuit in that it calls into question taken-for-granted assumptions about the overriding need for short-term profits and quick returns. It challenges long-held assumptions that shareholders' desires should always trump stakeholders' needs. Although it may not always go against received wisdom about a firm's purposes and means of achieving those purposes, it always calls them into question.

In his book, *Change the World: How Ordinary People Can Create Extra-ordinary Results*, Robert Quinn highlights the power of disruption as a force for positive change.[91] Bringing people face to face with the consequences of their actions can be a powerful way of waking people up. Such disruption does not have to have a negative feel. Barry and Meisiek recount a wonderful story of a CEO of a failing manufacturing company in Germany who demanded that the entire factory be painted white, thus transforming what had become a dark and depressing place in which to work into a bright and sparkling space.[92] This leader enacted his interpretation of CS by attending to the aesthetic needs of his workforce (and he was rewarded with improved performance).

The important point here is that the trickster archetype provides us with alternative approaches to influencing change that do not rely on measurement, ten-point plans and Gantt charts. The trickster comes up with ways of waking people up to their senses, to something that is real, here and now, and through that contact enables people's innate creativity to respond—not just their creativity but their hearts. The trickster can stir up a whole-bodied response, because he or she wakes us up out of our habitual ways of seeing and reacting to the world.

The trickster answers the question 'How should we do this?' by disruption, by waking people up, by bringing people to their 'senses'.

Leading for corporate sustainability

Here, we have explored three perhaps unlikely archetypes that might inform corporately sustainable leadership. Informed by the philosopher archetype, such leaders would engage the skills of encouraging collective inquiry into how the organisation might best respond to the changing context. Philosophical skills are particularly important for framing the way in which organisational members might make sense of a change towards more sustainable practices, thereby more adequately setting the scene for further action. Leaders wishing to enact the philosopher archetype might seek to understand existing ways of understanding concepts such as 'responsibility' and 'sustainability' and the ways in which organisational members are already enacting them. One organisational leader who put philosopher skills into practice in her organisation established enquiry groups in which people from a cross-section of the organisation discussed what sustainability meant to them. Remarking on the process, this leader reflected,

> When we first began the journey to embedding more sustainable practices, we thought it was about having recycling bins around the place and using less electricity. It was only when we began to talk about what really mattered to us, as parents, neighbours and friends, that we really began to see the changes we could collectively make.

Borrowing from poetic role models, such leaders would actively seek creative ways of connecting the deeply held values of the organisation and its current reality to salient aspects of the emerging environment. Poetic skills are crucial in helping people to make connections between their experience and the changing context, and to better understand their roles within that context. Adnams, the family brewery in East Anglia, provides an excellent example of a CEO who has engaged 'poetic' skills to encourage his workforce to embed sustainable working practices in their organisation. Initiatives taken by workers from all levels of the organisation have included offering customers locally produced blankets to wrap up in when sitting outdoors, rather than using heat lamps. By connecting closely to the particular context and history of the organisation, Adnams has been able to introduce innovative practices that are aligned to the specificity of their seaside location and genealogy. In this way, not only has the company introduced and embedded more sustainable practices, but it also resonates with an authenticity that suggests these changes are truly built in, rather than bolted on.

Finally, like the trickster, such leaders would experiment with disruption as a way of waking up individuals within their organisations to the reality of their impact on a wide net of both seen and unseen stakeholders. Such disruption is key to stimulating change by disturbing old patterns or behaviour and making apparent the need for new ways of operating. A wonderful example of the way in which 'disruption' can be used to bring about greater appreciation of the impact organisational decisions have on often silent stakeholders is to produce photos of the actual workers, community members or others affected. This has the effect of increasing moral intensity, and as such can at least cause decisions to be revisited and re-evaluated in the light of increased insight into the impact of those decisions.

Table 3.1 depicts the relationship between different archetypes and the strengths they bring to different phases of the process of embedding more responsible, sustainable ways of operating.

Finally, these archetypes offer the possibility that individuals do not have to occupy the top of organisational hierarchies in order to make 'leaderly' impact. The power of philosophers, poets and tricksters can be felt from wherever they are located within organisational structures. Asking good questions, using poetic means of connecting with others and instigating generative disruption have long been exercised by those in positions of less power to influence and subvert organisational momentum. Similarly, they can be potent means by which those occupying more junior organisational ranks might exercise leadership, resulting in new levels of corporately sustainable ways of operating. Wherever people are located in their organisational hierarchies, whether in the middle and enacting leadership informally, or from the top where leading is an expected part of the role, these archetypes provide new insights into how individuals might find novel ways of creating responsible, sustainable organisations.

Table 3.1 **Aligning leader archetypes with phases of CS**

	Setting the scene	Linking with the context	Stimulating the change
Philosopher	X		
Poet		X	
Trickster			X

4

Embedding the governance of responsibility in the business of the board

Andrew Kakabadse
Professor of International Management Development

David Grayson
Professor of Corporate Responsibility

> Corporate governance is concerned with holding the balance between economic and social goals and between individual and communal goals. The governance framework is there to encourage the efficient use of resources and equally to require accountability for the stewardship of those resources. The aim is to align as nearly as possible the interests of individuals, corporations and society (Sir Adrian Cadbury, Chair of the UK Commission on Corporate Governance, 1992).[93]

A series of corporate scandals, blue-ribbon commissions, stock exchange listings' requirements and legislation have combined to make corporate governance more important over the last couple of decades. Effective corporate governance is a critical aspect of what it is to be a responsible business: 'the responsibility of governance'; but nowadays it is also becoming more widely recognised that boards have to be fully engaged in the governance of responsibility: in overseeing a company's commitment to sustainability. Indeed, we would argue that if boards are doing their job properly (setting strategy, checking on progress and holding executives to account for their performance), sustainability cannot be fully embedded in a company *unless* the board has ensured that it is integrated into overall purpose and strategy; and unless the board is ensuring effective oversight that this is being implemented. Thus, boards need to be paying increasing attention to the environmental, social and governance (ESG) performance of their firms. Climate change, water shortages, resource depletion and human rights abuses could all affect the value of businesses. Research published in 2009 by three leading international business schools—Bocconi, Cranfield and Vlerick on behalf of the Academy for Business in Society (EABIS)—showed how ESG can affect each of the classic drivers of business value.[94] Embedding sustainability within core business strategy is not just good for the planet, but also good for businesses.

The role of the board in corporate sustainability

Good corporate governance suggests that the role of the board is to set the strategic direction of the company, check on progress, hold management to account for their performance against the strategy, appoint and if necessary remove the CEO, ensure effective succession-planning, and be the guardians of the corporate values—for 'the way we do business around here'.

The veteran corporate accountability campaigner Allen White has written:

> In the dynamic world of corporate social responsibility
> (CSR), remarkably little attention has been focused on
> the role of corporate boards. This is at once unfortunate,
> unsurprising and unacceptable: unfortunate because the
> board is the supreme governing entity of the corporation
> and should be a major actor in shaping the firm's CSR strat-
> egy; unsurprising because the board, by virtue of law and
> tradition, perceives its role in CSR to be either negligible
> or contradictory to its mandate; and unacceptable because
> the board, the ultimate steward of the well-being and per-
> formance of the organization, cannot afford to be a passive
> bystander in shaping the organization's CSR strategy.[95]

Yet White has elsewhere said, when addressing the USA Global Compact network: 'Boards must recognize that a company's long-term
wealth comes from a range of capital providers, including human
capital, natural capital and social capital.'

In 2008 a survey of 1,040 directors of US companies found that
39% of respondents expected that the board would spend more
time on sustainability issues during the current year than in the past.
Similarly, in their 2010 survey of global CEOs for the UN Global
Compact (UNGC), Accenture found that 93% of CEOs agreed that
boards need to discuss and act on sustainability issues (up from 69%
in a similar survey in 2007); and 75% of CEOs said that their own
company's board does discuss and act on sustainability issues as part
of its agenda (up from 45% in 2007). The Economist Intelligence
Unit (EIU) says that globally 26% of companies locate responsibility
for sustainability performance with the board.[96]

The UNGC's 2010 annual survey of signatory companies found
that 39% of the 1,300 companies responding to the survey have
boards that 'routinely address corporate sustainability issues' with
the mechanism used by companies varying widely. Research by Cranfield's Doughty Centre for Corporate Responsibility, using data from
Business in the Community's annual Corporate Responsibility Index,
revealed positive signs that more large companies are starting to do
this.[97]

How a board addresses sustainability will depend on its and, therefore, the company's, stage of corporate responsibility maturity (see Ch. 1, Fig. 1.2). Stage 1 boards or companies ('deniers') will not deal with sustainability; Stage 2 boards ('compliers'), if they tackle sustainability at all, will do so spasmodically and from a risk perspective; Stage 3 boards ('risk mitigators') may have a lead non-executive director (NED) or even a board committee and may be linking sustainability performance to the corporate risk register etc.; Stage 4 boards ('opportunity maximisers') will have linked to strategy and new business/value-enhancement and will have effective governance of risks and opportunities; and at Stage 5 ('champions') the company will also be getting regular stakeholder feedback, engaging in collaborations with other organisations and sharing its experiences and learning.

Board structures

Formal board oversight can take different forms: an NED for sustainability; a formal board committee; extending the remit of an existing board committee such as Audit and Risk to include ESG; reserved for regular and substantive discussion by the full board; a hybrid board–executive committee, typically chaired by the CEO; or a committee immediately below the board and reporting to it. See Table 4.1 for examples.

There are potential advantages and disadvantages associated with each model. We suspect there is no particular model that is preferable, and that what is more important is the degree of CR commitment and maturity of the company, and whether the CR governance model chosen fits within the corporate culture and practice (see Table 4.2).

Table 4.1 FTSE 100 models of board oversight of sustainability

Structure	Examples from FTSE 100
Dedicated board CR (or sustainability or similar) committee	Aviva, BAE, Barclays, BHP Billiton, BT, Legal & General
CR is part of extended remit of existing board committee such as Audit and risk or Reputation	Admiral, GKN, National Grid
CR is reserved to main board	Anglian Water, Ashmore, Hargreaves Lansdown, Kingfisher
Lead NED for CR/sustainability with or without non-board executive committee	Astra Zeneca, Bunzl, Lloyds Banking Group, Rexam
Mixed CR committee of NED and non-board executives	Anglo-American, Eurasian, GSK, Reed Elsevier
Executive CR committee reporting to board through chair, CEO or lead NED	British Land, Capita, GKN, Experian

Table 4.2 Potential advantages and disadvantages of different models of governance of corporate responsibility

Structure	Potential advantages	Potential disadvantages
Organisation makes no provision for CR	If ESG impacts are genuinely considered in each board discussion it can improve decision-making	Given ESG risks and unexploited opportunities most companies face, having no specific structure at this stage of CR maturity may be short-sighted and problematic

Structure	Potential advantages	Potential disadvantages
Dedicated board CR (or sustainability or similar) committee	Sends clear signals internally and externally about seriousness with which company treats subject	Risks reinforcing silo mentality
CR is part of extended remit of existing board committee such as Audit and Risk or Reputation	Ensures greater likelihood of joined-up strategy and implementation	CR may struggle for attention within a well-established committee with a well-established annual work agenda
CR is reserved to main board	If board experienced and properly trained in CR and sustainability, and consciously consider CR and sustainability dimensions of every discussion, ensures holistic approach	If board not experienced and trained, may not surface ESG issues sufficiently or at all
Lead NED for CR/ sustainability	Offers a focal point for CR/ sustainability on board	But depends on authority and credibility of that individual and how well supported by executive
Mixed CR committee of NED and non-board executives	Effective link between strategy and implementation	May confuse roles between non-executive and executive functions
Executive CR committee reporting to board through chair, CEO or lead NED	Ensures operational awareness	May mean board divorced from issues

According to the UNGC, the three models that are encountered most frequently among their signatory member companies are: (1) tasking the entire board with oversight, (2) creating new committees dedicated exclusively to sustainability, and (3) using existing committees that assume responsibility for sustainability as one aspect of their activities.

In a discussion paper prepared by the business-led CR coalition Business for Social Responsibility for the UNGC's LEAD Network, the authors say:

> While the numbers of large companies resting responsibility for oversight of sustainability continue to grow, there is no current consensus about the best model to apply. In a 2009 survey by Deloitte of 220 directors of American companies with over $1billion in revenues, 37% of respondents thought that some committee should have oversight responsibility of sustainability. When asked which committee should have oversight, Risk and Governance committees were each chosen by 24% of respondents, 22% chose the Strategy committee, and 15% chose the audit committee. For those companies preferring existing committees, similar numbers expressed support for risk, governance and strategy committees. These figures suggest that thinking continues to evolve, and that the future may deliver not a single model, but rather a range of options for companies.[98]

Whatever structure is favoured, a commitment to corporate sustainability creates an added dimension for boards—embedding sustainability within overall strategy, overseeing specific sustainability initiatives and approving major sustainability public commitments—and, therefore, for existing board committees.

Audit and risk committee. How will regular work to keep the corporate risk register up to date adapt to the need for a more comprehensive definition of material future risks to the company, which embraces environmental, social and economic impacts?

Remuneration committee. How will the performance of senior executives on sustainability be appraised, what key performance indicators will be used and how will this long-term performance be reflected in executive compensation, including bonuses?

Nominations committee. How will understanding of how sustainability affects the future of the business be reflected in the generic and specific skills matrix and, therefore, in the mandate to headhunters and the criteria for appointment of new board members?

Strategy/business development committee. How does commitment to sustainability change overall corporate strategy and the relative attractiveness of different business projects?

Investment committee (or equivalent where it exists). How will sustainability factors be incorporated in all corporate investment criteria, and how will specific sustainability investment proposals be appraised? Will this be to the same or enhanced evaluation?

In practice, we suspect that in the longer term the particular board structure is less important than the mind-set with which the board approaches sustainability. In the short to medium term, there is probably value both in a board committee (whether extending the remit of one of the existing committees or a separate sustainability committee) *and* regular discussion in the full board. As the *Moving Upwards* report quotes:

- The breadth of challenges requires both means of oversight.
- Where there is no full Board oversight, several things fail to happen:
  a) Sustainability issues are not addressed in annual meetings and annual reports
  b) No criteria or performance measures are set
  c) Issues and goals are not embedded in Board calendars with incentives.
- At the same time, sustainability subcommittees of the Board can be effective because they will meet and

> deliberate for longer periods of time, and then distill
> information for the full board.[99]

We share this view and that of Aron Cramer, CEO of BSR, 'Ideally, dedicated board committees would be seen as redundant in a decade's time . . . but they might be needed now to catalyze the transition.'[100]

A number of companies supplement this with formal stakeholder-engagement mechanisms—including in some cases, a stakeholder or external sustainability experts panel to advise the board or the CEO.[101] These may be stakeholder advisory boards or panels (SABs) consisting solely of external stakeholders or joint management–stakeholder committees (JMSCs), that is, formal bodies that consist of a number of company representatives as well as internal/external stakeholders that meet regularly.

An analysis of the submissions made by 51 companies that completed the Business in the Community Corporate Responsibility Index every year between 2002 and 2007 shows a steady growth in the use of JMSCs.[102]

While the experience of this sub-group is over too short a timeframe to enable definitive conclusions, the development of JMSCs suggests that for some companies this may become a more important instrument of stakeholder governance. The use of JMSCs leads primarily to alterations of measurement, monitoring, policy development and reporting.

BSR and the UN Global Compact also say that the use of external advisory panels is growing and argue that:

> while they do not qualify as formal governance mechanisms,
> they represent an interesting innovation that in effect create
> a 'soft governance' model in cases where they serve in an
> advisory role and/or provide a public oversight mechanism.
> These panels are generally comprised of experts either on
> sustainability in general, or on specific topics of particular
> interest to a company, such as health, nutrition, renewable
> energy, etc. Where such bodies are established with a direct
> line to company Boards, they augment formal governance
> processes, and provide a direct means through which Boards

can implement their mandate to consider stakeholder opinions about sustainability performance and strategy. Over the coming decade, it is possible that this mechanism will develop further, with some companies experimenting with a further melding of the 'soft governance' of external panels with the 'hard governance' undertaken by the formal Board of Directors.[103]

As Ruth Bender writes in Chapter 12, companies are increasingly issuing specific sustainability or CR reports. As the topics these reports cover are becoming more material to long-term business success, and especially with moves towards **integrated reporting**, where companies issue a single report integrating sustainability within the overall company report, boards will be expected to pay more attention to the contents of these reports, and to sign off on them.

Board composition

Important as these corporate governance innovations are, their impact on corporate behaviour will be limited without further action. Nominations committees of boards need to be more proactive in requiring basic knowledge and experience of ESG performance as a specification for all new board members and ensuring that in-depth sustainability knowledge is included in the essential skills matrix among the board members as a whole. Headhunters asked to find new board members should be screening for sustainability awareness. Our initial suggestions as to generic and specific NED sustainability skills are summarised in Box 4.1.

Box 4.1 NED recruitment: CR and sustainability as part of skills/experiences requirement

Generic skills all board members should have

- Basic awareness of sustainable development and how it affects the organisation
- Basic understanding of what corporate sustainability and responsibility are
- Ability to identify at a high level the most material ESG impacts of the organisation
- Understanding of how poor ESG performance can create reputational and other risks and conversely how good performance can add value
- Ability to articulate how corporate sustainability and responsibility relates to the purpose and strategy of the organisation
- Understanding of sustainable development/CR trends generally and as they affect the industry, and their impact on the company
- Understanding of the company's business case for sustainability
- Ability to hold executive to account for delivery of company's CR and sustainability strategy

Specialist skills within the board skills matrix

Among directors, there should be at least one director with the following skills or experience:

- Understanding of how organisations seek to embed corporate sustainability and responsibility
- Familiarity with some of the main organisations and individuals working in the corporate sustainability and responsibility field

➔

- Understanding of public commitments on corporate sustainability and responsibility and how to design appropriate public commitments for the organisation
- Experience of board oversight of corporate sustainability and responsibility and how to monitor implementation, measure and report
- Ability to fulfil a mandate to follow through and intervene to ensure implementation of strategy as agreed by the board
- Ability to make good use of stakeholder advice in order to advise the board

Legislation or the threat of legislation, stakeholder pressures and governance pressures have combined in recent years in many jurisdictions, and especially across Europe, to raise questions about board diversity. Gender diversity is one aspect, but it is best seen as part of a much broader issue of ensuring board diversity of views, experiences and backgrounds in which an understanding of how previously 'soft issues' such as the environment, human rights, health and well-being have become 'hard issues' for business and need to be handled as such. Some have suggested the introduction of 'stakeholder directors' for this purpose. This is not something we would favour. All directors should be concerned with the long-term interests of the company and not the immediate interests of one stakeholder group to the potential detriment of the overall organisation.

Board induction, training and continuous professional development

Sustainability and what it means for the board must be part of induction, and continuous professional development (not tokenistic, lip-service) should be provided for board members on corporate sustainability. Handling sustainability issues should be part of the regular appraisals of board effectiveness that good governance generally requires chairs and directors to do at least annually (for assessment of the effectiveness of both individual directors and the collective board). A series of searching, open questions, such as the Arcturus questionnaire[104] developed by the Caux Round Table specifically for NEDs to discuss their perceptions of risks and opportunities for the company, can provide a structured process for identifying business-critical issues.

Sustainability should be included substantively within accredited director training programmes such as those of the National Association of Corporate Directors and the International Corporate Governance Network in the USA, and the Institute of Directors in the UK. In addition, certain business schools, such as Cranfield, provide training and development for newly appointed and experienced NEDs and sustainability and responsibility need to be more thoroughly covered in such programmes.

Developing board capacity

An important prerequisite to secure institutional involvement of boards in the sustainability agenda of the company is upgrading reporting mechanisms to 'capture materiality', that is, the tangible impact of the company's social and environmental commitments on financial and economic performance. Unless the company produces metrics and material evidence on non-financial aspects of performance, the board will not have a solid base to incorporate those concerns into its risk assessment or performance oversight. 'Plainly said, if there is no report to the Board on the financial aspects of non-financial concerns, Boards will not have much to think about.'[105]

Boards need to incorporate sustainability into their regular assessments of risk; but they should also be pushing hard for evidence of how it is being factored into new business development and innovation. They need to revisit what the principles are on which they aspire to do business, and what they expect from their employees and agents in terms of business behaviour.

However, above all else, the governance of responsibility needs to be neatly positioned as an integral part of the business of the board. Easy to recommend but, as other, new research from Cranfield School of Management highlights, this is not too easy to implement. A series of international surveys of over 3,000 board directors has identified NEDs as 'out of touch'.[106] For example, 85% of British NEDs have not been able to clearly state what the role, purpose and value of their colleagues on the board is. Equally, in the same surveys on each and every measure of board performance the full-time managers who sit on boards down rate their NED colleagues by some 40%. In effect, the managers who run the business find it difficult to identify what value the NEDs on the board provide.[107] Dominic Barton, Managing Director of McKinsey and Co. argues in the March 2011 edition of the *Harvard Business Review* that 'only 43% of the nonexecutive directors of public companies believe they significantly influence strategy'.[108] It is therefore of paramount importance to attend to the leadership of the board. The message from research is that little is accomplished until the board operates as a high-performing team, drawing together the capabilities of all board members. Unfortunately, approximately 20% of boards emerge as operating as fully functional entities.

The following checklist may serve as an aide-memoire for non-executive directors wishing to function effectively:

- Have we made a public commitment to sustainability and if so, what is this?

- Is this linked to business purpose and strategy?

- Is sustainability embedded within corporate values?

- Are senior executives committed to sustainability, and comfortable and credible in leading on that commitment?

- Do we have effective board oversight of sustainability?

- Does the company recruit, induct, train, appraise, reward, promote and take difficult decisions using the corporate values?

- Does the risk register incorporate risks and opportunities associated with social and environmental and economic impacts?

- Does the board regularly assess the company's environmental and economic impacts?

- Does the company have a process regularly to review emerging sustainability issues and surface them at board level?

- When did the board last have an open forward discussion about responsible business and sustainability issues and the implications for its business?

- Does the company have clear targets on sustainability and is it clear who has direct accountability for each target?

- Is board discussion of sustainability already aligned with board discussion of its annual business performance review?

- When did the board last discuss the company's talent development strategy, and is capacity to understand and deliver on responsible business and sustainability an integral part of that strategy?

- Does the company publish a responsible business and sustainability report? If so, did a board member as well as the CEO or Chair sign it off?

- Does understanding of responsible business and sustainability figure on the list of desired skills or areas of expertise for one or more of the NEDs?

The global financial crisis has stimulated various initiatives to improve corporate governance—particularly for banks but also for companies generally. We should get in front of the gathering 'global sustainability crisis' and check not just for the responsibility of governance—but also for the *governance of* responsibility. In other words, boards of companies need to take more direct responsibility for the governance of sustainability performance.

Ordinary savers who ultimately own companies through their pensions, life insurance and other savings, and other stakeholders whose activities are impacted on by the activities of corporations, should be demanding nothing less. They should therefore ensure that their agents—the fund managers and the institutional investors—check companies' performance on their behalf as to whether the governance of sustainability is embedded in the responsibility of the boards. This should now be treated as an essential part of active stewardship.

5

Strategic business performance for sustainability

Mike Bourne
Professor of Business Performance

Pippa Bourne
Regional Director, Institute of Chartered Accountants in England and Wales

David Ferguson
Visiting Fellow, Doughty Centre for Corporate Responsibility

A company's value and continuous performance cannot be effectively determined using established financial performance evaluations alone. Financial measures, for example, do not necessarily help identify key areas for improvement, do not always capture the true contribution of intangible assets, can in fact encourage poor management decisions, and can fail to really inform longer-term strategic goals.[109] Since the mid-1990s understanding and measuring non-financial performance have become much more mainstreamed, moving from a peripheral operational zone to serving as key performance indicators (KPIs).

Now these KPIs are being incorporated into strategic business performance assessments and are impacting on executive-level decision-making and performance reviews.[110] In addition, these KPIs are also impacting on investor relations, communications and the investment community's analytical assessments for clients.[111]

Corporate sustainability is clearly a strategic issue for leading companies and the measurement of non-financial business performance (the KPIs) can be an effective way of understanding the contribution that sustainability makes to business performance.[112] We believe there is a distinct link between corporate sustainability and good management;[113] taking a socially responsible position can be achieved without a negative effect on profitability and indeed among FTSE 350 companies it has proved to have a positive effect on performance in the longer term and when recovering from external shocks.[114] Therefore, such an approach—if used, for example, as an innovation—can enhance the company's strategic performance by differentiating the company from its competitors.[115]

This chapter provides an overview of tools for measuring sustainability business performance and demonstrates, using examples, how these tools are being used and can be developed within your company.

Realising sustainability as a strategic performance issue

Sustainability is the major issue for society and business today. Sustainability issues significantly impact on the current and future performance of a business, and therefore must be imported into the business objective, strategy and performance. If we use climate change as an example: 'Climate change and its potential impact on key sectors of the economy, such as agriculture, tourism, energy, transport and insurance, are dangers of the same order as the currency or interest rate risk' (Henri de Castries, Chief Executive, AXA).[116]

Around five years ago, the resistance to climate change started to diminish and be replaced by a growing realisation that a low-carbon economy is now a strategic performance transformational imperative for almost all business sectors. A McKinsey survey in 2007 revealed that 60% of the 2,192 executives who responded now view climate change as an important consideration within their company's overall strategy.[117] In the same year, Sir Terry Leahy, Chief Executive of Tesco, wrote:

> Scientists say with ever-increasing clarity that, if we fail to secure radical cuts in greenhouse gas emissions, the consequences for all of us could be severe. For each one of us this poses a challenge. I am determined that Tesco should meet this challenge by being a leader in helping to create a low-carbon economy.[118]

In their efforts to move from stated intent towards measurable performance Tesco (for example) joined an industry coalition to pioneer and launch a new Guideline Daily Allowance (GDA) food-labelling initiative,[119] and subsequently created a blueprint for future low-carbon-impact stores that have an impressive 70% lower carbon footprint than a comparable 2006 newly built facility.[120]

Embracing sustainability can help create:[121]

- A marketing imperative, especially for brand positioning

- A 'people' imperative, especially in recruitment and retention

- A financial imperative, for example with eco-efficiency

- A supplier imperative, especially in product design, new product development and supplier relationships

Developing a leadership position around sustainability is not only about risk mitigation; it is also about scanning the horizon for internal business developments, innovations and growth opportunities. According to a recent IBM survey of around 250 global company executives, 68% believe having a sustainability and corporate responsibility strategy in place gives them a competitive advantage over their peers that feeds straight into their bottom line.[122] Leading companies are seeking to capitalise on the various opportunities in their sustainability ambitions.

Quite simply, done right and with clear strategic intent, sustainability can offer a competitive edge. As such we are proposing that key sustainability dimensions should be treated like any other management issue and business development function; applying strategic business performance for sustainability should be perceived as just good management practice, another way of managing the long-term viability of the organisation.

What are KPIs?

Although KPIs (both strategic and operational) can be generic in their nature, to be effective they have to be relevant to the organisation's sector, goals and specific business environment. In effect, they have to capture the company's strategic imperatives. If they don't, the organisation will be in danger of following the KPIs and ignoring the strategy. Examples of KPIs may include:

- **Generic.** Customer satisfaction (e.g. retention/churn rates), health and safety of personnel (e.g. accidents/fatalities) and brand value and reputation (e.g. media coverage/legal issues)

- **Strategic.** Number of approved new drugs in pipeline over the next five years (pharmaceutical sector), number/type of recalls/incidents in the last three years (automotive industry), product portfolio range and market share over five years (healthcare industry), volumes of unexploited resources in new fields (oil and gas sector)

But if a company wishes to pursue a strategy of sustainability, it needs to create, implement and use KPIs that reflect this goal.

Identifying and measuring sustainable business performance

There are numerous frameworks (such as EFQM, performance prism and balanced scorecard) and publications describing approaches for performance measurement. What we propose here (Fig. 5.1) takes the essence of these approaches and adapts them to focus on sustainability. We have created a simple, iterative seven-step process through which you can build sustainability into your business as a performance-management approach, utilising the complementary tools, guidance and frameworks provided in each step.

First, however, you need to identify your business case for sustainability. Many leading companies have developed an explicit overarching strategic mission statement or aim around sustainability; this legitimises the orientation of the company around sustainability principles and supports the strategic operationalisation of activities. You need to define your mission and business case, which should be clearly linked to the business mission and strategy.

Establishing a business case is a core part of the strategic management and decision-making process; it also serves an important role within the development of KPIs. Some aspects of the sustainability business case, particularly in terms of waste reduction and energy efficiency, are more tangible and measurable; so are new asset investments that are designed to deliver cost savings. New market opportunities and R&D development/pilot projects are perhaps more challenging. These require judgement calls when considering the potential impact on market share, competitors, customers and consumers. Other business cases—such as brand development, customer retention, employee advocacy, knowledge retention and learning, improved supplier

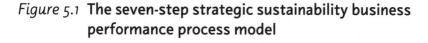

Figure 5.1 **The seven-step strategic sustainability business performance process model**

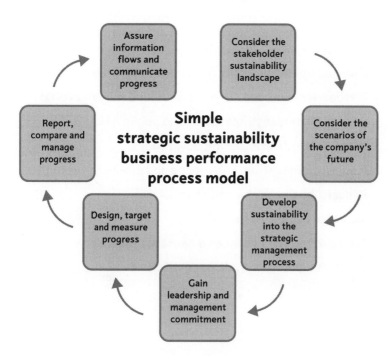

resilience and increased licence to operate—are less tangible and are sometimes more associated with providing business sense and sound business argument around business benefits than the more distinct, quantifiable and clear business case. However, leading companies already work with these value propositions within their traditional business-case justifications. See Box 5.1 as an example.

Whatever the challenges, the establishment of communicable strategic business benefits serves as a foundation for developing and establishing a workable strategic business performance approach towards sustainability and is an essential starting point for your journey through the seven-step process.

Box 5.1 **Some strategic business-case themes for sustainability**[123]

Business benefits and business cases around strategic sustainability and corporate responsibility

- *Reduced* **operating costs** from resource efficiency
- The development and *retention* of **valued human capital**
- *Improved* **company reputation** and public relations
- Brand **value differentiation** *advantages*
- *Increased* **innovation, knowledge** and product development
- *Reduced* **business risk** and financial risk
- *Increased* **access to capital**
- *Extended* business **licence to operate** timescales
- *Additional* business **trade opportunities**

The seven-step process

Step 1: Consider the stakeholders' sustainability landscape

Identify the stakeholders

Your stakeholders are those people that affect or are affected by your organisation. They include customers, employees, governments, regulators, investors, NGOs, the media and local communities. Each of these stakeholder groups will have opinions and information about the company's impact and track record on environmental, social and governance (ESG) issues. That is not to say that all opinions are correct or well informed but capturing this is an essential data-gathering process and helps you describe the sustainability landscape from the perceptions of your stakeholders.

Because each organisation has a huge range of stakeholders, it is important to identify those stakeholders that have the most significant relationship with your company, alongside those that have the most relevant issues around your company's impact and opportunities regarding the future. To capture this data you need to undertake a stakeholder mapping (to identify critical stakeholders) and consultation exercise to capture these different opinions and perceptions. As well as direct engagement, data collection from the Internet and from trade, competitors and non-trade sources serves to provide context to issues and support developing salience around different stakeholders.

Issues identification

Once you have identified the issues that relevant stakeholders have—both from their perspective (their wants and needs) and your perspective (your wants and needs)—you can prioritise the issues relevant to your organisation. The power and interest matrix is a useful mechanism to help do this[124] (see example in Fig. 5.2). Power means the actual power a stakeholder/group has over the business, and interest refers to their interest in using this power in relation to their issue.

As such, you should think about:

- Which stakeholders rely on your organisation most for their own success, such as employees, investors, suppliers and those that are most significantly affected by what you do. For companies that use significant local resources or have high concentrations of emissions for example, this might be the local community within which they operate. For those manufacturing consumer products, this would also be the end-user consumers

- Those stakeholders who are capable of affecting the business performance the most, for example, competitors or regulators

- As well as considering the most powerful and influential stakeholders, it is prudent to also consider who are pressing the most urgently and the most persistently. The fact that the issue may be urgent in itself is relevant; left unattended, it can suddenly come to a head. For example, a relatively small but issue-focused NGO may begin to engage with the media and expose or inflame an issue that has generally been ignored for a while, and this suddenly cascades into a government and regulatory issue. Shell faced this issue when it tried to dispose of an oil rig in the North Sea. So, be prepared

It is important, therefore, not only to consider the influence and impact experienced by a stakeholder, but also to be aware of the issue and the extent of the company's impact around an issue, compared to the sector or other comparably sized companies. This will give you context for the strategic relevance of the stakeholder's perspective on the landscape and your company's potential level of involvement and exposure compared with others.

Figure 5.2 **The power and interest matrix: stakeholder management model**

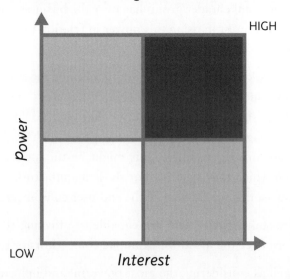

Step 2: Consider the future scenarios

Having identified your stakeholders and the key concerns, the next step is to use this information to develop and describe the potential future sustainability scenarios and their impacts and opportunities for the company. This will allow the development and scoping of organisational strategies around these issues.

There are a number of approaches to scenario building. We suggest you look at two specific time-horizons: medium-term and long-term. This will help structure your discussions and debates more effectively and give a better understanding of your planning horizons; by this we mean the time you have to respond to these changes.

Medium-term futures

Utilising your stakeholder inputs, here you should be looking at the possible sustainability impacts on and from your business in the five to ten years medium term.

- Will people want what you are selling or the service you are providing or will wants and needs change? In what way might it be different?

- Will what you are doing be more constrained legally or encompass more regulation? In what areas?

- Will what you are doing be socially and environmentally acceptable at that point in time? What may trigger this change and when?

- Will what you are doing still be the leading technology or approach? What alternatives are emerging out there now?

- What will your customers really want? (e.g. for a car manufacturer: does the customer really want to own a car or have a safe, effective and clean means of getting from A to B?) What might a consumer preference change mean?

- Is there another way of describing what you do? This will help you think about new opportunities that might be open to you. For example, you are providers of home comfort (heat and light) rather than retailers of electricity and gas. This may provide the impetus for exploring home insulation services with your extensive customer base. How might re-orientating the traditional view change the sustainability-offering proposition?

Similarly, you should also think about your stakeholder and your key inputs. How will changes in input affect your products and services? How will changes affect your future profitability?

- What are the key resources your business relies on? These include things such as raw materials, built assets, transport infrastructure, energy and fuels, as well as staff, suppliers, investors and cash

- What environmental and social issues might affect their availability, price and social acceptance in the future?

- What effect would this have on your cost base, on your company's reputation, and on your company's ability to produce quality goods or services consistently and reliably?

Long-term futures

An alternative method of scenario building is 'back-casting'. This involves taking the final scenarios, say in 50 years' time, and working backwards towards the present. This is one method adopted by The Natural Step for identifying the strategic sustainability for an individual company.[125]

For this method you take a more 'out-of-the box thinking' approach to possible scenarios that can be developed with a bearing on the company's future. Using specific issues identified from stakeholders in Step 1 (e.g. around some key themes and issues) a small group from around the company take part in a brainstorming session or workshop programme. The group blend some of the future issues and develop this into a possible scenario for the distant future. This method is potentially an easier process to understand, calling on imagination and creative thinking, free from the immediate issues and operational constraints in the company. Then, with the identified possible scenario, the group 'roll back' the years—each time adding a little more detail of the activities in and around the company—until they get almost to the present day. This is iterative; however, it tends to allow a funnelling back to the detail of the issues and context for change in the present.

We suggest that both approaches to futures identification be utilised, as each has its strengths and limitations, and together they can help avoid missing any interesting and potentially highly relevant strategic business performance dimension. These medium- and long-term futures and scenarios should be summarised and fully documented, with supporting evidence and with access to the stakeholder profiles and issues. This is vital for Step 3 of this process.

Step 3: Develop sustainability for your strategic management processes

As we explained earlier, it is vital to have developed your strategic business case around the relevant sustainability issues. The business case can now be completed using the scenario insights identified in Step 2. We recommend you use your company's preferred language and terms wherever possible and that you familiarise yourself with some relevant sustainability business-case materials[126] as it is likely you will be asked questions by your peers and superiors.

Having said that, the following key business-case guidance and tactics should be considered at all times:

- Have you ensured your plans for sustainability are totally aligned with existing organisational strategies and that some top management are involved in/debriefed on your developments?

- Could embracing sustainability within your strategy help build reputation with key stakeholder groups?

- Are there any opportunities to gain access to new markets? For example, offering a new environmentally friendly product or socially welcomed service

- Could sustainability actually provide solutions to current business problems?

- Could this be an opportunity to build on internal company competences? For example, a law firm gains extra on-the-job training for their employees by encouraging them to serve as volunteers at community-based law centres

It is essential you identify the issues that are likely to have a major impact on your business *and* have a high probability of occurring. A useful approach to identify this combination is to plot the key issues you have identified on an impact assessment matrix, as illustrated in Figure 5.3, and develop clear and detailed plans for the issues that appear in the top right-hand box called 'Action zone' as these are issues that are most likely to happen and have the highest scale of impact.

This matrix can also be utilised with management teams, not only for raising awareness and eliciting discussions, but also as a consensus-building tool around the key immediate issues. This should draw on stakeholder issues identified in Step 1 and the scenarios and futures from Step 2. At this point you should be quite clear about the strategic sustainability issues affecting your future business performance. Articulating this in a document and making this assessment clear for other managers to read and make their own assessment is essential for gaining the necessary commitment for progress.

Figure 5.3 **Impact assessment matrix**

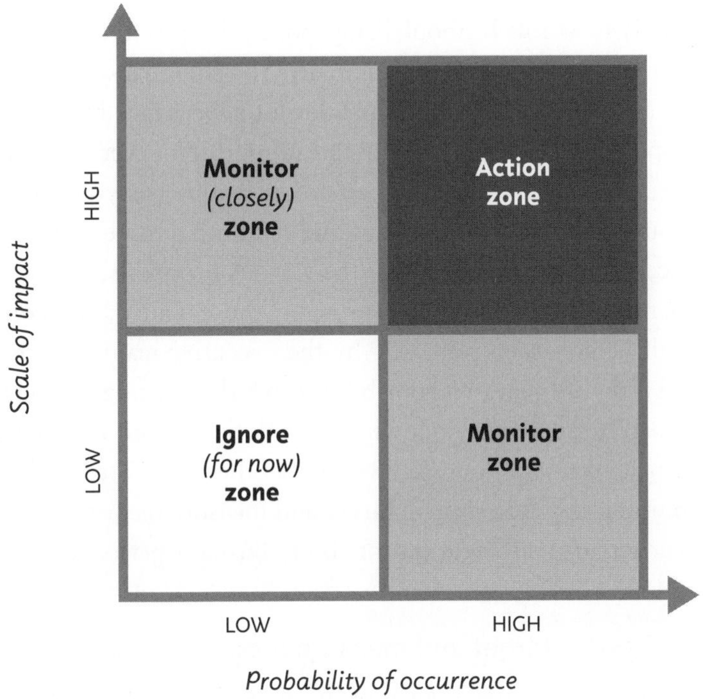

Scale of impact

HIGH

Monitor
(closely)
zone

**Action
zone**

LOW

Ignore
(for now)
zone

**Monitor
zone**

LOW   HIGH

Probability of occurrence

Step 4: Gain commitment internally

You need commitment from your colleagues for your plans to be successful. Involving a representative group of staff from your business at the outset will help, as will involving them in reviewing and commenting on the emerging aspects of each of the steps. You may also at this point decide to include again people from other stakeholder groups (such as your suppliers) who were involved in your stakeholder consultation process in Step 1, to review and comment on your final strategic planning outputs (around areas where there are no confidentiality issues).

Ideally you will have a sponsor at the senior management, if not executive, level, who can ensure this reaches, and solicits responses from, the right people in your organisation. At the very least, you should have involved those persons with responsibilities in the key areas. This is as much about being politically astute as it is about sustainability issues within the company. You should also be prepared to make brief presentations to the relevant governance bodies within the company to gain their interest and support. Not everyone is going to agree, and not everyone will come on board, but you should be endeavouring to recruit supporters and establish a route to executive-level access and exposure around the various proposals.

With respect to gaining commitment, the extent of the commitment will be governed primarily by the executive team, as it is they who have the ultimate responsibility towards enacting and managing such strategic issues. Following their decisions and recommendations to your strategy document created at the end of Step 3, the next underpinning step is to design, target and measure the progress of the agreed criteria for strategic sustainability business performance.

Step 5: Design, target and measure progress

In this step, you need to design appropriate KPIs or performance measures. Choose a few key measures that reflect what you need to achieve and that will track progress towards reaching the sustainability goals. They can be used to measure the creation and implementation of policies and procedures, as well as the management of materially important sustainability issues. Working with HR to include measures of sustainability in regular individual performance reviews will also communicate to your employees how important this is.

The KPIs for each identified strategic issue should be designed and developed to meet the following criteria:[127]

- Measurable

- Consistently measured across the company

- Collected and reviewed on a regular basis so they can feed into the management process while not being too onerous

- Limited to those that really matter, otherwise the system will become unwieldy

- Performance is compared to a baseline or starting point as a reference, therefore the starting point has to be measured

- Assured internally or externally

- Understandable and meaningful

- Expressed in terms relevant to the audience

- Connected to future performance targets

- Worthwhile—with the benefits of measuring outweighing the costs

- Able to be acted upon

- Encourage the right behaviour

- Owned by an individual or team

Additionally, considering the number of measures, the different sustainability criteria and the different personnel involved in managing and acting on the performance measures, you might like to use a performance record table for each issue to help in the design, implementation and monitoring of your measurement system.

Not only is this useful as a reference for new personnel, it also focuses minds on the important areas of detail required in its development of appropriate measures. See Figure 5.4 for what to ask and as an example.

Figure 5.4 **Performance measurement record sheet**[128]

Category	Description	Completed example
Measure	A good self-explanatory title	Waste-to-Landfill Management: Zero-Waste Reduction
Purpose	Why are we measuring this?	To avoid (escalating) landfill charges and to reduce our environmental impact on local communities regarding key operational sites
Relates to	Which strategic sustainability objective does this relate to?	New Zero Waste Initiative
Target	What specifically is to be achieved and by when?	Reduction of ALL landfill waste: 25% of 2009 baseline by 2012; 50% reduction 2015 to 2020 Zero Waste (global target)
Formula	How is this to be measured—precisely (any recognised standards)?	Absolute terms: kg as well as intensity terms (kg/total volume production) split into hazardous (controlled) and non-hazardous waste streams excluding electronic goods (covered separately under the WEE policy)
Frequency	How often is this to be measured and how often is it to be reviewed?	Measured daily, collated weekly, reported monthly
Who measures?	Who specifically collects the data and who reports on the data (to whom)?	Shift controller collects data. Site's environmental officer reports data and comments to the operations manager who reports these to the operations director
Source of data	Where exactly does the data come from? Is it an automated measure, etc.?	Data comes from the Controlled Hazardous Waste register, and from the daily (electronically weighed) collections from the waste management company
Who acts on the data?	Who is responsible for taking action around the data? Be precise	Operations manager is responsible for making recommendations around improvements, and operations director is responsible for final approval

→

Category	Description	Completed example
What do they do?	What are the general steps to be taken?	Operations director is to work with the shift managers to identify waste reductions generally, to explore process improvements, and in the case of hazardous waste to work with the environmental officer to identify suitable less hazardous alternatives. Proposals above £10,000 and less than £25,000 are to be made into project investment appraisals for the operations manager to review and submit to the operations director. Projects over this amount must go through the full project investment process via the site's operations manager and ultimately via the operations director
Notes and comments	Additional notes that are useful for anyone picking up the responsibility for elements of this performance measure. Also use to document any changes to the process etc. as document control information	Initiative launched in February 2010. Process upgrades part of general maintenance programme reduced 10% waste in extrusion and 8% in cold rolling processes. Waste management scales must be checked for calibration every 2 months. A check on monthly charge with daily collections must be completed. Shift manager's process change recommendations have brought about a further 3% waste savings and a re-granulating plant at £40,000 was approved and installed in September 2010, bringing the extrusion waste down by 40%. Experiments with less hazardous materials are ongoing, with only 3% waste reductions to date. Cold mill roll investment scheduled for September 2011 of £150,000 with £75,000 in electronic trimmer expected to reduce waste by 30%. Consider implementing the BERR waste management process, environmental officer approval re: change of measurement process for April 2011

There will be circumstances where the performance criterion requires measurements from different areas of the company to become aggregated. For example, for RWE Thames Water's Climate Change KPI they collated measurements from different data sets and sources from different managerial accountability across different business units (see Fig. 5.5).

Figure 5.5 **Aggregated performance measures within a strategic sustainability KPI**[129]

RWE Thames Water's Strategic Climate Change KPI and Measures

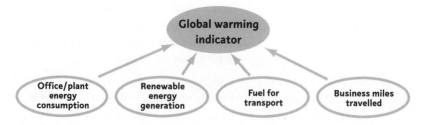

As such, when constructing the strategic sustainability perform-ance KPI a number of measurement record sheets are required to be developed and verified for different types of measurements. The colla-tion of these record sheets into a controlled master reference file will be useful in maintaining a coherent understanding of the system and adapting it to the changing business dimensions, for example, in cases of business-unit acquisitions and mergers, while maintaining assur-ances of its level of relevance, scope and coverage of the company as a whole.

Having now designed the measures, developed the monitoring and performance-management infrastructure, established the baselines and the targets and started the measurement system implementation, it is assumed that the relevant action plans are now incorporated within the strategic planning process and included within operational management review systems; this is vital to the strategic management focus. To bring this all into closer scrutiny and effective implementation, the penultimate step in our seven-step process model is the all-important reporting step.

Step 6: Internal reporting and comparing progress

Reporting appropriately helps focus efforts on assessing status, implementing improvements and maintaining commitment towards the goals.

In the first instance, you need to consider carefully how you will present the various data sets. Your prime company-centred audience will include executives and senior managers with very limited time. They need to receive a summary of key points around progress as well as the main areas requiring their attention. Your audience could also include relevant operations managers who are probably more focused on their particular area of responsibility. With this in mind the following pointers should be considered:

- Present data graphically against targets and with projections. These graphs should include short summaries about the current situation, future projects and activities that are being undertaken to deliver performance

- Separately from this presentation, and more from the operational perspective (although still clearly feeding into the strategic performance outcomes), report data in as much detail as possible on the areas of operations of the relevant managers and staff. This audience is more interested in their particular areas of work and how much they have affected or need to affect the performance dimensions

- Comparisons can be a useful way for staff at different levels within the company to get an idea of the achievements and challenges and a sense of scale of the activities and requirements. For example, at the executive level a comparison with the published sustainability reports of industry peers can provide added relevance and focus. Similarly, providing internal comparisons on the level of contribution from each business unit, department and even shop-floor level, can be very useful—if such granular data can be collated. This friendly competition can spur on action in less responsive areas as well as with those who have already been pioneering progress

You must integrate your sustainability goals and initiatives into existing management processes, for example:

- Include sustainability KPIs in your regular business management reporting pack

- Ensure sustainability projects and performances are reviewed as part of your monthly management meetings across the company

- Post the sustainability KPIs with your other KPIs on the notice boards, intranet or other relevant places where employees can generally get access, ensuring they are regularly and consistently reported

- Include sustainability issues in your staff briefings and provide relevant information to your colleagues with respect to their staff briefings

If such goals don't become part of the everyday management of the company the effort required will be unsustainable. Remember too that one key benefit of reporting and reviewing the measures is to encourage discussion about the present performance status and how it can be improved to achieve targets. This engagement with senior and middle managers, as well as staff, raises awareness and encourages thinking beyond the previous, more limited, requirements about strategic performance in the company. Use this reporting process as a tool for stimulating the engagement and strategic-thinking activity around sustainability as much as for purely informing your audiences.

Step 7: Assure information flows and communicate progress

Assuring that the information being collected, analysed and reported is accurate, comprehensive and consistently reliable is an essential foundation for both the internal and external credibility of your strategic sustainability performance measurement and management system. This underpins the data for use in internal management decisions and performance appraisals, as well as for enabling employee engagement. It is also an imperative for external reporting as the public are sceptical of many claims and there is a growing use of the term 'greenwashing'. Considering the investment that has gone into this process to date, it might be considered foolish not to ensure it is of good quality.

First and foremost is ensuring that the internal reliability of the data measurement and management system is trustworthy and robust. In this context, internal data sampling and assurances should be conducted by semi-independent persons, potentially relying on those who have experience in assessing the company's internal financial data reporting processes. Process and policy improvements are to be expected in the early days of using a new system. In this context there should be an assurance report detailing the sampling, the level of conformance, with particular emphasis placed on detailing minor and major non-conformances alongside corrective actions for improving the level of assurance, and the time-frames for revisiting and checking these have been implemented.

Your final strategic sustainability business performance reporting should also take a form appropriate to your various external stakeholders. Although this is dealt with in more detail in Chapter 12 by Ruth Bender, there are a few strategic internal considerations:

- External format is expected to be considerably different from your internal reporting. The main contrasts will be in terms of commercial confidentiality, focused brevity and managerial comment

- Wherever possible the reporting of progress with targets should remain the same, to ensure consistency and credibility

- Reporting should also include more general operational, policy and strategic intentions to help improve the external stakeholders' awareness and understanding about the broader company's sustainability-related activities

- Other than the performance measurement and targeted performance criteria, the style, content and format of this reporting is very different for different audiences

- The reporting process will involve coordination and cooperation with various departments and because of the likely increased sensitivity around external disclosure, particularly in the early years, it is wise to have a senior executive sponsor this annual initiative specifically

- It is essential, however, to ensure the same figures and targets are discussed and highlighted to ensure reliable credibility and reputation are established within your communications on strategic sustainability business performance

You could consider having the external report content assured; assurance is as much about making sure that the information reported is accurate as it about ensuring it meets the user's needs. As in the case of financial reporting, an external assurance mechanism may be employed to complement your internal assurance process. It may be provided by stakeholder views, statements from consultancies or opinions from accounting organisations (audit reports).

Independent assurance of sustainability information should include the following:

- Clear, specific information on both the scope of the exercise undertaken and the areas not reviewed or assessed

- Level of assurance: whether the practitioner is providing reasonable assurance (by giving a positively worded opinion, such as the information is accurate in accordance with what the management says) or limited assurance (nothing indicates that the information is inaccurate or incomplete in the report prepared by the company)

- Criteria are used to assess the information, for example, whether the report has been assessed against a recognised standard such as Global Reporting Initiative reporting guidance or any other publicly available criteria, which could include the company's own criteria

- Work performed: an assessment of underlying processes, systems, reporting procedures and performance

- An opinion or conclusion from the auditing body or the stakeholder consultation group

Conclusion

Having completed this seven-step process you are now in charge of a performance-management system for business sustainability. However, this will require updating and reviewing if it is not to become out of date and irrelevant to the company. This must be done every time there is a significant review of strategy or a change in the environment. We recommend that a repeat of steps 1, 2 and 3 in particular, around strategic issue management, stakeholder engagement and prioritisation, are conducted at least on an annual basis, with the corresponding steps 4 to 7 employed to ensure the new direction is communicated to the whole business.

Developing a strategic approach to how you approach corporate sustainability is vital for engaging and embedding sustainability into the business. We have provided a seven-step process to enable this development of meaningful KPIs and measurements. The seven-step strategic sustainability business performance process creates identification, measurement and management. The following points summarise key components and important strategic considerations within this approach:

- Clarify the *key* strategic issues around sustainability in terms of impacts and opportunities for the business

- Engage with a broad range of stakeholders (internally and externally) to gain consensus and commitment around key strategic KPIs (ten maximum)

- Develop clear and well-documented measures and management processes, with emphasis on the methods employed and accountabilities within the company

- Report the performance criteria in a relevant and appropriate manner with the precise level of detail needed for different internal audiences, especially executive managers, operational/functional managers and general staff at the department/business unit or team levels

- Utilise all the internal communication mechanisms to provide access to the relevant data so as to reach and encourage improvement discussions with all the people in your company

- Internally assure and improve non-conformances and inconsistencies in the data, methods or system to ensure internal management that the data can be reliably acted on

- Undertake some internal due diligence and establish a minimum level of confidence before considering any external reporting and communications

- Maintain consistency for the strategic performance data sets, goals and achievements as far as practical

- Look at methods of independently and externally assuring your stakeholder report to maximise the credibility and reputational gains

- Update your approach. Your business operates within a dynamic environment, so don't become complacent. You will need to return to assess the strategic stakeholder management, sustainability issues and scenarios at least annually

6

Sustainability and new product development

Keith Goffin
Professor of Innovation and New Product Development

There is a growing consensus that 'there's no alternative to sustainable development'[130] and corporations must develop products and services that are both environmentally and socially acceptable. However, this consensus has taken a long time to emerge—leading researchers have lamented that the 'revolution' has taken decades.[131] Even today, some senior managers believe that if environmental and social concerns are the primary drivers of new product development (NPD), profits will be compromised.[132] Managers must take account of the growing evidence that a focus on sustainability can lead to increased revenues, create opportunities for new products and services,[133] strengthen reputations and ensure customer loyalty. It is at the operational level where corporate sustainability initiatives fail,[134] and so management teams that only concern themselves with the so-called 'corporate-level' issues will fail. Senior managers must take the time to understand the challenges in developing sustainable products and services.

The main focus of writings on corporate sustainability (CS) has been the need for top management leadership and support for corporate initiatives and, consequently, the challenges faced in trying to develop sustainable new products and services have been largely ignored. Organisations need to make significant modifications to NPD processes to achieve sustainable innovation. Product development teams already face the challenge of having to accommodate the many, often conflicting requirements of different functional areas, such as R&D, marketing and manufacturing. So adding a sustainability perspective to NPD complicates an already complex process. Consequently, the most effective way to introduce sustainability thinking into NPD is to build on existing techniques—in particular the **Stage-Gate™ process**. This chapter describes the Stage-Gate process and gives concrete recommendations for how it can be adapted to achieve **sustainable new product development** (SNPD).

In covering the factors that influence SNPD this chapter will:

- Explain the relationship between sustainability and new products

- Identify the barriers to introducing sustainability thinking in NPD

- Describe an approach for overcoming these barriers and integrating sustainability into NPD

- Present a case study on Unilever's current approaches

Sustainability and new products

There are three main elements to sustainability: economic, environmental, and societal. Companies can address these by using a triple-bottom-line approach,[135] which takes into account environmental and social impacts of products and services, as well as their profitability.

Product sustainability issues

The need to consider the environment and reduce manufacturing waste has been clear for a long time. From a management perspective it goes back to the work of polymath Charles Babbage (1791–1871; best known for his ground-breaking work on computing). His 1832 bestseller *On the Economy and Manufacture* was the first management text to consider how waste could be reduced (which today would be called 'lean manufacturing') and wealth created from by-products.[136]

One major issue is that as societies become more affluent the demand for products increases. This places a greater burden on the environment and the following equation[137] shows that environmental burden (EB) depends on the population (P), their affluence (A), and the technology (T) involved:

$$EB = P \times A \times T$$

The implication of this equation is that as the large populations of developing nations become more affluent, EB will rise significantly. The increasing demand for cars in China and India is often mentioned in the media and it illustrates that some current products that industry produces are not sustainable. Radically new technological solutions are required to reduce the magnitude of 'T' in the above equation to a fraction of today's values, and thus slash the environmental burden. Many products that are widely available today will need to be totally redesigned to drastically reduce their environmental 'footprint'.

It should also be remembered that service organisations need to consider how to reduce their environmental impact. An example of this is the FedEx Corporation, which encourages customers to provide electronic files so that FedEx can print locally, rather than shipping large volumes of paper documentation.[138]

As the impact that products have on the environment has become recognised, companies have focused on reducing its magnitude. This can involve both increasing efficiencies throughout manufacturing and the supply chain (see Chapter 9) and redesigning products.[139]

The energy required for producing products has been reduced and there have been many advances in the use of new technologies and materials in products and in their manufacturing.[140] Examples of technological advances include reduced water requirements in paper-making, lighter materials for cars (which reduces fuel requirements), and greater use of recycled materials.

Emerging challenges

Traditionally, companies have focused on the developed countries and the affluent. The world's poor rightly aspire to better lives and they require appropriate products—that is, products with appropriate features and that are affordable. The growing middle classes in these new markets will be purchasers of many of the goods and services already sold in developed markets. But in addition the poorer consumers, by their very numbers, provide huge new opportunities[141] that should spur innovation. In India there is enormous interest in innovation and the Hindi word for low-cost solutions made from available materials (often scrap) is *jugaad*.[142] The realisation that the poor of the world are a neglected market has led to the terms 'base of the pyramid' (BOP), which refers to the 4.5 billion people who have to survive on less than $3 a day,[143] and 'B4B' (business to 4 billion—poor people). The huge number of customers at the BOP means that creative, responsible companies can access unique revenue-generating opportunities. However, the types of product and service that need to be developed are so different that they dictate that companies must become much better at understanding customer needs, as some examples will show.

BOP products and services need to help people address the challenges of living in the developing world where infrastructure is poor or missing. Many people need to reduce the amount of time they spend on obtaining water and fuel or cut the cost of their power requirements. New technology can help in such cases as, for example, lighting. LED technology has low power requirements and so-called

'micro-solar power' is a highly viable alternative to expensive investments in electricity infrastructure in rural environments.[144] However,
product developers must understand the real needs of consumers in
the developing world, as these are not always obvious. The environment in which products are used can be very demanding. So new
products must be robust and achieving this is not easy, as evidenced
by the poor performance of solar-powered lights.[145] A difficulty with
developing products for BOP markets is that many product developers do not have an understanding of social and cultural factors that
influence the needs of customers (see Case study 6.1).

Case study 6.1 **The Jaipur Foot**

The Jaipur Foot[146] has become a household name, particularly in the
war zones of the world. Western bio-medical engineers have for many
years designed artificial limbs, many of which use expensive materials. The demand for prostheses in some countries is extremely high as
a result of the millions of anti-personnel mines that have been laid in
war zones. Civilian populations in countries such as Afghanistan continue to lose limbs as they return to their villages and agricultural fields
following conflict. However, these civilians do not have the money or
access to the high-tech devices developed in the West. The Jaipur Foot
was designed by an Indian craftsman working with a physician. It was
conceived to fit with lifestyles in Asia (where many people squat, eat
and sleep on the floor); to use readily available materials (rubber, wood
and aluminium); and to be easy for local craftsmen to make and repair.
It costs far less than the Western solutions; the Foot typically takes 45
minutes to build, lasts five years and costs about $30.

As we have seen, sustainability requires companies to consider not
only environmental but also economic, cultural and social factors
related to products and services and, with changing markets, this is
challenging. We will now discuss the reasons why, too often, sustainability is not fully considered during new product development.

Barriers to sustainability thinking in NPD

Research has shown that there is a gap in many organisations between the proponents of sustainability and those who develop the products and so are responsible for implementation.[147] Two aspects are particularly important: the negative impact on product development of shallow corporate initiatives; and the wider range of stakeholders to be considered.

Shallow corporate initiatives

The corporate journey to truly sustainable products and services is not an easy one, as many '[e]xecutives behave as though they have to choose between the largely social benefits of developing sustainable products or processes and the financial costs of doing so'.[148] Once senior executives have bought into the importance of sustainability they need to set appropriate targets and communicate these effectively throughout their organisations (see Chapters 4 and 5).

The next step, understanding how to embed social and environmental thinking at an operational level (i.e. into the NPD process) is a real challenge. For example, a recent survey of UK manufacturers showed that although significant numbers of corporations had environmental policies, many failed to match these with changes to their NPD processes.[149] Such corporations must make operational changes; otherwise they risk being accused of talking about environmentally friendly products but not delivering them. (Activists have coined the term 'greenwash' for companies where the public relations angle is addressed but appropriate actions are missing.) NPD processes need to be changed to take full account of sustainability.

More stakeholders

Traditionally, there has been a strong emphasis in NPD on both company-internal stakeholders (e.g. marketing, R&D and manufacturing) and the customer. The customer is perceived as the key stakeholder and so a key driver of NPD is the voice of the customer, as determined by market research. Identifying customer needs can be difficult, particularly with BOP markets,[150] and many companies will struggle to understand such needs. Intensifying the problem, sustainable NPD has a wider range of stakeholders than traditional product development. The additional stakeholders in SNPD are legislators and even activists. It is advisable for companies to listen and understand these groups' perspectives during NPD, although this is challenging.[151]

New product development and sustainability

New product development is where corporate sustainability initiatives succeed or fail. One challenge is that for busy NPD teams, sustainability is yet another competing requirement to consider. This can increase the tension within NPD teams and it is exacerbated by the additional need to consider external stakeholders' views. A study published in 2010 found that although Unilever had changed its NPD process to include a section on sustainability in every 'product brief' (a document summarising the scope and features of new products), this section was often left blank. As the authors of the study concluded, 'incorporating sustainability in the new product development briefs does not guarantee results'.[152] Within Unilever the approach has now changed significantly, but it demonstrates that management must ensure that sustainability is fully considered (e.g. by setting appropriate targets—see Case study 6.2 on Unilever at the end of this chapter).

Sustainable new product development (SNPD)

The consideration of sustainability in NPD has four elements: a broader consideration of customer needs; a focus on the whole life-cycle of a product from its manufacture to its end-of-life; planning for post-use; and ensuring that the supply chain is effective.[153] Increasingly, sustainability engineers are being added to NPD teams to ensure that these four elements are adequately considered.

Some researchers have started to define completely new processes by which they think sustainability can be integrated into NPD.[154] However, proposing a completely new process ignores the very comprehensive body of NPD knowledge that has been developed from practice and research over several decades. Other researchers have recognised that it is important to build on the existing body of innovation knowledge and adapt existing tools and techniques to sustainability issues.[155] Therefore, in recommending how to integrate sustainable thinking into NPD, the key findings of product development research will be considered.

The Stage-Gate process

New product development consists of a number of key stages, including identifying customer requirements, developing a product concept, generating a detailed design, testing, and launching the product to market. Extensive research has shown that at each of these stages, a number of functional areas are involved—including R&D, marketing, finance, industrial design and manufacturing—and effective communication and collaboration is fundamental to the development of successful products.

The most common way to manage the different stages and functions involved in NPD is the ubiquitous Stage-Gate methodology developed by Cooper and Kleinschmidt,[156] which specifies the responsibilities of each functional area at each 'stage' of the process and defines the goals that have to be met at each 'gate', before proceeding to the next stage. Most companies use a form of Stage-Gate process and the typical stages, based on Figure 6.1, are:

1. **Discovery.** During this stage the focus is on a fast identification of a number of opportunities for new products and services. These are screened and the best one is taken into Stage 1

2. **Stage 1: Scoping.** Here the scope of the selected idea is defined and market research conducted to identify specific customer needs. R&D considers how the customer needs can be addressed in the product design and manufacturing decide how the product will be produced

3. **Stage 2: Business case.** Building on the scoping stage, this stage identifies the size of the market, the way market requirements will be addressed, development costs, and the potential return on investment

4. **Stage 3: Development.** A major stage where R&D takes a leading role in designing the product and each of its features and solving the many technical issues that arise

5. **Stage 4: Testing and validation.** This involves testing the functionality of the product in the user's environment, verifying the marketing plan and ensuring that the manufacturing and delivery will run smoothly

6. **Stage 5: Launch.** Here the product is marketed and full production starts as the first units are sold

At each stage, every department has specific tasks to complete and the main benefit of Stage-Gate is that it ensures that different perspectives are considered when key decisions are made. Such decisions are often trade-offs, where the goals of every functional area cannot be met and so the best decision for the overall project needs to be made. Stage-Gate also helps prevent oversights, for example, failing to consider manufacturing early enough (which can lead to production problems).

Figure 6.1 **Key factors in embedding sustainability into NPD**[157]

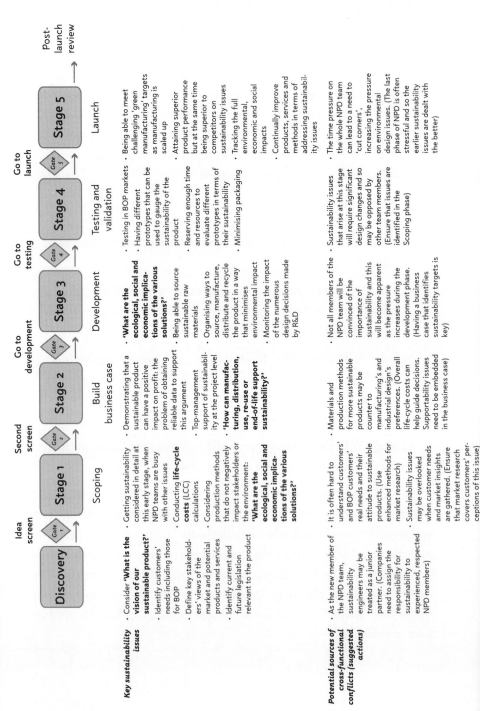

Stage-Gate and sustainability

Figure 6.1 illustrates how the Stage-Gate process can be enhanced to include sustainability issues. For example, it shows that at the discovery stage it is important that a vision for a sustainable product is developed. If this is not done by the sustainability engineer, then the buy-in from other members of the team is unlikely to be achieved. When, at later stages of the project, the pressures increase, sustainability may not be given sufficient emphasis in the many trade-off decisions to be made. Similarly, Figure 6.1 shows that senior management sponsorship is needed, particularly at the business-case stage. It is lack of top management involvement at this stage that can mean that sustainability strategy fails to become implemented at the project level, and strong business cases that articulate value are key.[158] Figure 6.1 indicates the potential cross-functional conflicts that can arise and so these are important points for those taking the responsibility for sustainability in NPD.

Figure 6.1 also identifies the potential cross-functional conflicts that will need to be managed. As we have stressed throughout this chapter, senior managers need to demonstrate leadership by becoming involved with NPD teams, understanding the challenges of embedding sustainability at the operational level, and solving the cross-functional conflicts that arise. Case study 6.2 shows how (after initial problems referred to earlier) Unilever has taken steps to ensure that sustainability is embedded in every new product development project. This involved making a clear link between corporate and project goals; developing suitable tools to assess the environmental impact of new products; and having champions to drive the adoption of the new approach.

Case study 6.2 **Sustainability and NPD at Unilever**[159]

Unilever is a large fast-moving consumer goods (FMCG) company, which employs over 167,000 people worldwide and produces a diverse range of food, home and personal care products including famous brand names such as PG Tips (tea), Flora (margarine), Signal (toothpaste), Vaseline (skin care), and Dove (hair shampoo). The company is aware that over 160 million people use its products every day. This massive level of consumption has led to the term 'small actions, big difference', which refers to the fact that even a small reduction in the environmental impact of a new product or process can result in a big difference when multiplied by the scale of Unilever's global sales.

In 2010, Unilever launched the Unilever Sustainable Living Plan (www.sustainable-living.unilever.com). This plan sets out specific commitments to reduce Unilever's environmental footprint, while increasing the social benefit arising from its activities. There are three overall themes: helping more than one billion people take action to improve their health and well-being; halving the environmental impact of the making and use of Unilever's products; and enhancing the livelihoods of thousands of people in the supply chain. It is recognised that these commitments will not be easy, and Unilever will need to work in partnership with governments, NGOs, suppliers and others to address the big challenges confronting the company. (Unilever's commitment to embedding sustainability has been discussed in detail in Chapter 1, Case study 1.1.)

To ensure the successful integration of environmental sustainability considerations into the product innovation process, Unilever has defined three product metrics (covering water, waste and greenhouse gases) and one supply-chain metric for sustainable sourcing. In order to monitor the impact of future innovations, it was important to first measure the impact of Unilever's existing product portfolio. This assessment set a baseline against which new products are compared. Based on this information, guidelines and tools were integrated into the Stage-Gate innovation process to guide decision-making and inform product developers of the impact of their new innovation versus an existing product.

→

It was essential to support the roll-out of this new approach with the appropriate training and the identification of 'champions' to drive the successful implementation within the business.

It was also important that this new approach was supported with rigorous scientific assessments, which were provided by a team of Unilever scientists responsible for conducting life-cycle assessments of Unilever's products. With more than ten years' experience of analysing the complex environmental impacts of products, this team is one of the most knowledgeable in the industry. Their work has been the drive behind some of the key innovations in Unilever's portfolio, such as concentrated laundry liquids (see Chapter 7, Case study 7.3) and the unit dose approach.

Campaigners have used the term 'greenwash' for the way some companies talk about sustainability but do little in reality to improve their products. Consequently, leading companies such as Unilever have recognised that it is important to gain external endorsement and recognition of their sustainability agenda. Unilever is doing this in two ways. First, it has a group of external advisers that comment on the company's progress each year. Second, Unilever has been very open in discussing its approach with external bodies and, for example, it has been recognised by the Dow Jones Sustainability World Indexes (named as food category leader ten years running) and the FTSE4Good (achieving a top environmental score of 5). Unilever has also developed the Unilever Sustainable Agriculture Code, which was developed with recommendations from the Unilever Sustainable Agriculture Advisory Board (SAAB), which included NGOs such as the Rainforest Alliance and WWF.

Summary and conclusions

In considering the leadership issues, the sustainability literature has largely ignored the challenges in creating sustainable new products. Organisations need to make significant modifications to their existing new product development processes and senior managers need to sponsor sustainability not only at the corporate but also at the project level. Otherwise sustainability will be difficult to achieve because product development teams already have to accommodate many, often conflicting aims from different functional areas, such as R&D and manufacturing. Embedding sustainability thinking into NPD should be achieved by:

- Using existing tools and techniques for managing product development—in particular the Stage-Gate process

- The active engagement of senior management to ensure that a clear process for sustainable new product development is defined and followed

- Senior management taking the responsibility for making balanced decisions when sustainability objectives appear to be in conflict with the objectives of specific functional areas

Without senior management driving the development of a sustainable NPD process, new products and services will not make the triple contribution to the bottom line that is essential.

7
Issues in sustainable marketing

Lynette Ryals
Professor of Strategic Sales and Account Management
*and colleagues Paul Baines, Radu Dimitriu, Simon Knox,
Emma Macdonald and Javier Marcos-Cuevas*

Sustainable marketing can be described as a development that recognises the limitations of marketing philosophy, acknowledging the need to impose (self-) regulatory constraints on the market mechanism in economic development.[160] It is the zeitgeist of the last few decades, with a growing recognition of societal and environmental problems, where the causes and solutions require joint and global action. It is an idea whose time has come. There is now increasing recognition that marketing activities can have a harmful impact on the environment and well-being of societies (issues that economists call 'externalities', i.e. problems created by companies that occur outside the company itself). Sustainable marketing is therefore an attempt to broaden the concept of marketing beyond simple economic (monetary) development; it seeks to give marketing a morality and accountability.

Three central ideas permeate sustainable marketing thinking, namely that:

- Marketing should not negatively impact on the environment (it should be ecological)

- Marketing should not allow or promote inequitable social practices (it should be equitable)

- Marketing should encourage long-term as opposed to short-term economic development (it should be economic)

Sustainable marketing has, however, not developed suddenly or in a vacuum. In fact, when looking specifically at environmental impact, sustainable marketing can be characterised as the 'third age' of green marketing:[161]

1. In the first age, ecological green marketing developed around the 1960s and 70s, and was concerned with automobile, oil and agrochemical companies encountering specific environmental problems in the production process

2. In the second age, environmental green marketing in the 1980s witnessed the arrival of the green consumer, who purchased goods to avoid negative environmental impacts, for example, cosmetic products not tested on animals. Some so-called 'green' products didn't work and companies faced a consumer backlash as a result[162]

3. The third age of green marketing is sustainable green marketing. In this third age, companies will need to do business differently, by lengthening their return on investment terms, working in greater and more equitable collaboration with supply-chain partners, adopting accepted environmental auditing methods (such as carbon labelling schemes that count carbon for disposal as well as development, delivery and consumption), and—shock horror for many marketers—companies may actually need to discourage consumption[163]

Figure 7.1 **The domain of sustainable marketing**

Marketing and sales overview

Given this great upheaval and change in marketing in the 21st century, how should a company incorporate the changing trend in sustainability into its marketing processes? Will the emergent marketing strategies promote efficiency in resource use, or brand leadership in sustainable products and services, or both?

In this chapter, we provide an overview of sustainable marketing management. We examine new insights into customer attitudes and behaviours and show how sustainable marketers are using them to create sustainable value propositions and communicate these to customers. In Chapter 8 we will examine how sustainable marketing ideas are influencing, sometimes profoundly changing, marketing practices. We call this 'the domain of sustainable marketing' (Fig. 7.1).

Customers say they want it, but will they really pay for it?

One of the first big challenges for organisations implementing sustainability marketing programmes is the attitude–behaviour gap. For example, 90% of customers might claim to be concerned about the environment but only 10% will be prepared to change their behaviour, such as paying a premium for sustainable products.[164] There is widespread (although not universal) acceptance that climate change is an important issue. Yet as individuals we still frequently engage in behaviours that are inconsistent with this belief. Studies show that, despite high awareness that driving our cars contributes to climate-change emissions, few of us alter our behaviour through, for example, changing our mode of transport (e.g. catching a train instead of driving our car) or changing our use of existing modes of transport (e.g. through car sharing).[165]

So, why is there a gap between customer attitudes and behaviours? In some cases individuals may feel unable to shift their own behaviour to reflect their attitudes due to practical issues (such as the unavailability of transport alternatives or the need to transport items or children). In other cases the perceived inability of individual actions to affect a global issue may also explain the attitude–behaviour gap. The theory of planned behaviour tells us that perceived self-efficacy is an important determinant of behaviour.[166] Perceived self-efficacy is the belief that you, the individual, can personally make a difference. Provision of information may help to empower individuals to act. For instance, a device that demonstrates energy use within the home can both inform and engage individuals to take action on their energy use. E.ON claims its Energy Fit campaign, which provides a monitoring device that shows the energy consumption of specific household appliances, reduces household consumption by 5%.[167] The theory of planned behaviour also tells us that social norms ('doing the right thing') can have a significant impact on our behaviour. Some energy companies have experimented with indicators on customer bills that tell households whether they are using more than the average power for their households: 'smiley faces' for below-average users and 'frowns' for above-average users. They have found that even this simple indicator of positive/negative attitudes shifts excessive users towards a drop in their consumption and encourages energy conservers to continue acting this way.[168]

Because changing people's attitudes is seen as a necessary precursor to behaviour change, many sustainable marketing campaigns aimed at changing customer behaviour focus on attitudes and attitude change. However, marketers have long understood that changing attitudes is no easy task; it is a process that requires a solid understanding of a customer's underlying goals as well as the communication of carefully crafted messages repeated over time.[169] Moreover, no matter how well-executed the communications campaign is, behaviour change is more likely to happen if it is consistent with multiple customer goals and can be easily incorporated into the customer's existing lifestyle.[170] What this tells us is that despite people's intentions, *context* has a big impact on their subsequent behaviour. If a situation makes it difficult for individuals to carry out their intended behaviour, they are likely to be put off course quite easily. By contrast, if it is easy for them to carry out their intentions, then it is more likely they will act in the way they intended. So for example, waste bins in a public park that make it easy to sort packaging for recycling will assist individuals in implementing behaviour consistent with their attitude that recycling is important for the environment.

The notion of 'choice architectures'[171] recently advocated by Thaler and Sunstein has long been in use by effective marketers.

These are process and design elements that make it easier for individuals to implement desirable behaviour. Marketers would not have called them 'choice architectures' but essentially that is what the marketer's toolkit, the marketing mix, enables. Marketers have always used this toolkit to design optimal market offerings that encourage certain consumer responses (e.g. product available in a *convenient* location, accessible in an *easy* packaging, available at an *achievable* price). However, these ideas have recently become very fashionable, particularly in political policy, as the result of the blockbuster book *Nudge*.[172] The nudge perspective takes into account the weak link between attitudes and behaviours in many contexts to suggest that the best way to change behaviours is . . . to change behaviour! There are several examples of 'nudges' that governments might implement to make it harder to carry out 'bad' behaviours and easier to implement 'good' behaviours. For instance, in Australia the government has recently legislated that cigarettes should be withdrawn from display in stores; the idea being that if cigarettes are out of sight under the counter they are less likely to be included in the shopping basket. Another way to 'nudge' behaviour is by linking it to entertainment.[173] A recent campaign by VW automobiles represents this latter approach via their website thefuntheory.com. This website shows multiple ways to encourage positive behaviours. In 'The World's Deepest Bin', technicians from VW installed a sensor and sound system into a regular public rubbish receptacle in a public park. As any piece of rubbish was dropped into the bin it emitted a sound that implied the rubbish was falling a very long way down a very deep hole. The novelty of this experience encouraged people to pick up and throw away more than double the amount of rubbish compared to any other day in the park.

Creating sustainable value propositions

Classic marketing theory tells managers that value propositions should be both believable and compelling, and that they should be either about some form of competitive differential or about something that resonates with the customer.[174] Many of these are, in practice, product-based; consider, for example, Dyson vacuum cleaners and the 'dual cyclone—no bag, no loss of suction' proposition. This is both competitive (since it implies that competing products *do* lose suction) and resonating (there is no bag to empty out, and the cleaner works as well when it is nearly full as it does when it is nearly empty). However, as sustainability becomes a bigger issue in consumers' minds, we find more value propositions that incorporate an ethical or sustainability dimension. We refer to this as 'choice influencing': when marketing and awareness campaigns try to enable and encourage customers to choose and use products more sustainably and efficiently. For example, there is an increasingly wide set of products and services that have emerged because of wider environmental concerns. These include Earthmate low mercury CFL light bulbs; Rix Biodiesel, reducing emission of particulates from vehicle exhausts; projects to reduce sulphur dioxide emissions from power plants in China and the USA; Poland's Południowy Koncern Energetyczny's recently-announced project aiming to reduce nitrogen dioxide emissions from Polish power plants by 60%; and the UK's SO2SAY project, which aims to reduce or remove sulphur dioxide from the food chain.

Some extremely effective examples of value propositions that are both powerful and sustainable come from business-to-business (B2B) situations where suppliers provide complex and extensive bundles of physical products and support services (product–service systems), often in collaboration with their customers. Product–service systems change the boundaries of production and consumption that exist in traditional production-focused 'pile it high and sell it cheap' business models. From a sustainability perspective these traditional models are heavy absorbers of natural resources and excessive producers of waste as the manufacturer has little incentive to maintain existing products in the customer's space. However, by shifting the boundary of responsibility to maintain and operate the product to the producer, benefits accrue in three ways: to the manufacturer, to the customer and to the environment. Two examples of this new kind of value proposition are DuPont automotive paint and Rolls-Royce aero-engine manufacturers (case studies 7.1 and 7.2).

Case study 7.1 **DuPont**

Under a traditional manufacturing model, DuPont sold 'paint for cars', so their business was to sell as much paint as possible. Under a product–service systems model, DuPont sells 'painted cars' to their customers, which means the manufacturer now has a stake in providing efficient methods for car painting that minimise the wastage of paint that is used. From the paint manufacturer's perspective the traditional approach aims to sell as much product as possible, whereas the newer product–service model aims to reduce the amount of product sold to minimise wastage.

Case study 7.2 **Rolls-Royce**

Working collaboratively with its customers, Rolls-Royce has introduced an offering called TotalCare®. TotalCare® customers pay by the hour of engine operation; Rolls-Royce collects detailed data on engine performance during flight and provides servicing and technical advice as necessary to keep the engine operational. The TotalCare® contract aligns the interests of Rolls-Royce and their customers (the aircraft operators). One factor that affects engine life is the way that airline pilots fly. Therefore, as Rolls-Royce moves towards 'engine life' deals with its customers, it is also building mechanisms within its contracts to incentivise use of the engine that promotes reliability, encouraging pilots to manage the use of thrust to enhance engine life. Rolls-Royce

→

now provides a flight operations adviser whose job is to go to airlines and spend time with pilots advising them on more efficient and safe flying methods. Not only does this reduce the need for unplanned maintenance (and hence reduce one cause of flight delays), there are also positive consequences for the airlines in terms of fuel economy.

These examples are held up as best practice because they offer both financial and sustainability benefits to suppliers and to customers. Major win–wins like these are perhaps more readily achievable in the B2B arena where long-term, close relationships on a substantial scale mean that the size of the prize is larger. However, there are a number of examples from consumer marketing where there are benefits in terms of sustainability, but the firm may also benefit financially. One such example is Unilever's Surf Small & Mighty, the first super-concentrated laundry liquid.[175] This example illustrates the striking role of brand positioning in sustainable marketing.

Case study 7.3 **Unilever's Surf Small & Mighty**

Surf Small & Mighty is a highly concentrated laundry liquid sold in a bottle that is about one-third the size of conventional laundry liquids. Unilever claims that Small & Mighty's highly concentrated format reduces the amount of water used in manufacturing, the amount of plastic used in packaging and the lorry miles to deliver it. As the website says, 'Almost 30 million bottles were sold in 2007, with savings of 33 million litres of water, plastic equivalent to 262 million shopping bags and 665 tonnes of CO_2'.

Therefore, Unilever reduces environmental impact and reduces some of its costs—a win–win for the company. But are these gains passed on to consumers, or are environmentally conscious consumers expected to pay more? A price comparison using mysupermarket.co.uk (as at October 2010) gave the following prices on medium-sized laundry powders and liquids* (Table 7.1).

→

Table 7.1 **Price comparison of 'environmentally friendly' and standard laundry products**

Product	No. of washes	Retail price	Price per wash
Surf Small & Mighty concentrated liquid 1 litre	28	£4.49	16.0p
Surf Essential Oils powder 2 kg	25	£4.48	17.9p
Persil Small & Mighty concentrated liquid 1 litre	28	£6.30	22.5p
Persil washing powder 2.125 kg	25	£6.78	27.1p
Fairy washing powder 2 kg	25	£5.98	23.9p
Ecover laundry liquid 1.5 litre	17	£4.48	26.4p
Ariel washing powder with Fabreze 2 kg	25	£6.96	27.8p

* Special offers and special products such as gels, colourfast or biological, as well as non-branded, excluded from comparison.

Table 7.1 shows that, excluding special offers and supermarket own-brand products, consumers were 1.9p (11%) per wash better off if they chose Surf Small & Mighty over the similar wash-capacity Surf powder. The same holds true of the comparison with the only other super-concentrated product available at that time, Persil Small & Mighty. The consumer is almost 5p per wash better off buying Persil Small & Mighty than Persil powder (17%). In both cases there is an additional saving as the consumer should get three more washes (28 compared to 25), giving a total saving of 96p per bottle of Surf and £1.83 per bottle of Persil Small & Mighty over the standard product. (Chapter 1, Case study 1.1 looks at how one of Unilever's customers, Walmart, supported the sustainability message by stocking liquid detergents only in concentrate form. Chapter 9 examines the sustainability impact of product-design decisions.)

Delivering and communicating the value of the sustainable brand

Brand managers of the 21st century increasingly have to address issues of sustainability as part of their job. They are required to undertake effective stakeholder communications in their endeavours if sustainable brand positioning is to be developed successfully in today's business environment, which demands greater transparency and more responsible decision-making. This importance of sustainability to brand managers has been evolving for a number of reasons, including the need to address climate change and pressing societal issues, the action of NGO pressure groups (e.g. Greenpeace) and legislation (e.g. on CO_2 emissions) or, simply, the corporate belief in the importance of building a more sustainable future. As a consequence, many established brands have attempted to build connections with sustainable issues, such as environmental leadership, cause-related marketing, NGO sponsorship and fair trade. For instance, UK-based chocolate manufacturer Cadbury's Dairy Milk chocolate has recently engaged in Fairtrade and the brand now features the Fairtrade mark with its associated commitments. US coffee store chain Starbucks promotes the 'Make your mark' programme, through which the company donates $10 for every hour that baristas or customers volunteer for community projects. The premium ice cream maker, Ben & Jerry's, uses certified organic ingredients that are environmentally sustainable and has launched the 'Lick global warming' initiative aimed at fighting global warming.[176]

In addition to these established brands, there has been an emergence of new brands positioned on a sustainability platform. In North America, the Whole Foods retail chain sells healthy products based on sustainable agriculture, while striving to recycle, re-use and reduce waste whenever possible. USA-based company Vivavi produces and designs furniture and furnishings that use environmentally sound materials, including recycled materials and organic cotton.[177]

What do sustainable brands offer to customers?

As brands are attempting to address the sustainability challenges that society and the environment are facing today, the question is whether they can also achieve enduring competitive advantage in the value they create for customers. As a starting point, sustainable brands need to build the necessary 'fit-for-purpose' associations, such as product quality. When US sandwich store chain Subway positioned itself as the healthy fast-food chain, it realised that communicating good taste alongside healthiness was essential for ensuring market success. Similarly, Ben & Jerry's and Starbucks have been admired from when they were relatively new to the market for the quality of the products they offer.

Once such necessary functional associations are established, other attributes, including fairness, low ecological footprint and ethics, can be used to differentiate and deliver specific value for customers. For instance, certain sustainable brands can create symbolic value by allowing customers to express themselves or communicate their group belonging. Being a customer of the American apparel brand Wildlife Works represents a statement that one is involved in the fight against the extinction of endangered species. Similarly, by shopping at the UK beauty-store chain Body Shop, people can signal their disapproval of animal testing and their wish to protect the environment through the personal care products they purchase there. Other suitable brands can create experiential value for their customers through sustainability. At Starbucks, the in-store visuals portraying coffee growers symbolise the commitment to Fairtrade coffee, encouraging customers to feel they are part of an authentic and unspoiled coffee-consumption experience (although the claim that Starbucks is grower-friendly has been challenged by Oxfam).[178]

However, the brand manager cannot expect the value of sustainable brands to resonate with all the customers in a market. Rather, specific customer segments may find them more appealing, depending on their personal values and involvement with environmental and societal issues. The chances are that a sizeable portion of the customers in a market are primarily concerned about price levels or luxury status rather than sustainability. However, with the backing of governments through climate legislation and the 'push' of NGOs both in appealing to consumers to boycott certain products and forcing multinationals to change their supply-chain policies, it is possible that the 'editing' of consumer choices may become a sufficient social pressure for households to actively monitor their carbon footprint and ethical purchases.

An early example of an NGO 'push' in the 1990s was the initiation of the fair trade movement by a number of UK-based NGOs aimed at offering better trading conditions for subsistence farmers in third-world countries and securing the rights of marginalised producers and workers. Ever since then, the Fairtrade mark (Fig. 7.2) has evolved into a recognisable symbol through which certified brands can signal to customers that they are committed to offering fair commercial terms and know-how to the producers at the back-end of the value chain. Sometimes companies themselves can be the force behind changing consumers' values and behaviour. For example, the Wales-based apparel company Howies has built its value proposition around the offering of quality, durable clothing that is said to last at least ten years.[179] Howies actively communicates to its customers that the best way in which it can help protect the environment is by making their products last a really long time; thus attempting to persuade their customers to buy fewer (other) products in the long term.

Figure 7.2 **The Fairtrade mark**

So, are sustainable brands really sustainable?

Experience shows that walking 'the sustainability way' in a timely fashion can pay off. The UK coffee brand Cafédirect was a promoter of the fair trade movement and of the Fairtrade mark, and has enjoyed significant growth rates in the last ten years. However, the positioning advantage of Cafédirect has recently been challenged as other brands also received the Fairtrade certification or competing ethical claim certification marks. In general, brands can expect to be challenged in defending their sustainability differentiation in the long term. For instance, Toyota is no longer the only automotive brand in the marketplace associated with 'low emissions'.

Over time, sustainability is likely to develop from a compelling point of difference into a necessary point of parity or 'hygiene factor' in many markets. This is likely to be the case in situations where sustainability can bring about other positive business outcomes and is part of a coherent strategy. For instance, according to a recent update of Tesco's cost savings based on their strategic commitment to sustainability[180] not only does eco-efficient sourcing seem to involve fewer ingredients and less embedded energy, but it can also lead to overall reductions in design, supply chain and display costs.

With the convergence of societal trends combined with the efforts by governments, NGOs and businesses, it is highly likely that customers will emphasise sustainability and ethics more when making purchasing choices in the future. Eventually, we can expect sustainability to become 'the way of doing business of the 21st century' to which all companies will have to adhere. In the following chapter we examine how some trailblazing companies have implemented sustainability and are integrating it into their core business practices: they are trying to make sustainability sustainable.

8

Implementing sustainable marketing

Lynette Ryals
Professor of Strategic Sales and Account Management
and colleagues Shahpar Abdollahi, Stan Maklan and Hugh Wilson

Sustainable marketing planning

Case study 8.1 Iceland

Malcolm Walker, the founder of UK supermarket Iceland, had two bright ideas at the end of the 1990s. The first was to make the whole of its own-brand frozen vegetable range organic, which took effect in 2000. The second was to launch an online supermarket in 1999. Neither was demonstrably successful: by December 2000, sales were down by 5.5%, as the supermarket's shoppers—generally in the more price-sensitive demographics—went elsewhere for their Christmas dinner. Stuart Rose came in as chief executive, took one look and moved briskly on to Arcadia. By 2001, the *Independent* was reporting: 'In allowing the company to push ahead with its strategy of going fully organic on frozen

veg, Mr Rose seems to have forgotten about his most precious asset—
Iceland's customers . . . As for Mr Rose, well, he talks the talk, but can
he also walk it? So far he's never stayed anywhere long enough to find
out . . .' [181] Stuart Rose did indeed stick around elsewhere, becoming
the boss of sustainability champions Marks & Spencer, and he clearly
learnt the lesson well: that to fulfil sustainability aims the customer
must be carried along too.

The difficulties encountered by pioneers such as Iceland supermar-
kets in the 2000s revealed some powerful lessons for early adopters.
Building on those lessons, subsequent successes have confirmed that
there is a UK market for both organics and online shopping, but Iceland's conservative, lower socioeconomic group customer base was
never going to be the right place to start.

Iceland's strategy, while commendable in its attempt to lead the
market, was seen as foolhardy at the time even without the benefit of
hindsight. Nonetheless, this incident shows clearly the importance of
two crucial skills in marketing planning, without which any sustainability objective will fail in the marketplace:

- The first is choosing the right customers: an online organics
  business would clearly need a different target demographic from
  Iceland's traditional base

- The second is ensuring a competitive value proposition on the
  customer's buying criteria, whatever they are

These key tasks are summarised in the two axes of the directional
policy matrix, illustrated in Figure 8.1.

Figure 8.1 **Sustainability aims and the directional policy matrix**[182]

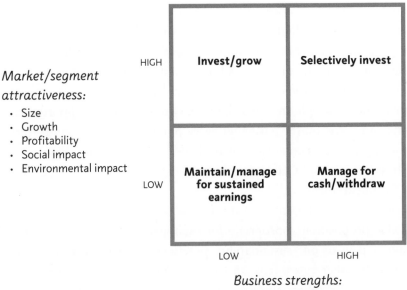

Market/segment attractiveness:
- Size
- Growth
- Profitability
- Social impact
- Environmental impact

Business strengths:
- Product efficacy
- Service quality
- Relationship quality
- Price
- Impact on environment
- Etc.

Strategy guru Henry Mintzberg famously defines strategy as a sustained pattern of resource allocation.[183] The best companies have always been clear on who their target customers are and what value they require relative to the competition, and allocate resources accordingly. This matrix is a simple way of making sure that the executive have a common understanding on these crucial questions.

What makes a segment or product group attractive? Well, for most firms, the size of the profit pool comes into this judgement, and so the attractiveness criteria on the vertical axis of Figure 8.1 include segment size, growth and margins. But they can also include the fit of the segment with other aspects of the firm's mission, such as social and environmental objectives. The London Symphony Orchestra consciously prioritises activities that fit its educational mission. So does Cranfield School of Management, for that matter. Nestlé's Nespresso brand is targeted at corporates and richer individuals who are prepared to pay for the higher cost not just of its coffee quality but also of its fair trade practices (see Chapter 9, Case study 9.1). If Iceland was determined to build an organics business, it clearly needed to choose some different customers ... which would probably require a separate brand. In tough times it's all too easy to chase every opportunity that's out there, on the basis that every pound is a good pound—but choosing which customers we want is just as important a dimension of business success as satisfying the customers we've got (as evidenced by Cranfield research).[184]

Once we have chosen the customers we want, we then need to craft a value proposition appropriate for each group. This may explicitly make a play of our sustainability practices, as in the case of Nespresso. In other cases, it is up to us to translate our sustainability objectives into utilitarian or hedonic benefits for the customer, such as lower costs and hence lower prices.

Channel design

Channel design is a good case in point. Should we cut costs and carbon footprint through the use of new channels, or do our customers demand high-cost, high-carbon face-to-face contact? The good news is that with careful thought, it is generally possible to reduce both carbon footprint *and* costs *at the same time as* improving the customer experience! The trick that achieves this is combining multiple channels in the customer journey, which we call channel combining for wealth. As Alan Hughes, former CEO of First Direct, put it in a recent Cranfield book on the subject:

> Customers are only too delighted to use a low-cost channel when it's right for the job, but there are other times—such as when they have a complaint—when we would be mad not to roll out the cavalry of warm human contact. [185]

And under Alan Hughes's direction, First Direct shifted 80% of customer transactions online, with no loss in its stellar satisfaction and advocacy ratings.

Such channel shifts can be a significant contributor to environmental objectives, in business-to-business (B2B) contexts as well as business-to-consumer (B2C) ones. BT's Major Customers division used to have 2,000 high-carbon field salespeople. It used a coverage map to shift simpler transactions to direct channels, as shown in Figure 8.2.

Figure 8.2 **Keeping high-carbon face-to-face contact for when it's needed: coverage map for BT major customers**[186]

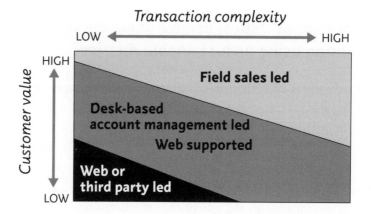

The company reasoned that while selling complex solutions such as an outsourced call centre is bound to require extensive face-to-face contact, many simpler queries or indeed sales transactions can be handled happily through call centres or the Internet—helping both parties with their environmental objectives. After a successful pilot, the scheme was rolled out, replacing 400 field salespeople by desk-based account managers, with an *increase* in revenue and satisfaction as well as a reduction in cost and carbon.

In other cases, though, the marketer might reasonably judge that the customer is prepared to pay just a little more for a sustainable offer, however that is defined in the particular context. Here, though, we need to be careful: consistency of message is as important in sustainability as in any other aspect of integrated marketing communications. And in a Web 2.0 age, that includes consistency with the employee experience, often the target group who are most passionately prepared to take decisions based on a firm's sustainability practices. It is no coincidence that BT worked hard to engage employees in its sustainability practices before worrying too much about the customers (see Chapter 10, Case study 10.1); Rolls-Royce is following a similar trajectory in its low-profile public relations on environmental impact.

Measurement issues: can we generate sustainable marketing using unsustainable metrics?

Some advocates of responsible business have long claimed that the business case for corporate responsibility is unquestionable; you 'do good by doing good'. In fact, the evidence is not as clear-cut as this phrase suggests, but a more fundamental question for managers is whether framing sustainability in terms of the business case is the wrong discourse. By doing this, managers implicitly accept that they are only responsible to the extent that the bottom line permits; this limits ambition and the definition of sustainable business.

In this section we will challenge the business case as the ultimate arbiter for determining policy. Pressure groups, even government agencies, provide anecdotes that by responding to the responsibility agenda XYZ Co. created a new product that makes money and reduces harm: case proven! However, creating offers for unique market segments assessed through environmental or social scanning predates, and is larger than, the sustainability movement. If companies have failed systematically to identify and exploit such opportunities, perhaps they have been looking for innovation in all the wrong places?

In a similar vein we hear anecdotes about companies, motivated by environmental targets, that have found ways to reduce waste and save money while making their offer more attractive. Surely, though, 'meeting customer needs profitably' is a 50-year-old definition of marketing and surely any good manager seeks to eliminate non-value-adding costs? Is this really a definition of *sustainable* marketing, or simply a definition of good marketing practice? Many advocates of sustainability say that sustainability is not a proxy for good management—it is simply about good management, it is essential management.[187]

Part of the business case used by some for adopting sustainable business practices is that firms that do so will enjoy a form of first-mover advantage and thus build brand preference, but we may need to revisit this as responsible practices permeate business. Consider Fairtrade coffee—it was a unique selling point five years ago, but now every major UK grocer claims fair trade on their coffees. These practices are easily imitated and the advantage that they confer quickly dissipates. That said, we believe that responsible corporate behaviour is quickly becoming the norm and while adopting sustainable business practices may no longer differentiate you, the failure to meet institutional norms will surely inhibit the business to which you can aspire.

Aside from challenging the business-case argument on technical grounds, we maintain that the business-case discourse alone is too limiting. Firms embrace sustainable business practices along a continuum anchored at one end by conforming to social norms and, at the other end, by transforming the manner in which they do business. Normally the former is the lower-cost option in terms of cash and organisational development. At the low-cost end of the continuum, firms balance reputational risks to their business against identifiable costs of making changes to their practices. Reputational risk increases when you are visibly 'behind the pack' in embracing responsible practices that stakeholders demand or that pressure groups publicise. At the opposite end, some firms have made a policy decision to embrace responsible business practices fully, well in excess of social expectations and foreseeable regulatory demands. What determines a firm's position on this continuum? For those that define the firm in terms of short- or mid-term shareholder value alone, the choice is easy. That a number of firms make a conscious decision to move further to a short-term, high-cost, transformational objective means that either the management is failing in its duties to shareholders in the short term *or* that there is another dimension to the issue.

This other dimension is often discussed in terms of ethics: 'getting ahead of the game'; building relationships with stakeholders vital to the long-term future of the organisation or long-term reputational benefits. However one defines this other dimension, its essence is based on having benefits that are hard to assess in short-term monetary terms using current business-case methodologies.

Most management theorists would argue that decision-making under uncertainty defines all management activities. Therefore, expected-value decision-making using probability theory and cash-flow discounting with appropriate risk adjustments remains valid in the context of sustainable marketing. However, the tyranny of traditional single financial metrics can lead to 'inventing' business cases for every responsible practice, such as ascribing to responsible investments all sorts of benefits that represent good practice. Discounted cash flows and variants thereof are useful but do not eliminate that other dimension. Therefore, managers face two aspects of sustainable marketing policy: where they fall on the continuum of cost–effort; and what immediate and tangible business benefits they insist on. This can be illustrated as a two-by-two matrix (Fig. 8.3).

Figure 8.3 **Strategic choices in making the sustainable business case**

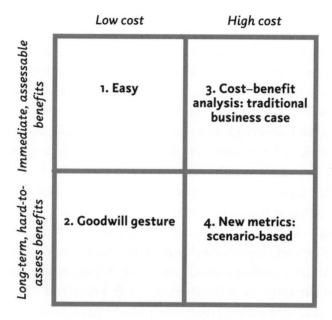

	Low cost	*High cost*
Immediate, assessable benefits	1. Easy	3. Cost–benefit analysis: traditional business case
Long-term, hard-to-assess benefits	2. Goodwill gesture	4. New metrics: scenario-based

There is plenty of evidence for easy, low-cost activities, particularly in supply-chain optimisation: fair trade coffee, chocolate and cotton, for example, are becoming commonplace across major retailers and brands. Excess packaging is being eliminated where it adds costs but little value. Apple's dramatically reduced packaging programme is a case in point. Such activities are relatively easy (although if you work in that supply chain you might not think so!) and they provide immediate benefit in terms of reduced carbon, material and cost.

In other cases, low-cost activities generate benefits that are longer term and harder to assess, but as they don't bankrupt the business are done as 'goodwill gestures' or leaps of faith often ascribed to meeting the values of the firm. You may hear managers justify the cost in such terms as 'our brand values' or that 'customers expect' or 'we live in a new world'.

In Figure 8.3 the top right-hand area (Cost–benefit approach) is challenging but can be managed through traditional financial analysis as the costs and benefits are amenable to quantification and the timeframe is reasonable.

It is the bottom right quadrant that will challenge us: large-scale, costly change in business practices justified by long-term, hard-to-assess benefits. Here we argue against trying to shoehorn discounted cash-flow analysis where the assumptions underlying that method are contestable. Cadbury earns plaudits for its responsible sourcing practices, but should it promote chocolate to young people in an era where obesity is a major health concern? Could it build a healthy snack business even if the competences required and the business model are totally different from those of confectionery? Should food retailers offer high-fat, high-salt food under the auspices of offering consumers choice? BP's previous 'beyond petroleum' vision is another example. Commercially, nothing seemed more intuitively appealing than to find and exploit more oil, given shortages, high prices and BP's business know-how. Yet for a time there was a small part of BP that wanted to move beyond that which would sustain it profitably for the foreseeable future and explore very controversial and difficult investments in other energy platforms such as solar. The Gulf oil spill, however, has greatly complicated matters for BP and one wonders if it can return to its 'beyond petroleum' evangelism. GE has deployed its considerable intellectual resources and balance-sheet strength to reducing the carbon footprint of the heavy capital equipment it makes, yet it has been criticised for its tax position in the USA. Bottom-right quadrant strategies are proving difficult to sustain and act on consistently across all policy areas. We believe that the lack of a widely accepted basis for evaluating this strategy is an obstacle to its long-term deployment and highlights the need for industry and academia to develop new, more sensitive measures. Promising avenues include scenario-based techniques and real options.

The notion that new metrics will be needed to measure the longer-term impact of some sustainable marketing and sales initiatives brings us to the final section of this chapter, in which we consider the future of sustainable marketing and explore the challenge raised above as to whether sustainable marketing is truly sustainable.

The future of sustainable marketing

In this section we look to the future and take a business-to-business (B2B) perspective to consider how a focus on responsibility and sustainability might affect marketing and sales. We identify two clear trends that, to some extent, conflict. These are the pressures for increasing accountability in marketing spending, and the trend towards collaboration between companies. We explore the implications of both these trends for sustainability practices in marketing and sales, and indicate some wider implications for supply chains in general.

Sustainability and customer profitability

One of the hottest topics in contemporary marketing concerns the accountability of marketing and the return on marketing spend. A considerable debate is raging among academics and practitioners about the best way to measure marketing. This debate is particularly relevant to the sustainability agenda because of the shift that seems to be taking place from measuring product profitability to measuring customer profitability. A focus purely on product profitability tends to lead to marketing and sales efforts that 'push' higher product sales, which may conflict with wider environmental and sustainability issues. The emerging focus on customer profitability, however, allows organisations to think longer term about the value of their relationships with customers. As we have already seen, this is linked to notions of 'servitisation' (providing increased services to customers). The development of longer-term relationships with customers also allows organisations to benefit through lower costs, not just through higher sales. In other words, longer-term relationships provide the potential for profit improvement in more sustainable ways, including reduced inventories and lower waste.

Since the mid-1990s there has been a growing body of evidence from both the USA and the UK that companies that are more oriented towards longer-term customer relationships tend to be more profitable.[188] In fact, in the B2B context, our research shows that both sides—customers as well as suppliers—benefit from collaborative relationships. Figure 8.4 illustrates this mutual benefit. Customers benefit from, for example, continuity of supply and tailored products and services, while suppliers benefit from a higher share of their customers' spend and from positive word of mouth.

Figure 8.4 **How collaboration between customers and suppliers affects the bottom line**

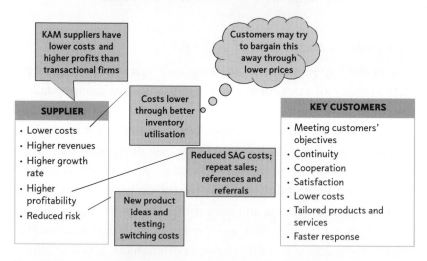

Note: KAM key account management; SAG sales, administration and general.

How does this affect the sustainability agenda? Figure 8.4 indicates that there are some efficiencies that result for both parties from collaborative relationships. Better inventory utilisation is a case in point. Where companies in a supply chain collaborate, inventory levels tend to be lower because they share information about market trends and this can improve their forecasting. Not having to hold safety stocks means that less storage space is needed, reducing the need for warehousing and handling facilities. Less inventory also means less spoilage and less obsolete inventory ending up in landfill.

Figure 8.4 also illustrates the powerful impact that long-term customer relationships can have on the profitability of supplier companies. As the figure shows, this is not only about inventory reductions; it also works for service firms. Customer profitability tends to be higher in long-term relationships because suppliers can focus their sales and marketing effort on their most valuable customers; this means that they do less wasteful prospecting, such as producing marketing brochures that are simply thrown away. These suppliers also benefit from relational benefits such as learning and innovation; working closely with customers means that new product or service ideas are more likely to be market-relevant and less likely to fail. Moreover, where customers give positive word of mouth, suppliers find it easier to recruit new customers; this reduces their cost of sales and cuts wasted effort by their sales team.

Therefore, in a sustainable world, we can say that the lifetime value of a customer is:

Financial value + Relational value (Learning + Innovation + Recommendations + Referrals)

Network power and organisational sustainability

It is not just the relationships between supplier and customer companies that are important; increasingly, organisations are thinking in terms of the power of their networks. In this context it is important to note that:

1. Environmental and social management and sustainable development require companies to acquire knowledge that is not ordinarily found within one single firm

2. Aligning environmental and social management with business management requires companies to participate in collaborative action that links their traditional business setting to new environmental and social concerns

3. The development of this knowledge requires the focal firm to be connected to a broad set of actors outside the firm

4. Social connections could contribute to both competitive and intellectual capital gain

When we think about networks, value can be attributed to different types of relations including buyer–seller relationships, strategic alliances and joint memberships in industry associations. These ties enable firms to exchange and acquire a broad level of tangible and intangible assets (knowledge, capital etc.). Thus, external social ties could contribute both to a firm's competitive advantage and to its intellectual capital and 'know-how'.

The role of networks in creating competitive advantage and intellectual capital

By selecting influential allies (suppliers, professional/non-professional network association or public and press relations partner) firms can influence and be influenced by these focal relationships. However, the key to managing these relations is to adopt a strategic stance. Those companies that share common goals and interests (e.g. ethical or environmental) could (and some do) join forces to leverage market dynamics to their benefits and advantage. Two examples are the joint ventures between Norwegian Telenor and Grameen Bank in Bangladesh in the late 1990s: Grameen Phone and Grameen Telecom. At that time, Telenor was facing saturation in its home country and was seeking market expansion opportunities. The Grameen Bank, founded in 1983 by Nobel Laureate Professor Muhammad Yunus, provides microfinance to millions of the poor in Bangladesh. A joint venture would enable Telenor to provide telephony to one of the world's least developed countries, in partnership with a highly reputable and ethical bank.

The objectives of the two ventures were slightly different. Grameen Phone, operated by experienced Telenor managers, aimed to maximise financial returns. Grameen Telecom on the other hand was set up to maximise the number of jobs created for the rural poor and had a different organisational culture and management structure.

On its launch in 1997, Grameen Phone was one of four companies to receive a licence to operate a mobile network in Bangladesh. By 2004 the company had surpassed expectations and was not only profitable but had over 2 million subscribers and a major market share. By 2006 it had 6 million subscribers. It is now one of the largest private companies in Bangladesh and the second largest tax-payer in the country, reflecting its profitability. At the same time, Grameen Telecom had created over a quarter of a million jobs for micro entrepreneurs, better known as 'village phone ladies'. These are poor rural women who generate income through operating these phones. Grameen Telecom is financially and socially sustainable and creates over 10% of Grameen Phone revenues, and is expected to increase this proportion.

Network connectivity can also contribute to intellectual capital gain by enabling access to knowledge and information that can help support a firm's sustainability. Access to intellectual capital can be particularly useful for small firms or firms entering new markets with limited access to resources. Many companies active in fair trade or environmental-economic sustainability areas come from the not-for-profit or social enterprise sector and may find it challenging to enter profit-oriented industries. By tapping into existing knowledge through trading and non-trading organisational networks they can gain momentum and create added value to their business.

A good example of this is the non-trading alliance between Christian Aid and Divine Chocolate. Divine is a manufacturer of Fairtrade chocolate products in the UK and USA. In 1997, Kuappa Kokoo set up a chocolate company that could offer high-quality chocolate from cocoa beans produced by its members. In partnership with Twin Trading and supported by the Body Shop, Christian Aid and Comic Relief, the then Day Chocolate company (now Divine) was formed in the UK in 1998 with Kuappa Kokoo owning a third share. Christian Aid, which has over 200,000 members and over 35,000 active campaigners, plays the role of a main information partner for Divine. Both organisations have worked together from the very early days of Day and continue to do so. Through an initiative called Choc Shop, Christian Aid supporters sell Divine chocolates to friends and family. More importantly, as a competitive source of intellectual capital, Christian Aid backs Divine with press and public relations. Christian Aid's rich intellectual capital has helped Divine to stay sustainable while achieving profitability and gaining market share in a competitive market.

As these examples illustrate, implementing sustainable marketing frequently requires collaboration with supply chain partners. In the following chapter we move on to consider some new models for sustainable supply chain management.

9

Towards more sustainable supply-chain management

Mike Bernon, Peter Baker, Carlos Mena, Andrew Palmer,
Heather Skipworth, Alan Smart and Simon Templar
Department of Logistics and Supply Chain Management

'Supply-chain operations' refers to 'a set of three or more entities (organisations or individuals) directly involved in the upstream and downstream flows of products, services, finances, and/or information from a source to a customer'.[189] Supply-chain operations have significant impact on sustainability and therefore managing them in an environmentally and socially responsible way has now become a key management concern. Examples of environmental impacts include CO_2 emissions from the transportation of goods, resource depletion, pollution and waste. However, social factors such as child labour, the right of association and a fair wage have also become prominent. The complexity involved means that effectively embedding sustainability across supply-chain partners requires a high degree of commitment and deep understanding of the issues.

Over the past decade, supply chains have been evolving dramatically; many have become geographically dispersed and truly global in nature, often consisting of complex networks. In addition, the trend towards outsourcing—especially to low-cost economies—means that operations previously done in-house are now performed by third-party organisations and no longer under a company's direct control. Therefore, building sustainability into supply chains requires new thinking that involves embracing a holistic and integrated way of doing business. Companies that fail to take this approach will, at a minimum, leave themselves vulnerable to business risk. Those who embrace sustainability can achieve a significant reduction in operating costs which can lead to competitive advantage through innovative new networks.

The economic realities for moving towards sustainable supply chains also need careful consideration. Academics and practitioners alike agree that there is an important relationship between the management of supply-chain activities and organisational performance (financial and non-financial). Supply-chain decisions have an impact on the returns, earnings or profit of the organisation as they can affect both sales revenue and operating costs that are included in the organisation's income statement. Supply-chain decisions are typically based on an appraisal of the costs and benefits and will be measured against a predetermined standard relating to return, payback and risk. However, the ability to quantify and measure the costs and benefits of a sustainable supply-chain initiative is essential for gaining stakeholder support and competing against other corporate initiatives for finite financial resources. Through their Plan A programme, Marks & Spencer have shown that there is a financial incentive to develop and implement a sustainable supply chain and report a net benefit of over £70 million delivered as a result of Plan A activities (see Chapter 11, Case study 11.2) in 2010/2011, compared to £50 million in 2009/2010.[190]

To understand sustainability in a supply-chain context, it is useful to define its scope or the 'system boundary'. The Supply Chain Council's

Supply Chain Operations Reference (SCOR) model[191] describes the five principle processes of supply-chain management as being plan, source, make, deliver and return. This is a good place to start—however, for supply-chain sustainability we need to encapsulate the *full* product life-cycle (PLC) from 'cradle to cradle'.[192] Hence three further elements need to be considered, namely: design, consumer use and end-of-life management. The proceeding sections explore some of the emerging issues that supply-chain professionals need to consider within the scope of a sustainability strategy.

Design and planning

During the product-design process many decisions are made that have major implications for the sustainability of the supply chain that ultimately delivers the said product to market. For example, 75% of life-cycle costs—incurred largely through consumption of resources—are determined by product design. This emphasises that the design and planning stages should consider the implications of the design on the resources required in the supply chain.

The need to connect the design of a product with its supply chain has led to a number of design approaches and we review those most relevant to sustainability here. Design for manufacture and assembly, where products are designed with significant consideration given not just to customer need, cost and legislation, but also to how the product is physically manufactured and assembled. This approach requires the careful consideration of component manufacture and assembly early in the product-design cycle, resulting in simplification of design in terms of fewer components, materials and manufacturing processes; thus reducing the resources required for the product's manufacture in terms of materials, labour, equipment and rework, and ultimately energy consumption and its related emissions.

The concern for the environmental impact of products extends beyond their useful life. Further, European legislation is guided by the German originator principle, 'he who inflicts harm on the environment should pay for fixing the damage', which implies that products should be designed for recycling.[193] It is widely believed that 80–90% of the recycling costs and benefits are determined by the product-design stage, compared with only 10–20% that are driven by the recycling processes, such as separation and purifying techniques.[194] Mangun and Thurston present a model for making decisions regarding component re-use, remanufacturing, recycling or disposal over several product life-cycles for a portfolio of products.[195] A case study of personal computers demonstrates that allowing the possibility of re-use, remanufacture or recycling simultaneously improves cost, environmental impact and customer satisfaction. In the automotive sector, BMW have led the way in design for recycling. In 1991, BMW initiated the BMW Recycling Programme, which oversees standards to dismantle vehicles to obtain the maximum amount of re-usable materials in hundreds of recycling centres throughout the USA, Japan and Europe.[196] The programme complements BMW's Design for Disassembly programme, which has a goal of manufacturing cars in a way that minimises the end-of-life effort needed to separate materials for recycling and to use as few different types of materials as possible.

Returning to the environmental impact during a product's production, it has been recognised that product variety throughout the supply chain, involving a high number of components, sub-assemblies and finished products, adds complexity and increases the resources required due to proliferating inventories and low transport efficiencies increasing relative CO_2 emissions.[197] Consequently, it is desirable to delay the differentiation (increase in variety) in the manufacturing process, and associated supply chain, in order to simultaneously improve customer service and efficiencies—thus reducing resource requirement while improving value delivered to the customer. This approach to product design is referred to as 'design for supply chain' or 'design for logistics' and includes increasing product and process modularisation, increased product standardisation and re-sequencing operations.

More recently a new business model for the provision of products has been shown to deliver significant environmental and social gains. Product–service systems (PSS) is the integration of product and service offerings that delivers value in use and involves the delivery of an offering where the product is central to the provision of an integrated set of services, such as maintenance, repair and support. The most famous example is Rolls-Royce's 'Power by the Hour' and 'TotalCare' contracts, which provide the airline operator with fixed engine maintenance costs, over an extended period of time, for example, ten years (discussed in Chapter 7, Case study 7.2). Other prominent examples include Xerox's change of business model from selling printers and copiers to delivering 'document management'.[198] In these scenarios the manufacturer is motivated to minimise the resource required to maintain and repair the product throughout its useful life, because the revenue stream is constant regardless of the level of intervention.

Consistent with the above approaches, concurrent engineering (CE) proposes that different functions work concurrently on the design of the product. This approach is a more efficient approach to bringing new products to market than the traditional sequential approach, where product designs are passed 'over the wall' from the designers to other functions who are then faced with the issue of how to manufacture and distribute the product in an efficient way. A lack of concurrency can lead to excessive transportation and unresponsive supply chains that fail to meet end-customer needs—in short an unsustainable supply chain. Despite this, there is still currently a lack of inclusion of supply-chain decisions in product design.

Sourcing and procurement

In recent years there has been a significant development in procurement operations, especially in the increasing use of overseas suppliers. Many European and North American firms have increased their purchasing from developing nations, in Asia in particular, because of the lower costs of production, labour and materials. This trend raises two key issues that have an impact on the sustainability debate: carbon footprints, and human rights ethics and reporting.

The surge in overseas sourcing has led many organisations to consider in more detail the impact of procurement on their carbon footprint. For instance, UK retailers Marks & Spencer and Tesco are evaluating the CO_2 impact of purchasing from overseas suppliers;[199] their increased carbon impact comes primarily from additional transportation when moving products between continents.

Human rights ethics is similarly an issue of concern in overseas sourcing. In the UK, the Ethical Trading Initiative (ETI) was established in the 1990s to improve the employment conditions of workers in the food sector's global supply chain.[200] According to the ETI members' code:

- Employment should be freely chosen

- There should be freedom of association and the right to collective bargaining

- Working conditions should be safe and hygienic

- Child labour should not be used

- A living wage should be paid

- No discrimination should be practised

- No harsh or inhumane treatment is allowed

These issues remain of concern across all business sectors. In 2009, the UK retailer Primark (along with Tesco, John Lewis and Asda) were accused of using factories in Asia that employed child labour—they were obliged to review their overseas sourcing procedures.

As overseas suppliers provide an increasing proportion of the final product, buyers must also consider suppliers' impact on their corporate social responsibility (CSR) reporting requirements. Most buying firms already conduct supplier assessments and increasingly environmental impact and human rights are part of the assessment process. For example, buyers will seek information on suppliers' current environmental reporting, use of sustainable materials and their attitude to recycling. This allows an understanding, or a scorecard, of a supplier's sustainability record to be built. US retailer Walmart for example requires all its suppliers to assess the environmental impact of producing their goods, and from this Walmart gives each product an eco-rating.[201] (See also Case study 1.1 in Chapter 1.)

The concern regarding sustainable procurement is not limited to a few firms—a 2009 EcoVadis survey found that 75% of firms surveyed were incorporating sustainability criteria into their procurement bidding processes.[202]

These three issues are just some of the considerations needed for sustainable sourcing and procurement. The issue of socioeconomic impact of sourcing from developing nations, especially when the raw material is scarce, is also one that needs to be addressed—the Nespresso Case study 9.1 shows how multiple sourcing and procurement issues can affect a single product or brand.[203]

Case study 9.1 A call for action in the coffee supply chain

Coffee is one of the most widely traded agricultural commodities in the world, with the coffee industry having yearly retail sales of US$45 billion. Coffee consumption is concentrated in the developed economies, while production takes place in smallholder farms in more than 50 developing nations, with over 20 million families depending on this crop.

➜

The coffee crisis of 2001, when the price of coffee dropped substantially, hit coffee producers especially hard as many of them were subsistence farmers. The crisis was a 'call to action' for activist organisations such as Oxfam and Equal Exchange, which organised campaigns to inform consumers and the media of the precarious conditions of coffee growers, and to question the sourcing practices of the large and powerful coffee buyers.[204]

At the same time, while demand for average coffee was slowing down, consumer appetite for high-quality coffees was on the rise and Nespresso's coffee capsules were enjoying great success, pressuring supply-chain operations to manage a continually rising demand for high-quality coffee. Nestlé Nespresso focuses on premium single-portion coffee at the high end of the market, with a patented coffee-capsule technology, associated machinery and coffee capsules. Sensitive to the difficult conditions—and concerned about the sustainability of the long-term supply of high-quality coffee needed to support an aggressive growth strategy—in 2003 Nestlé Nespresso launched the Nespresso AAA Sustainable Quality™ Program.

According to the firm, the programme represented an 'effort to secure highest quality coffee while promoting environmental, social and economic sustainability along the entire value chain, from the farmer to the consumer'. The programme was driven by Nespresso, but developed through collaboration with green coffee suppliers, Nestlé internal resources and the Rainforest Alliance (RA), an agricultural production sustainability non-governmental organisation (NGO). The programme elements included assessing the sustainability practices of farms and designing a 'continuous improvement' process while at the same time providing a premium price to farmers for their coffee. During its inception and initial activities in 2003, the programme operated in two geographic clusters and involved the RA and two traders. But over time the programme expanded, and by the end of 2007, it was operating in 10 clusters in five different countries, involving 14 organisations and approximately 12,000 farmers.[205]

Manufacturing

The manufacturing of products is where materials are transformed into finished goods. A number of issues affect sustainable manufacturing, including land usage, the consumption of natural resources, the nature of the materials embedded in products, energy consumed in manufacturing, and pollution caused (including greenhouse gas emissions). The production of internationally traded goods, for example, is associated with significant environmental impacts, attributable to 30% of global CO_2 emissions.[206]

Due to the range of processes that exist in manufacturing operations, an exhaustive discussion of the impacts is beyond the scope of this chapter. However, by looking at three sectors—cement, electronics and beverages—we can illustrate a number of the important considerations. Cement has been associated with a number of adverse impacts in the production process itself. During quarrying there can be significant land and wildlife degradation from the extraction of raw material and hence a major environmental consideration has been the regeneration of sites back into natural habitats. Moreover, the cement manufacturing process produces large volumes of CO_2 emissions—with varying reports suggesting that it is responsible for as high as 5–10% of total man-made emissions.[207]

For a number of products, the concern is the materials that are contained within them. In the electronics industry the nature of the materials used has been a major environmental concern for many years due to the heavy metals and hazardous chemicals they contain. This has been highlighted by numerous campaigns by NGOs,[208] notably Greenpeace, which publishes *Guide to Greener Electronics*, which scores individual manufacturers on their performance.[209] Such concerns in Europe have led to the introduction of legislation, including the European Union Restriction of Hazardous Substances (RoHS), which came into force in July 2006. The directive is designed to minimise toxic materials contained in products by restricting the usage levels in the use of a number of substances, including lead, cadmium, mercury, chromium and polybrominated diphenyl ethers (PBDE) flame retardants. Hewlett Packard is one company that has sought not just compliance, but has voluntarily gone beyond this requirement by identifying two further substances that have negative impacts and reducing their use in their products.[210]

The final example of a key manufacturing issue is the use and conservation of natural resources. Water, as the key to life on our planet, is one of the most fundamental elements of our natural resources. It is also in scarce supply, and conflict exists between water use for survival and water use for commerce. For example, fresh water is one of the key ingredients in the production of soft drinks. Water is also used for flushing through and cleaning various production systems. Additionally, if we consider the wider supply chain, water is also used for irrigation purposes for raw material production, for example, for growing sugar beet. For companies such as Coca-Cola, with sugar beet as an essential raw material, they face the challenge of meeting their increasing need for good-quality fresh water with the impact this use has on surrounding environments and societies. A recent study undertaken by Coca-Cola estimated that the green water footprint (water contained in the ground) of the 0.5 litre Coca-Cola beverage is 15 litres; the blue water footprint (surface and ground water) is 1 litre; and the grey water footprint (water used to assimilate pollutants) is 12 litres[211]—a significant use of water (and release of waste water) especially given that the company sells over 1.7 billion servings of drink across their product range per day.[212] How sustainable is this in different countries, with different levels of water scarcity? How might climate change affect irrigation needs and domestic requirements in the future in regions where their products are manufactured? Cotton production is another example of this conflict, where about 84% of the water footprint of cotton growing and production, for its consumption in the European Union, is located outside Europe—with major impacts, particularly in India and Uzbekistan.[213]

Delivery

The aim of nearly all companies with a logistics operation is to minimise costs in a supply chain while achieving the desired levels of service within legislative requirements such as the EU 'working time directive' (which restricts the number of hours employees or contractors can work and, significantly, also driving hours). There is a delicate balance to manage across total transport, warehousing and inventory costs in order to achieve this cost equilibrium. Over the last two or three decades, this equilibrium has been achieved by many companies by reducing and centralising the warehousing function; this reduces the levels of stockholding, and therefore the cost of holding stock, to a minimum. European retailer Zara now uses two central super warehouses to stock its 1,500 stores worldwide.[214] However, the result of this cost-balancing exercise has meant an increase in primary and secondary transport costs. Furthermore, other needs—including the significant rise in Internet home deliveries, the increase in global sourcing resulting in longer delivery distances, restrictions being placed on deliveries in urban areas and issues such as delivery reliability and congestion—have meant that logistics management has needed to evolve.

As consumer awareness of the link between global warming and CO_2 emissions from vehicles has been increasing, companies are now responding by implementing initiatives to mitigate the emissions from freight transport. To reduce CO_2 emissions it is necessary to run fewer, more efficient, miles; increase the use of more environmentally friendly modes of transport such as rail; and make warehouses more environmentally efficient in the way they are constructed and operated, and how different types of stocked and stockless facilities are used.

Key initiatives and collaborations set up by many organisations are addressing the issue of emissions from deliveries. The Efficient Consumer Response (ECR) (a European trade and industry body for the grocery sector) UK Sustainable Distribution Initiative has resulted in a reduction of 120 million road miles over four years, the equivalent of removing 2,000 lorries from Britain's roads—also conserving 60 million litres of diesel fuel per year.[215] These types of initiative have included collaboration between companies to maximise vehicle fill and reduce the amount of empty running. These collaborations have even seen competitors such as Nestlé and United Biscuits overcoming significant barriers and merging aspects of their transport operations, resulting in a saving of over 175,000 miles driven.

The design of the physical supply chain has also come under scrutiny. As the price of a barrel of oil is consistently increasing, the cost and environmental impact of transport becomes more important relative to manufacturing, inventory and facility costs. With the rapid increase in the price of fuel in 2009, and the possibility of the peak oil concept being a reality, companies are looking at reducing transport and delivery distances by moving production and storage facilities nearer to customers. The concept of a global supply chain may have developed as a result of cheaper wages and production methods, but the price of oil, which is inextricably linked with CO_2 emissions from transport, is having an impact on this approach:

- Procter & Gamble recently launched a comprehensive review of the design of its entire supply operations in response to rising energy costs and its plans for global expansion[216]

- Sharp, a consumer electronics company, recently started moving its flatscreen TV manufacturing facilities from Asia to Mexico to better serve customers in North and South America[217]

There have been many predictions about a reduction in offshore production and an increase in local sourcing of goods, driven by higher fuel prices. Environmentally, this is a complex issue because it relies on a life-cycle analysis of CO_2 emissions. For instance, tomatoes grown in Spain can be more environmentally beneficial than British-grown tomatoes because they do not require the artificial heat that is required to grow tomatoes in Britain. A study by the UK Department for Environment, Food and Rural Affairs (Defra) found that British farmers generated three to four times as much CO_2 during the production of a tonne of tomatoes than their Spanish counterparts. The additional emissions from transport in moving the goods from Spain to Britain are more than offset by the savings in growing the produce. Thus, the 'food miles' emissions argument when it is broadened to include production in addition to transportation becomes more complex and relative.[218]

In the light of such pressures and issues surrounding delivery, in many instances a company's physical supply-chain network infrastructure has been in place for a number years and could now be inefficient. A study in 2007 examined the opportunity to reduce the external costs of food transport in the UK by 20%.[219] It showed that optimising a supply-chain network could reduce CO_2 emissions by 2.8% and using longer vehicles would enable CO_2 to be reduced by 6.5%. Aerodynamic design has also been shown to provide 9% CO_2 reduction alone, and by choosing the most efficient vehicle to use, combined with aerodynamic features and fuel-efficient driver training, CO_2 emissions could be reduced by as much as 18%.[220] Marks & Spencer, for example, has started using the 'teardrop' design for their haulage fleet in an effort to reduce their climate-change impact by 20%,[221] and Tesco has adopted double-deck trailers.[222] The introduction of telematic systems such as satellite navigation and vehicle routing and scheduling has been suggested to additionally reduce the distances travelled by vehicles and save about 10% in CO_2 emissions.

Sustainable distribution centre design

In the design of the distribution centre buildings themselves, there have been significant steps in recent years to improve their environmental impact. Water recycling is now commonplace in new buildings with rainwater from the roofs being collected and recycled for 'grey water' uses (e.g. for washing lorries and flushing toilets). Much more consideration is given to materials used in construction, such as using wooden frames from sustainable sources. The US Postal Service dedicated its first, and New York City's largest, green roof high atop the Morgan mail processing facility on 22 July 2009.[223] Energy conservation is an important consideration with sealed vehicle doors and high levels of insulating materials now being normal; 'air flow' systems, for example, may be incorporated that direct the inflow of air underground keeping buildings cool in summer and warm in winter. Energy is often generated now at distribution centre sites by incorporating solar panels on the roof and installing wind turbines around the perimeter. Nike, whose Air suspension product design already considers climate-change neutral material, also had a commitment towards green power to underpin over 35% of its major owned and operated facilities by 2006; their major European distribution centre at Laakdal in Belgium now has six large wind turbines, as well as solar panels, to provide its power needs.[224]

Managing product returns and end-of-life

For some organisations, notably catalogue retailers, the level of returns can be as high as 30% of volume, while one study in the USA estimated the annual value of returned goods to be around $100 billion.[225]

The effective management of returns is not only a cost consideration to organisations but also represents a significant burden to the environment from the waste of natural resources and from the distances returned products travel and the low vehicle utilisation experienced (which means they also incur disproportionately higher levels of vehicle emissions than products in the outbound supply chain). Despite the fact that managing these returns incurs substantial costs through logistics, inventory, and disposal, many companies appear to employ inadequate processes for dealing with returns. Given the tightness of margins in many organisations, it is worth emphasising that the improved management of returns can have a significant impact on bottom-line performance. As a consequence, a number of retailers and manufacturers are now evaluating their supply-chain return processes in a more sophisticated way, recognising that the key drivers of returns exist within their own processes and therefore are within their control. Simple examples range from better forecasting techniques to customer on-line help desks. In addition, at the disposal end, a range of techniques are now being employed to maximise the residual asset value and minimise waste. These include reselling via eBay, TV price-drop channels, and factory-outlet stores.

However, customer returns are not the only problem. The emergence of producer-responsibility legislation—for example, the EU Waste of Electrical and Electronic Equipment Directive—now places a legal obligation on producers to recycle their products at the end of their product life. In the short term most companies have defaulted to solving the problem by joining a compliance scheme where third-party organisations manage the collection and proper recycling operations for a fee. However, a small but growing number of companies see that there is competitive advantage to be gained by setting up their own compliance schemes. These companies, such as Hewlett Packard,[226] typically design their products with recycling in mind (called reverse logistics), have high residual values, and can retrieve their products from the market place at relatively low cost.

Managing waste

Waste arising from supply-chain operations has a direct and broad impact on the three pillars of sustainability: economically, environmentally and socially. Economically, it involves the loss of the value of the product and any disposal costs. Environmentally, it involves a loss of natural resources and unnecessary emissions of greenhouse gases. Socially, it involves a loss to humanity, one that is particularly regrettable in industries such as food or pharmaceuticals where scarcity can have a direct impact on people's lives.

Waste can arise at any stage in the supply chain, including from the final consumer, and the further downstream in the chain an item is wasted the greater the loss in terms of value of natural resources. However, efforts to tackle waste often lack traction because the total cost of waste is often undervalued as costs, such as energy and water use, are 'hidden' in other stages of the chain. Furthermore, actions in one stage of the chain can affect waste in other stages. This complexity means that the waste problem requires holistic solutions.

The waste hierarchy[227] provides a five-level structure for managing waste: waste prevention, re-use, recycle, energy recovery and disposal. However, to prevent waste it is necessary to understand its root causes. A recent study focused on the UK food industry revealed a number of root causes that are applicable to most other industries:[228]

- **Lack of waste management responsibilities.** Organisations lacking clear responsibility for waste usually do not measure and manage waste systematically

- **Performance measurement.** Waste has to be measured to be managed. Ideally it should be reported alongside other KPIs such as cost, efficiency and availability

- **Inaccurate forecasting.** Although estimating sales is a complex and inherently inaccurate task, a scientific approach to forecasting can help reduce forecast error and waste

- **Poor information sharing.** When information is limited, variations between forecast and orders can increase and this can lead to waste. Furthermore, uncertainty caused by poor information sharing can amplify across the supply chain creating a 'bullwhip' effect[229]

- **Inappropriate packaging.** In terms of waste, packaging is a double-edged sword. On the one hand it protects the products from damage; on the other it generates waste unless it is re-used and recycled. The decisions concerning how much and what type of packaging to use are critical for reducing waste

- **Inappropriate quality management.** Quality issues can lead to rework, rejections and even product recalls. These situations can often lead to waste, particularly for products with a short shelf-life

- **Insufficient awareness and training.** Employees are often unaware of the implications of their actions on waste and sometimes do not have the skills to allow them to minimise waste

We argue that although it is more than a decade since Lovins *et al.*[230] challenged business to 'restore, sustain and expand the planet's ecosystems so that they can produce their vital services and biological resources even more abundantly', we have still not achieved this goal. Hopefully, as raising awareness of the causes and the hidden costs of waste are better understood, this will serve as a catalyst for resolving the problem.

Conclusion

It is clear that supply chains have significant importance in driving forward sustainability. It is an extremely complex process and organisations need to think beyond their own boundaries and take a full product life-cycle view. To minimise their impacts, companies need to carefully consider the design of their products as this creates the foundations for reducing the burdens throughout the supply chain, during consumer use, and when the product needs to be recycled at end-of-life. Achieving the goal of supply-chain sustainability cannot be done in isolation; there is a role for policy-makers to provide the direction but organisations will need to work collaboratively with both competitors and suppliers and, when necessary, take an industry-wide perspective to mitigating the issues.

As this chapter has demonstrated, corporate sustainability activities are alive and developing within supply-chain management. We have mapped a number of key aspects for consideration in our sustainable supply-chain management processes. We have not been able to cover all the issues, but suffice it to say, sustainable supply-chain management involves considerable longer-term financial infrastructural investment, operable governmental incentives and effective informed managerial trade-offs between the various environmental and social concerns, against a backdrop of maintaining financial and economic competitiveness.

10

Enabling the change

Corporate sustainability and employee engagement

David Ferguson
Visiting Doctoral Fellow, Doughty Centre for Corporate Responsibility

Martin Clarke
Programmes and Business Director, Centre for General Management Development

> Each of our sustainability priorities represents an opportunity to engage employees, as we collectively contribute to a more sustainable world and benefit our business (Robert L. Parkinson Jr, Baxter International Inc. Chairman and Chief Executive Officer).[231]

There is an obvious intuitive appeal in the synergy between employee engagement and sustainability. The engagement of all employees in embedding corporate sustainability is essential for leveraging corporate sustainability's competitive advantages and business benefits. A number of organisations, including high-profile companies (such as Sky, Coca-Cola Enterprises, IBM, Cisco Systems, General Electric, Walmart, BT Group, RWE npower and Sun Microsystems [now part of Oracle America]) already formally recognise employee engagement as an essential element of their corporate sustainability activities.[232] When employees are engaged with corporate sustainability it is believed to result in improvements in staff productivity, better resource efficiency, reduction of environmental impact, better retention of a more committed workforce, and provide a stronger internal corporate identity and reputational brand.[233]

However, despite a decade of endeavours, the challenge for many organisations is still that 'best practice' approaches for engaging employees in corporate sustainability have not truly delivered the needed benefits. Assuming executive management have woven sustainability into the company's strategic aims, how is it therefore enacted and transformed into actual corporate business performance improvements? With no obvious silver bullet for establishing corporate sustainability into the culture and mind-set of the organisation, the companies that do get it right have a unique and powerful resource that competitors will find difficult to imitate.[234]

In this chapter we highlight some of the shortcomings in alleged 'best practices' for engaging employees in sustainability, as adopted by many organisations, and highlight both alternative and complementary approaches that can be harnessed to improve the effectiveness of engagement strategies designed to create a culture of sustainability.

Employee engagement: clarifying the concept

The topic of employee engagement is not new. Although studies have identified a strong connection between high employee engagement and a firm's performance—particularly around innovation, problem-solving and higher financial returns[235]—management has been wrestling with the issue of employee engagement for years. Most employers have only recently started engaging with employees around corporate sustainability and, to date, few companies have managed to harness the real benefits,[236] with the most recent study indicating there is still considerable room for improvement.[237]

Although employee engagement is a term readily used in conversation, like many aspects of management practice, it reflects a degree of ambiguity with different meanings, interpretations and ways of working. The term 'employee engagement' has been used to describe employee job-centred involvement and satisfaction[238] as well as the broader organisational commitment orientation.[239] A distinction has been proposed that 'commitment' serves purely as an emotional connection, whereas engagement—as an advance on this characteristic—generates discretionary effort and activity towards the organisation's goals;[240] the caveat being that you cannot have engagement without having first generated commitment. With respect to the term 'employees', this description of engagement is equally as applicable to executive and senior management as it is to middle management, line managers and staff.[241]

TowersPerrin's influential 2003 study describes two key engagement distinctions, namely the rational and the emotional aspects of employee engagement. The first relates to the extent to which employees can understand their role and how that relates to their organisation, and the second encompasses a more inspirational and passionate employee response about their work and their organisation.[242] Gallup has categorised the field as the 'actively disengaged', the 'not engaged' and the 'engaged'.[243] The 'not engaged' possess a more neutral stance and exhibit no measurable dissatisfaction in their job or with the company (i.e. they turn up and do their job as requested and that is that), whereas it is the 'engaged' that will go that 'extra mile' for the company's best interests.[244] Gallup and others concur that over three-quarters (75%) of employees are not engaged with their organisations.[245]

But what about those employees who may be dissatisfied with existing aspects of the business but are motivated to challenge accepted activity or introduce their local (sustainability) processes? Does this make them disruptive and therefore disengaged, or engaged because they will go the extra mile to make their business a better place to work—from *their* point of view? Organisations today are complicated and messy places with both competing and mutual interest groups. If an alternative view challenges the existing strategy does that make their orientation wrong? Much depends on their motives being seen as legitimate by other influential people in the business. A more sophisticated definition of engagement then, and the interpretation we seek to develop here, is: 'A positive set of attitudes and behaviours enabling high job performance which is in tune with the organization's mission'.[246]

This definition allows for a more pluralistic assessment of engagement, in which attitudes and behaviour may be in line with an organisation's overall mission but which at any one time might still challenge existing strategy, process and values.

Engagement 'best practice': the 'top-down' approach

A number of strategic and tactical process aspects of employee engagement around corporate sustainability have been developed. Many of these can be described as top-down 'best practice' mechanisms and are already employed by many corporate sustainability leaders across different industrial sectors (see Box 10.1).

From this perspective, leaders provide clarity of vision and purpose behind corporate sustainability. Without their highly visible commitment, the deeper engagement of employees will not gain traction. Similarly, without references to codes of conduct, policies, and codified strategies and objectives, there will be few reference points from which employees can draw explicit company expectations. The creation of measurable key performance indicators (KPIs) provides a route for evaluating managerial performance in operationalising sustainability. Processes for altruistic voluntary engagement outside

Box 10.1 **Top-down tactics for enabling employee engagement in corporate sustainability**

- **Leadership.** Executive/senior level commitment, with highly visible and consistent behaviour around the company's corporate sustainability approaches
- **Strategies.** Clear and regularly communicated strategy, missions, values and aims for the different business constituents
- **Policies.** Prominent business standards, ethical policies, affiliated codes of conduct and relevant industry practices
- **Objectives.** Stated, codified and measurable objectives (key performance indicators [KPIs])
- **Structures.** Specific management structures with relevant employee/union/independent expert representation
- **Processes.** Bonus systems, reward and recognition processes, KPI monitoring and reporting and employment engagement assessments
- **Training.** Sustainability knowledge and skills training, alongside induction and engagement training workshops
- **Employee advocacy programmes.** Dedicated employee volunteering programmes on in-house/external activities related to corporate sustainability

core job requirements, and the provision of reward and incentive mechanisms, bring added emphasis to corporate sustainability as an objective alongside other company priorities. Together, these top-down approaches and management systems provide the legitimacy and impetus for a range of employees to engage with sustainability. Organisations that are serious about bringing corporate sustainability into the heart of their business will have put considerable resources and effort into this approach, and certainly this is the position of most, if not all, leading corporate sustainability companies.

'Top-down' is not the only approach

We have referred to the above mechanisms as a top-down approach, and believe a company that has introduced this suite of managerial approaches has provided an encouraging starting point for enabling employee engagement. However, such is the dominance of this top-down mind-set in the management of many organisations that it can saturate executive time and attention at the expense of alternative and complementary approaches to change. What has been found is that although these aspects are being adopted by many leading companies, there is still 'considerable room for improvement'.[247] 'The millions of dollars being spent on employee engagement programs may be wasted money.'[248]

Why is this the case? What is missing? The first obvious question that comes to mind is, rather than beginning with a senior management strategy, have we asked our employees that we want to engage with what it means to them in the first place? How does it fit their work, motivations and values? This is a conversation that is needed at the beginning of a strategy, not once the board have signed off the budget. If the company's employee engagement is not happening effectively, have we actually asked our employees for a reason? Senior managers and specialist managers focused on corporate sustainability are known to have a rosier view of their company's performance than others in their organisation.[249] Have we actually sought out the 'real' views of our employees behind their engagement (or not) with the company's corporate sustainability vision? Why is it that it appears that some teams, departments and business units are engaged proactively in the corporate sustainability agenda, while others, compared to their peers, are not really delivering anything substantive?

The top-down approach, therefore, should not be the only approach to engagement. We question the effectiveness, comprehensiveness and pervasiveness of these programmes as the sole attributes of successful employee engagement. 'A top-down transformational approach reflects a simplistic view of the way organisations work.'[250]

A number of barriers and inhibitors have been identified, as listed in Box 10.2. Sustainability encouraged through a top-down mindset can too easily fall into a one-way engagement process. Although many executives sincerely seek open debate about sustainability, the pressure to meet stretch targets and cope with competing demands can detract from the need to engage with managers who might not necessarily believe in, or know how to engage employees with, sustainability. At the individual managerial level there are issues around confidence and skills to enact engagement. Coupled with senior- and middle-management cynicism towards engagement generally and a passive resistance to corporate sustainability it is not surprising to find that one of the most fundamental barriers to genuine employee engagement is the lack of cooperation by senior managers. For example, for some managers, genuine two-way engagement may suggest a loss of control in getting things achieved efficiently. With more views to consider, for others it may be seen as increasing the complexity of their work. This lack of support may appear as withholding information or delaying action.

Poor communication processes and an over-reliance on measurable results-based management can dominate managerial behaviour and have also been identified as impediments for engagement. Competing priorities and change initiatives can also serve to counter a corporation's genuine employee-engagement process at different levels of the business. This behaviour should be seen as an inevitable aspect of contemporary organisations rather than an aberration. Managers will have differing views on the priority of sustainability objectives when compared with what may seem to them more pressing short-term issues.

We are suggesting that unless the corporate sustainability engagement programme has been introduced as a new 'greenfield' approach,[251] via a detailed and robust engagement process, then some, not necessarily all, of the above elements will surface, even if it is not an enterprise-wide phenomenon. However, alternative mechanisms exist that allow astute employees to enact change through a more 'informal'

Box 10.2 **Inhibitors and barriers of employee engagement**

Strategic leadership barriers

- Mandatory top-down process with lack of employee value-base inclusion
- Leaders not confronting others to 'walk the talk'
- Lack of HR department recognition of engagement as a strategic issue
- Leaders are not skilled in developing and applying employee engagement
- Many leaders do not yet fully believe in employee engagement
- Organisational culture cannot at present deliver employee engagement
- Low employee perceptions around senior management visibility

Management barriers

- Senior managers' views of engagement are negative
- Senior managers inhibit their middle manager's engagement towards employees
- Management reluctance to relinquish control
- Management's perceived 'loss of control and power'
- Lack of managerial 'coaching' skills to enable engagement
- Inconsistent management behaviour creating sense of unfairness
- Lack of managerial action following preliminary survey and consultations

Line management issues

- Line management behaviour and lack of engagement
- Employees do not trust their line managers

Performance measurement issues

- Too much management focus on KPI results than teamwork and engagement results
- Focus on measurement, with engagement getting lip-service
- A focus on technical performance over teamwork performance

Communication issues

- Restrictive information dissemination
- Lack of communication and knowledge sharing
- Poor communication content and consistency

Personal capability issues

- Managers are not confident to go outside their comfort zones and overcome initial cynicism
- Managers don't have natural communication skills
- Managers revert to command-and-control and micro-management approaches

Employee issues

- Employees' lack of awareness and involvement in corporate sustainability
- Poor understanding of employee returns to corporate sustainability
- Limited understanding of employee needs fulfilled by corporate sustainability

employee-engagement approach. These 'pockets of good practice' can and are developed by employees who are adept at understanding how to enact change processes from within.[252]

We therefore now discuss complementary and alternative employee-engagement mechanisms that are to be found in most organisations. Although employees as individuals can use top-down mechanisms as a way to legitimise their own approach to corporate sustainability, they have to deal with this ambition inside a complex web of competing priorities, where organisational politics may (or may not) be hostile to corporate sustainability. These influence the effective enablement of employees to actively engage. And therefore these influences need to be explored.

Reading the organisational success criteria: harnessing organisational politics

For most employees, organisations are not one homogeneous entity with a synchronised value base. If they were, then the failure rates from implementing change initiatives and business transformations would not be so high. In reality large corporations are composed of heterogeneous groups with various power bases, functioning with a diverse range of political affiliations across the business units and within the managerial layers of each organisation. This in itself needs to be recognised as a potentially powerful barrier to *and* enabler of engagement.

We define organisational politics here as the competitive positioning of causes, using power in the pursuit of individual interests. But those vested interests do not need to be at odds with organisational effectiveness; rather, they potentially enable an understanding of how to get things done more adroitly. Given that organisations are composed of small 'politicised' entities that form constituencies within the business, and that these form into networks of relationships, then proactive managers have to become good at reading the organisation's success criteria and balancing these with the organisational politics within the company. In reality this management attribute must be harnessed and developed to stand any real chance of embedding changes to the status quo.

Implementing corporate sustainability within the organisation is therefore best achieved through applying **constructive political leadership**—a disposition in which managers recognise the need to engage in debate and action about sustainability, irrespective of hierarchical position or explicit authority.[253] Often this may involve challenging rather than following formal strategy. For the political leader this irreverent behaviour is enabled through effectively positioning ideas within the 'unwritten rules' and the very real self-interests of peers, subordinates and superiors. However, such behaviour can only be predicated on the assumption that political leaders possess 'civic virtue'; the ability to forgo, at least on some occasions, self-interest on behalf of others or on behalf of a wider common good. Being seen by others as having balanced motives is critical here.

Creating pockets of good practice: irreverent agents of change?

Corporate sustainability strategy, policies, and performance-management frameworks and processes do help legitimise key corporate sustainability activity. Particularly in the early days however, there is also a need to develop and establish 'pockets of good practice'. The recognition and endorsement of these 'pockets of good practice', using effective communication and knowledge sharing, serve as a nucleus and focus from which other actions crystallise, develop and spread within the company. As such, they are essential mechanisms for helping to change the status quo and to establish further innovations and new standards of practice within the organisation. This is achieved because these individuals act as catalysts and enablers, balancing and integrating individual interests with those of other constituencies. Especially at the beginning of the change process, both in terms of early adopters of the initiative and through the progressive operationalisation stages, they serve as important—if not essential—agents of change 'from within' and should be actively sought out and encouraged.

Who are these agents of change?

In reality, agents of change need to have political astuteness and the capacity to read and understand other people's behaviours.[254] As well as being able to translate the corporate sustainability strategy into relevant areas of self-interest, these potential agents of change are able to understand where the relevant power structures lie and how to use them to enable the change. They can assess the level of genuine interest in different priorities and access alternative networks and relationships that support the development of initiatives, thereby balancing different interests in a mutually acceptable manner. Along with being able to develop the vision of what can be achieved, they possess the capacity to innovate and are prepared to take risks. They are also capable of engaging with their peers, superiors and subordinates to develop specific actions.

It is vital to support these individuals formally and informally, and to allow what may seem like subversive activities to take place in the pursuit of longer-term sustainability goals. Particularly if the initiative has emerged as a top-down approach, these agents of change are crucial first-movers within the company. It would therefore be tactically prudent to develop methods for identifying and recruiting these potential agents of change, as well as nurturing, guiding and assisting them to be successful in their role.

Enabling, engaging and empowering: employee engagement and the democratisation of corporate sustainability

Traditional forms of engagement encourage a top-down, almost one-way transactional engagement of employees within corporate strategic rhetoric. Processes such as the medium-term planning process, objectives, budgets and KPIs are then expected to do the rest.

The alternative, and complementary, approach to engagement is to involve all employees at the beginning, encouraging them to provide solutions and commitments around what should and can be achieved (see Box 10.3). Although this may mean the strategy production is delayed, this would be a small sacrifice compared to a more engaged and involved employee base, and a higher probability for a more expedient and successful implementation of the necessary changes of behaviour.

- Although to some managers, particular corporate sustainability activities may appear as 'no-brainers',[255] it is still essential that ideas are developed bottom-up from the real and relevant issues that individuals face. This more democratised form of engagement encourages personal agendas and self-interests to coalesce around what *employees* see as important

- It means not launching rigid, detailed, prescriptive corporate sustainability targets or measurement-bound objectives; rather it means allowing for more equifinality around the vision, that is, allowing there to be more than one way of reaching the stated goals. This provides individuals with freedom of interpretation as how best to achieve sustainability goals

- As corporate sustainability is a somewhat nebulous concept, still undergoing definition in many organisations, this approach encourages and supports different levels of understanding about the sustainability challenge

- By enabling a 'loose fit', more employees can be encouraged to broadly participate in corporate sustainability, as each can engage in a way that is appropriate for his or her understanding of the issues

- Finally, it is vital also to recognise the cooperation and participation of those who have helped make it happen. This is not necessarily in terms of financial reward and bonuses, but also in terms of responding to different needs in this recognition process, for example, public profile, 'time off' to support/develop 'pet projects' or involvement in other high-profile or personally interesting initiatives

Box 10.3 **Management from within**

- Read and manage the politics in a constructive manner
- Seek to listen and balance line manager's self-interests with organisational sustainability objectives
- Engage and involve employees in the issue and respond to/ accommodate their solutions
- Recruit, train, guide and support agents of change
- Accommodate the flexibility of multiple trajectories towards reaching the corporate sustainability goals
- Identify, endorse and communicate pockets of good practice
- Consistently engage and discuss corporate sustainability strategy and operational actions with employees on a regular basis
- Recognise and 'reward' individuals in a flexible manner

Although the results may not be instantaneous, in time—and through progressive debate, the development of 'pockets of good practice', improved knowledge sharing, and continuous multi-channel, two-way engagement—new culture will coalesce around corporate sustainability that can become embedded within the fabric of the company.

The ten factors for fostering employee engagement in corporate sustainability

In summary, when seeking to optimise employee engagement and participation to operationalise corporate sustainability deep within the company, the following ten factors are deemed essential contributors for enabling the change and 'making it happen':

1. Clear corporate vision around corporate sustainability and connectivity to consistently 'excellent' leadership behaviour

2. Encouragement of distinctive formal and informal employee involvement towards shaping and framing the corporate sustainability value base and strategic/operational issues at the enterprise and local business/team/department level

3. Provision of 'public' formal commitments and endorsements to corporate sustainability strategy and planned objectives from executive and senior managers

4. Factoring in the inevitable political nature of the change, stimulating and protecting innovative pockets of good practice at different levels around the company

5. Transparently balanced and open organisational governance structures with employee-level representations, debate and discussion forums that are empowered and acted on

6. Regular and fully accessible 'integrated' communications from executive/senior management, middle management and staff around existing performance, good practices and inno-

vations to adopt, with discussion and engagement around key problems and future directions

7. Debating and communicating to formulate consistent management decision-making around good and poor corporate sustainability performance across the company and employee levels

8. Individual, team and cross-functional levels of recognition and 'personalised' flexible rewards for contributions to the company's corporate sustainability strategy

9. Providing individuals with information around their local performance criteria, with knowledge-transfer opportunities around good practices, company approaches, subject-specific knowledge and contemporary thinking

10. Management development for key individuals to lead engagement in sustainability with political acumen

Sustainability and employee engagement: mini-cases

Case study 10.1   BT's balanced CSR and employee engagement

Being ranked the number one telecoms company in the Dow Jones Sustainability Index for the last seven years running, BT has maintained a long-standing commitment to corporate sustainability. Employee engagement is important for the company and has been an important success factor in its achievement of a 60% reduction in CO_2 emissions since 1996.

> For me, the most important decision for a CR practitioner involved in employee engagement is whether you want to take a 'policing' approach or a 'releasing' approach. I have found it most fruitful (and certainly more fulfilling!) to take a 'releasing' approach to my role. Use communications to give people permission to get involved. That serves to release the pent up demand that I find is nearly always present amongst employees. Then our role as CR practitioners is to harness that energy by helping our people understand what is really material and how to apply their core competencies.
>
> As CR practitioners we should be in the business of releasing, rather than policing, the potential of our people to support society and the environment. (Kevin Moss, Head of CSR, BT Americas).[256]

As such, the company supported employees in their focus on aspects such as disposable cup and single-sided paper reduction initiatives, alongside more pressing corporate energy-consumption initiatives that were clearly a strategic priority area. This serves as a good example of releasing employees' engagement energy, rather than a top-down controlling or 'policing' approach; providing a more productive balance of motivational employee-based interests and strategic corporate interests around sustainability performance improvement.

Case study 10.2 **Diageo's innovative GREENiQ employee-engagement programme**

Diageo, a global drinks company, has sought a more fun-filled approach to inspire its employees to engage with sustainability. It has harnessed the Olympic Games as a thematic global business covering 80 sites across 40 countries. Its aim is to encourage its 20,000 employees to start initiatives and share them across the business.

Using the intranet, site-based green teams can be set up and registered. Along with online networking and a news portal, there are guidelines on how they can compete to win bronze, silver and gold medals towards a raft of environmental initiatives including, for example, bronze projects centring on setting of targets, with gold being recognisable for the achievement of challenging environmental targets. As an additional recognition and reward aspect, the site with greatest medal rankings each year is awarded a cash prize that can be spent at the site or local level. From a list including Shanghai, Buenos Aires and Dublin, Menstrie in Scotland won the £15,000 prize, which it can spend on a site-based or local environmental initiative of its choosing.

Diageo's new approach is clearly driven through a top-down executive-level-supported global programme, with easily accessible information and initiative-sharing infrastructures and a clear reward process that legitimises and encourages engagement with different types of initiatives. This is combined with a flexible, local voluntary uptake and participation mechanism, as well as local, site-based recognition for different achievements and involvement.

11
Sense and sustainability

Sharon Jackson
Associate at the Centre for Customised Executive Development

Understanding how managers in organisations make sense of corporate sustainability (CS) is an essential, but overlooked, component for embedding sustainability-related behaviours in organisations. Sustainability is a complex, subjective topic about which people have multiple, different interpretations and understanding. These interpretations are developed through sense-making; a conversational and narrative process that draws on storytelling, conversations and written narratives. It is this thinking process that people engage with to find meaning and to create a subjective world reality that is meaningful to them.[257]

Organisational sense-making has been identified as being fundamental to the development of organisational consciousness.[258] Furthermore, conversations facilitate change in organisations and through conversations sense-making plays a central role in shifting organisational thinking patterns and collective stories.[259]

Through drawing on new research, this chapter addresses the role of middle managers in terms of how they make sense of and therefore enact their organisation's collectively espoused sustainability principles. In my view there can be multiple interpretations of corporate sustainability, and different individuals hold different 'world realities' that are equally valid and real to them. This chapter discusses how people make sense of their organisations' expectations of them to deliver on sustainability aspirations, and explores how their sense-making and interpretation impacts on what they do.

The role of middle managers

There was a time, not so long ago, when business managers understood their daily responsibilities in the context of their role. When people are employed in specific roles because of their skills, knowledge and experience related to that role this makes sense, and managers can understand what their organisation expects them to do.

This changed at the turn of the millennium when high-profile corporate crashes such as Enron and WorldCom placed a global spotlight on corporate responsibilities towards the environment and society. This brought new expectations of responsibility for employees, at all levels, to be the guardians of their organisations' responsible conduct and image in society.

As well as conducting daily decision-making and actions necessary for carrying out role-related duties and objectives, these days managers are also expected to volunteer in the community, recycle waste, reduce energy and water consumption and carry out a host of other environmental and community-related activities.

Generally, organisations expect managers to contribute to espoused sustainability aspirations; however, the role of middle managers as change agents is frequently undervalued in terms of their role as connectors between an organisation's strategic and operational levels.

Also overlooked is managers' contribution to shifting organisational conversations and shared organisational interpretative systems necessary to create change[260]—and very necessary for collective understanding of the meaning of CS.

Gaps between good intentions and actions

In terms of embedding sustainability in an organisation, there can be a general, simplistic assumption that a well-constructed sustainability aspiration, with polished and attractive marketing materials, will lead to managers engaging in the aspiration, and through their decisions and actions contribute to a sustainable business culture. If this assumption were correct, how then can we explain the behaviour of some managers in (for example) some UK banks with espoused commitments to CS, acting in a way that was at odds with the publicly stated CS aspirations—so much so that their daily operational behaviour nearly destroyed the UK banking sector in 2008.

Further examples of this apparent disconnect between intent and action can be seen in the news all too frequently. Globally dominant energy and extractives companies, for example, publicly espouse CS principles as being vital to their 'licence to operate', yet many are repeatedly at the centre of allegations of commercial espionage, bribery and overlooking health, safety and maintenance short cuts leading to human injury and environmental damage.

In my own work helping organisations to engage managers in embedding their CS aspirations, I have seen many examples of organisations boasting sustainability awards and CS network membership affiliation, yet inside the organisation has existed a culture that does not enable truthful conversations or space for any form of reflective organisational learning. One example is a global information communications technology (ICT) business that appeared to be unaware of how its 70-hour-a-week work culture was resulting in exhausted managers who spent very little time with their families or paying attention to their own health.

The managers proudly told me about their latest award as an ethical company to work for, so I asked them how this aligned with the 70-hour work culture they had discussed with me earlier. The response was: 'If we do not put in the hours we will get overlooked for promotion.' I asked how many hours they planned on working after promotion . . . reflective silence followed.

Do these managers have a professional blind spot? How could they not realise the incongruence between the concept of a good place to work and an exhausting working week that kept them from their families? With such incongruence, how can managers make sense of what they are expected to do in terms of their organisations' commitment to society and the environment?

When I asked the managers at the ICT firm to give examples of CS in their organisation their response was: 'The company provides free coffee, day and night', and 'On hot days the boss gives ice creams to employees in return for business ideas'.

This is the managers' own world-view, their own interpretation of CS in their organisation—these were the 'cues' that they noticed and interpreted as being CS. However, as an outsider I noticed different 'cues'. I noticed that this organisation fosters (probably unconsciously) a culture, from the CEO down, of an implicit expectation for managers to work 70 hours a week for a 40-hour-a-week salary, justified by the promise of promotion in the future. The managers and I had *completely different interpretations of exactly the same scenario*. Herein lays the fundamental difficulty in making sense of sustainable business or CS.

The Doughty Centre for Corporate Responsibility defines a responsible business as a business that has a commitment to deliver sustainable value to society at large built into its purpose and strategy. Many companies state similar definitions and a commitment to this definition. Yet, somehow, in the ICT firm what we actually have is volunteering outside the organisation and free coffee inside. In my own view of reality, these tactical activities are far from 'purpose and strategy' and simply not enough if we are to truly embed sustainability in corporations.

The contemporary challenge organisations are facing is how to integrate their espoused sustainability aspirations into their mainstream business strategy and how to truly engage their managers in doing so on a daily business, operational basis.[261]

We have come to an important time in organisational learning where it is essential for managers, at all levels, to be honest about the gap between rhetoric and action around sustainable business and to face up to the tectonic shift in thinking patterns and behaviour change that is necessary to create truly sustainable businesses.

Bridging the gap between intent and action

A fundamental problem to overcome is that the notion of a shared meaning of CS is hard to communicate through a strategy or policy without losing the 'spirit' of the aspirations. The difficulty then arising is how managers, who are expected to enact these intentions, interpret the espoused aspirations. An added complexity is answering why people should do anything more than the daily roles that they are paid for, measured and rewarded against.

BT has been a global leader in responsible telecommunications (see, e.g. Case study 10.1 in Chapter 10); however, a BT manager said recently: 'One of our biggest challenges is overcoming why should our employees be interested in doing any of our CS?' I have heard this refrain many times in organisations that appear to genuinely want to be a good corporation at all levels.

A starting point to help managers make sense of their organisations' sustainability aspirations is to understand how the aspirations have been crafted, whether the managers have been involved and if the messaging is congruent with what the business does. If the sustainable business intentions have been written by an external marketing and communications firm it is highly unlikely that managers will feel connected to the espoused aspirations.

Congruent narratives

Alignment of language used in an organisation's guiding sustainability principles and internal identity is a critical factor in enabling congruent sense-making and interpretation. Where the language is considered to be 'woolly' and the messages do not fit, managers follow their own 'script' of interpretation aligned with their own tacit knowledge and experience.

Sustainability can start to have shared sense and meaning when it is explicitly linked through narratives and labels that connect with a collective identity with which people in the company passionately associate themselves.

Panasonic, for example, has a deeply embedded 70-year business philosophy emanating from its Japanese founder. Today this philosophy is congruent with the organisation's sustainability aspirations and has been highly influential in creating a shared organisational interpretive system and collective identity. This appears to impact on managers' individual sense-making, in that, when managers talk about Panasonic's sustainability aspirations they tell similar stories and subconsciously refer to similar information. They tend to refer to 'labels and cues' from their underlying organisational culture to make sense of sustainability in a daily context.

Research suggests that managers try to find a meaning of sustainability that is aligned with the organisation's culture and prevailing organisational sense-making systems.[262] They select information from the dominant organisational narratives, storytelling and language used in daily conversations. Conversely, where the language and messages around sustainability are not aligned, managers struggle to make sense of what is expected of them.

Patterns emerging through a growing body of research suggest that managers enact their organisation's sustainability intentions when their **individual sense-making is aligned with the collective organisational sense-making**. This means that managers' sense-making of sustainability must create a 'story' that is aligned with the prevailing organisational narratives and stories.

When this alignment does *not* happen, managers' own sense-making process can draw on a different set of personal sense-making influencing factors to create an alternative story, which is plausible in their own world reality. This could be described as managers 'reading a different script' from the collective organisational sense-making script. This can lead them to a different view of reality, or interpretation of the organisation's sustainability aspirations, which impacts on what they do, or do not do.

It is very important that sustainability aspirations make sense to managers in the context of the business. Here follows three examples.

Case study 11.1 **IAG Australia**

Directors of IAG identified a direct correlation between climate change and the 'health' of the insurance industry. From the start, they used clear messages, endorsed by the CEO, both inside and outside the organisation, saying business sustainability must be the intended outcome of a successful business strategy, not as a separate initiative or something that is discretionary.

IAG was a co-founder of the climate-change round table that lobbied the Australian government to introduce climate-change policies. Then, IAG moved proactively beyond climate-change advocacy to definitive action, which focused on mitigation and adaptation to ensure the resilience of IAG business, customers and the communities in which IAG operates. For example, as a major car insurer, IAG drew significant insights from its claims data that was used to improve road safety. IAG refined itself as more than just an insurance business.

Case study 11.2 **Marks & Spencer UK, Plan A**

Described as 'the way we do business', through written and verbal communications, Marks & Spencer provides clear links between Plan A and most areas of the business. This initiative has been endorsed by a high-profile CEO.

Plan A is based around five pillars of action, each with a branding and 'labels' with congruent messaging integral to the core business operation. Each pillar has clearly defined objectives and outcomes, including, for example a customer-focused 'do you need a bag?' campaign with targets for bag-use reduction, and innovative transportation 'teardrop' designed trailers to reduce fuel consumption by 20% and gain 10% in load space.

Case study 11.3 **InterfaceFLOR USA**

InterfaceFLOR has redefined itself as more than a carpet-tile business, claiming on its website to be 'the first company that, by its deeds, shows the entire industrial world what sustainability is in all its dimensions— and in doing so we will become restorative through the power of influence'. Led by its figurehead founder and CEO, Interface communicates internally and externally its mission to 'climb Mount Sustainability' to achieve zero waste by 2020. This message has become a very strong commercial differentiator, a platform for innovation and cost saving.

Interface puts organisational learning at the core of its sustainability journey, for example, by engaging teachers and thought-leaders in sustainability to educate the management, challenge their thinking and create a culture of reflective practice of accountability.

These three examples have sustainable business aspirations that are driven by different reasons; however, the outputs are similar in that all three organisations achieved broad engagement of managers enacting the aspirations in daily operational roles.

The leaders of all three businesses have a strong commitment and the storytelling and messaging in each firm is congruent from the top through into daily, routine narratives. The communications demonstrate a clear link between sustainability aspirations and business success, therefore contributing to aligned sense-making.

Common elements in the three examples are:

- Sustainability aspirations are aligned with the business objectives
- Congruent leadership messaging
- Investment in organisational learning
- Communications story is congruent and makes sense

While I am not suggesting that these three organisations have everything right, they do appear to be on a committed and congruent journey towards a model of sustainable business that makes sense, inside and outside the organisation. To summarise the similarities in these examples, Figure 11.1 illustrates the impacts on making sense of CS.

Figure 11.1 **Impacts of sense-making**

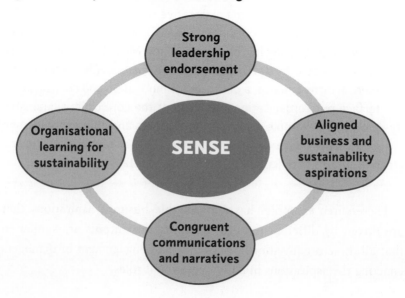

When sense gets derailed

To understand more about joined-up sense-making between 'intent and action', we need to understand how sense-making can become derailed so that action is not aligned with espoused intent.

My own management research into how managers make sense of sustainability in their organisation suggests that managers, subconsciously, expect someone else to enact sustainability.[263] The following observations provide new insight into the sense-making dynamics associated with engaging managers to enact sustainable business ambitions.

We will do it in five years' time . . .

The following examples from my research illustrate a subconscious sense-making process that can result in an interpretation that 'we will do it in five years' time'.

During a 90-minute research focus group, ten managers, all representatives of their organisation's green initiatives, mentioned ten times that there were too many lights on in the room. They all agreed that their organisation expected them to reduce energy consumption and CO_2 emissions as a commitment to reduce their impact on climate change. *Yet not one person turned off the extra lights.* The group discussed how three years ago nobody would have noticed that there were too many lights on and that in five years' time someone would turn them off. *They discounted the thought that they could act to turn off the lights today!*

The managers appeared to be unaware that through their conversations and storytelling they 'deselected' the reality of present-day action. Two weeks after the focus group the participants were interviewed one-on-one and asked why they thought nobody had turned off the lights. They were not aware of what they had said, which suggests that sense-making is a subconscious process that is only noticed through retrospective reflection.

One of the quotes from the interviews was: 'That is quite interesting actually isn't it . . . ? It kind of shows that although we are thinking about it we are not actually doing anything about it.'

Sense-making theory[264] suggests that to find their own meaning of reality, people notice and select different 'cues' to build a story of interpretation that impacts on their behaviour. Figure 11.2 illustrates how 'we will do it in the future' became the outcome of the managers' sense-making process, as observed through their conversation.

Figure 11.2 **'We will do it in five years' time'**

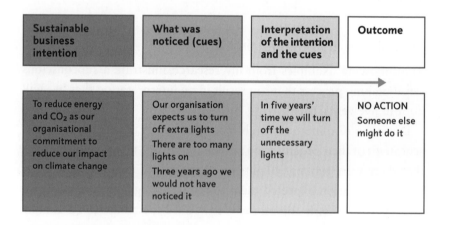

Sustainable business intention	What was noticed (cues)	Interpretation of the intention and the cues	Outcome
To reduce energy and CO$_2$ as our organisational commitment to reduce our impact on climate change	Our organisation expects us to turn off extra lights. There are too many lights on. Three years ago we would not have noticed it	In five years' time we will turn off the unnecessary lights	NO ACTION. Someone else might do it

Not my responsibility . . .

The same group were asked how they enact their organisation's sustainability intentions in their daily role. The IT Manager said, 'in IT we do not have any influence on sustainability'. Her interpretation was that her role was strictly around business performance and cost management. Her colleagues had an alternative interpretation that the IT function could make a significant contribution to the company's reduction in energy-use targets. The IT Manager deflected every comment from her colleagues and stuck very firmly to her interpretation of what was expected of her in her role and the key performance indicators (KPI) against which she was measured.

Using the theoretical sense-making model, Figure 11.3 illustrates how the IT Manager's sense-making process resulted in an interpretation of 'it is not my responsibility'. The manager did not process her interpretation of the organisation's espoused sustainability into action relevant for her.

Figure 11.3 **'Not my responsibility'**

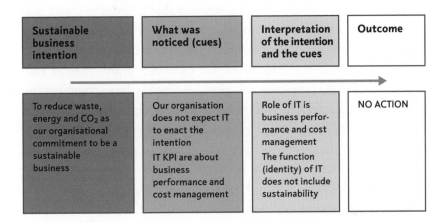

Sustainable business intention	What was noticed (cues)	Interpretation of the intention and the cues	Outcome
To reduce waste, energy and CO_2 as our organisational commitment to be a sustainable business	Our organisation does not expect IT to enact the intention IT KPI are about business performance and cost management	Role of IT is business performance and cost management The function (identity) of IT does not include sustainability	NO ACTION

Managers struggle to find meaning about who is expected to do what in terms of sustainability when the messages are conflicting. It is very important that communication is clear about *who* is expected to be 'doing sustainability' in an organisation.

Sense-making starts with asking 'what is the story here?' and congruent messaging across the organisation is essential to avoid everybody thinking someone else is doing 'it'. Otherwise, managers can often take 'no action', because their sense-making process leads them to 'deselect' information of their present-day personal responsibility.

This story of the lights and the IT manager may seem small and unimportant, but referring to both examples—figures 11.2 and 11.3—a poignant issue is that the managers from both firms were passionate about their organisation's responsible business reputation and awards for ethical business, and were proud to be the 'good guys'. These two research examples deselected the 'elephant in the room' as not relevant to CS and instead, free coffee and 'not my responsibility' were the preferred, noticed 'cues'.

Implications for organisational learning

Practitioner and academic writing suggests that in order to create sustainable businesses the operational managers of organisations need to enact the espoused sustainability aspirations through their daily decisions and actions.[265] However, the examples in this chapter suggest that in many companies this may not actually be happening. The noticing and deselecting process of sense-making can create an 'out of sight, out of mind' world reality. In many organisations there is reluctance for managers to have honest, organisation-wide conversations about the congruence between publicly stated sustainability intentions and what is actually happening in daily business activities.

Identifying chasms between rhetoric and action, through noticing which cues managers are selecting and deselecting, should be the first step in enabling many to make sense of sustainability in their organisation and therefore act in a sustainable way. However, this requires new skills and a new organisational approach that embraces the notion of multiple world realities. Currently, most managers are, in general, not required to operate in this area and therefore for this new approach to happen more investment in management development training is required that covers fundamental skills in reflective learning, communication and organisational change in the specific context of sustainability and CS.[266]

Conclusion

Sense-making is a human process of finding meaning that is reached primarily through narratives. Through conversations and stories people seek meaning that fits with their own interpretation of reality, even though their reality may be different from the organisation's intended collective reality. Because this is a subconscious phenomenon, 'sense-making fault-lines'[267] go unnoticed and un-discussed and remain unchallenged in organisations.

This chapter gives some insight into the existence of multiple interpretations of sustainability, depending on an individual's sense of reality. The challenge is to find the alignment between managers' frames of sense-making and the collective interpretations of sustainability to capture a shared meaning and action.

This requires a new approach to organisational learning and individual reflective learning to overcome sense-making fault lines. It is necessary to raise managers' awareness of their own sustainability sense-making process in terms of what information they notice and deselect.

Three suggested steps forward:

1. Become aware of, and accept, the problem of incongruent sense-making

2. Train new skills for recognising sense-making fault lines

3. Develop new skills and techniques for addressing the fault lines

For the radical and the brave . . .

In my view much of the marketing gloss has taken the sense out of sustainable business from a daily organisational perspective, leading to a gap between rhetoric and operational action. To address this, you could:

- Take an honest look at your sustainable business/corporate responsibility (CR) department. If it is simply an extension of a marketing function then *either* upgrade the budget, invest in skills training and increase the empowerment of the people, *or* close the department (being sure to re-employ loyal people in different roles)

- Pull sustainability and CR sense-making away from an elite few by allowing space and time for more collaborative cross-functional reflective conversations

- Develop a very clear story-line about what sustainability means in the company to assist with the sense-making process . . . and repeat, repeat and repeat the story, linking real examples of senior management behavioural leadership, middle manager 'best practices' etc. to help managers with their sense-making

- Utilise collaborative discussion and exchanges around the key story-line as to what that can mean for each business unit, team etc.

- Be prepared to intervene and change someone's misplaced sense-making mechanism. Encourage challenge within the ranks to enable re-evaluations of sense-making by those in power within the organisation's hierarchy

- Encourage bottom-up initiatives and projects to allow those with useful contributions to be able to make and create new stories within the organisation

And finally, not for the faint hearted:

- Throw away the glossy CR reports written by marketing consultants and start again with a fresh approach. There used to be a raw passion and authentic feeling around sustainable business, but sterile identical reports are less than inspiring

I hope this makes sense to you.

12
Telling it like it is
Reporting sustainability performance

Ruth Bender
Reader in Corporate Financial Strategy

To an accountant, accustomed to the standards and regulatory frameworks that surround financial reporting, the field of corporate sustainability (CS) reporting can be uncomfortably ambiguous. Sustainability reports, when they exist, take a variety of formats and report a miscellany of different indicators, mostly in different ways. In this chapter we will set out some of the questions an organisation needs to address when introducing sustainability reporting or developing its existing reporting structures.

First, what is meant by sustainability reporting? A useful definition is:

> SER [social and environmental reporting] is the predominantly voluntary, self-reporting of an organisation's social and environmental interactions. Such reporting is increasingly undertaken in stand-alone reports—some in hard copy, many on the organisation's website—and represents

an organisation's understanding of what it is to be environmentally and/or socially responsible and (potentially at
least) sustainable.[268]

Several points in this definition are worth noting. SER is currently
voluntary (although many jurisdictions demand some form of disclosure of an organisation's CS activities). It is **self-reporting**: the
company controls what is reported, and how. And it represents the
organisation's understanding of what is relevant, rather than merely
following boilerplate disclosures.

The rest of this chapter is structured around the questions that need
to be asked in preparing a CS report:

- Why should we prepare and publish a report?

- Who should prepare the report? Who will be reading it? Who (if
  anyone) will verify its accuracy?

- What should be disclosed?

- How should the data be presented?

- When and where should the report be published?

Why prepare a sustainability report?

There are broadly three reasons for an organisation to make sustainability disclosures: because they want to; because they see commercial
advantage in it; or because it is required.

Companies rarely jump in at the deep end of CS, becoming instant
advocates; their journey tends to be gradual. The attitude towards
reporting and the volume of disclosure will reflect this progression.
Companies in the early stages of this life-cycle may typically give
minimal disclosures, perhaps bold statements with little supporting
or validated information. As the company's approach to CS changes,

so will its reporting and the transparency of its operations—including its CS weaknesses and aspirations—will tend to increase.

Even a company not wishing to live and breathe sustainability may see merit in voluntary disclosure of CS activities. This can be understood in terms of institutional theory, which considers why companies' practices tend to become similar.[269] It suggests that practices converge for three reasons:

- Coercive reasons relate to adopting practices due to regulatory pressure, discussed below

- Normative reasons reflect practices passed on by the professionals advising the business, and here we can see the influence of consultants, accountants, investor-relations professionals and others who determine and promote 'best practice' (or at least, common practice) in disclosure

- Finally, and importantly, mimetic pressures are in play—companies do things because they see them working for other companies, and so have no reason not to do them

All three reasons are significant, and as it becomes more common for companies to make CS disclosures, *not* doing so might be seen as reducing a company's legitimacy in the eyes of society (particularly a society feeling wary of 'business as usual' due to a global downturn). Thus, adopting some form of CS reporting is also protective camouflage to ensure legitimacy.

Should the internal forces for disclosure not be sufficient, there is a growing body of both regulation and investor/shareholder pressure to encourage disclosure. Investor pressure comes from shareholders, lenders and analysts. For many years there have been investing institutions taking a proactive stance on sustainability in their investee companies. This was formalised in 2006 with the launch of the UN Principles of Responsible Investment (UN-PRI).

> The Principles for Responsible Investment aim to help integrate consideration of environmental, social and governance

> (ESG) issues by institutional investors into investment deci-
> sion-making and ownership practices, and thereby improve
> long-term returns to beneficiaries.[270]

Of the six principles underlying the UN-PRI it is the third principle that is of relevance to ESG disclosure: 'We will seek appropriate disclosure on ESG issues by the entities in which we invest.' Underlying this, the document suggests that signatories ask their investee companies for standardised disclosure of ESG matters, integrated into the annual financial reports.

Investors are also increasingly becoming aware that ESG matters and can be an indicator of performance. For example, in 2008 the Chartered Financial Analysts Institute published an ESG 'manual for investors' that pointed out the need to incorporate ESG issues into their corporate assessments and valuations.[271] For this to be done well, companies need to improve their disclosures.

In addition to these investor-related pressures, regulators in many jurisdictions are demanding more ESG disclosure. For example, since 2010 the King III Code of Governance Principles for South Africa has required companies listed on the Johannesburg Stock Exchange to publish 'integrated reports' (discussed later) that include both financial and sustainability information.[272] The European Union is considering whether to promote the concept of integrated reporting, but many of its member countries already demand significant CS disclosure.[273] The UK Companies Act 2006 (section 417) requires listed companies to disclose information about their environmental impact as well as details of employees and social and community activities, with relevant key performance indicators.[274] In the USA, Securities and Exchange Commission (SEC) guidance requires disclosure of legal or business developments as they relate to climate change. This includes a variety of matters, from the cost of complying with environmental regulation through to the risks associated with products that have significant greenhouse gas emissions.[275]

Companies choosing to make voluntary disclosures above and beyond their regulatory requirements have to consider a cost–benefit trade-off. The business-case benefits of transparency can include an easier relationship with stakeholders and better investor understanding, possibly leading to a lower cost of capital and thus higher performance for shareholders. However, some companies might see competitive disadvantage in making additional disclosures, and in all organisations there will be a cost involved in collecting and presenting the data. It is for the organisation to determine the additional benefit, tangible and intangible, of each separate disclosure.

Who is involved?

Who should prepare the sustainability report?

In much the same way as a company's finance department takes responsibility for the preparation and collation of its annual report, an individual or department needs to take responsibility for the CS report. However, CS is an activity that, done properly, involves the whole organisation, and although CS specialists can coordinate and compile the basic report, they will need significant contributions from other business units in the organisation. The final report should have input from the organisation's communications and finance functions, and will need the sign-off of an executive-level sponsor.

Who will read the sustainability report?

Fundamental to the need to prepare the report, and the determination of its content, is the understanding of who will be reading it: the range of users and scope of their interest is vastly broader than that of a financial report. However, a report that covered the needs of *all* the stakeholder groups would be a massive tome, seen as cumbersome and irrelevant by all. For example, employees will have different concerns from, say, environmental NGOs, and it can be difficult to satisfy both. One way in which companies deal with this is by web-based reporting, with stakeholder-specific sections highlighted.

Who, if anyone, will verify the report?

A company's financial statements are subject to statutory audit by a qualified auditor. However, there is, at the moment, no regulatory requirement for most CS disclosures to be submitted to any such assurance process. Nevertheless, many organisations choose to employ an outside body to provide a level of assurance, which provides comfort to the reporting organisation and may increase the legitimacy of the report in the eyes of stakeholders.

Verification can relate to compliance with reporting standards, or to the processes used in compiling the report, or indeed to some or all of the underlying data.

In employing external assurers, companies should be aware that there is a multitude of organisations offering such assurance, not all of which will have sufficient qualifications or experience to do a credible job. The reporting organisation should determine their competence and also consider what standards and principles are to be used in the verification process. (See, for example, AccountAbility's AA1000AS series of assurance standards [see Table 12.1].)

What should the report cover?

Although some disclosures are mandatory, as mentioned earlier the content of the report will depend on the stakeholders being addressed, and should reflect what they see as relevant. It may be useful to involve stakeholders in determining the subject matter (e.g. through questionnaires or focus groups): some standards (e.g. Global Reporting Initiative (GRI), see Table 12.1) adopt this practice. The content should relate specifically to the activities of the business rather than being generic.

A further issue to consider is what organisations the report should cover. The boundaries of responsibility for CS can be 'fuzzier' than for financial reporting. For example, often the whole supply chain is alive with potential CS issues and it might be appropriate for the organisation to include information about CS practices in its suppliers' businesses. If a company works with joint ventures, they might also be included in the report. Alternatively, organisations that are immature in their CS reporting may prefer to limit their output just to core activities or geographies until they have become more familiar with what is required.

Case study 12.1 sets out the boundaries used by Puma SE, the 'sport-lifestyle' company, which for 2010 produced what they refer to as 'the world's first environmental profit & loss account'.[276] This set out a cost for their water use, land use, emissions etc. throughout the company's supply chain.

Case study 12.1 **Puma's value chain**

Tier 1	Manufacturing	Footwear, apparel, accessories
Tier 2	Outsourcing	Embroidery, cutting, printing
Tier 3	Processing	Dye houses, tanneries, packaging
Tier 4	Raw material	Cotton fields, cattle farms, rubber plantations

The environmental cost of Puma's operations is relatively small for the company itself but increases significantly at each tier. The environmental profit-and-loss statement sets this out, and accompanying narrative explains that the metrics will be used to benchmark performance improvements in future years.

Puma is a long way down the development cycle for CS reporting, way ahead of most organisations. At the other end of the reporting life-cycle, Case study 12.2 sets out the process adopted by a UK company, Solarcentury, when it first introduced sustainability reporting. One key learning for the company was that the data-gathering task is large, and it is best to start with some of the easier indicators, rather than attempting to do everything in one 'big bang'.

Case study 12.2 **Preparing Solarcentury's first sustainability report**

Solarcentury, a UK-based private company providing solar energy, published its first sustainability report in 2008. The task of putting together the report involved advice and assistance from outside consultants and took a significant amount of internal resource.

The consultant provided a perspective on what other companies were doing and guidance on which of the multitude of available templates might be appropriate for the company's needs. Having determined the outline for the disclosures, significant effort was put into determining what underlying data was needed and how it could be collected. Then systems were set up to facilitate this data collection and analysis. For such a time-intensive task, the authority and encouragement of top management was essential, and supported both the data-gathering exercise and the resultant change in attitudes as the data was collected and published.

Solarcentury has continued to report its sustainability activities, and the report and data indicators have become more sophisticated as the company has become more used to the process and its data-gathering systems have matured.[277]

How should we report?

One format for CS reporting is the integrated report. The concept behind **integrated reporting** (IR) is twofold: first, companies often publish *comprehensive* data, rather than *comprehensible* information;

and second, companies need to improve how they report their CS activities. From this developed the notion of a report that would link key financial, strategic and CS factors, with supporting data available to users who chose to access it. Many definitions of integrated reporting exist, but one of the simplest is: 'a holistic and integrated representation of the company's performance in terms of both its finance and its sustainability'.[278] The leading bodies in the sustainability reporting arena are all part of the International Integrated Reporting Committee (IIRC), which produces research and resources to develop and support the adoption of an IR framework.

One problem with CS reports is that it is difficult to compare one company with another, as (possibly for good reasons) they report different things. Even within one company it can be difficult to get a sense of the trend in CS activities; many instances can be seen where a company's reporting changes radically from one year to the next, which limits comparability. (If a measure proves inadequate a change may be appropriate, but unless this is clearly explained, this can be frustrating to the reader.) It is always valuable to disclose trends and to explain them clearly to the reader. Providing absolute numbers and ratios or indexed data is also useful.

Another significant 'How' question is: How do we get the data? As indicated above, the difficulties surrounding this should not be underestimated. A company that has not been reporting its CS activities has probably not been recording them. Thus, having determined *what* should be reported, systems need to be developed for data collection. This is a time-consuming task, which needs the backing of top management to ensure that it is given appropriate resources.

CS disclosures can be quantitative (e.g. volume of emissions) or qualitative (e.g. policies on employing local labour). Both types of disclosure are appropriate, and the organisation—knowing its stakeholders' needs—has to determine where an appropriate balance lies.

When and where do we report?

A lot of work is involved in producing a sustainability report, and organisations need to determine whether their reporting is a once-a-year activity or done more frequently. This decision will be linked to their choice of format for the report—a hard copy report is static and expensive to produce and there is a movement towards web-based reporting, which is more flexible and more frequent.

A related issue is whether the CS report is made an integral part of the statutory financial statements, or whether it is produced as a separate document (this obviously links back to the integrated reporting movement). An advantage of integrating the reporting is that it reflects and encourages the integration of CS principles into the organisation—'built in' rather than 'bolted on'. But the sheer size of the regulated content of the financial statements generally makes it unwieldy to combine the documents, so a compromise needs to be found. Case study 12.3 illustrates one solution to this.

Case study 12.3 Henkel's sustainability report

In 2009 Henkel, the German-based multinational, produced a comprehensive annual financial report and a sustainability report. They were presented in almost identical covers, to highlight the link between the documents. The two were issued at the same time, in a joint binder, and each report included cross-references to the other. Thus, a lot of sustainability information could be published without increasing the length of the annual report. Investors signing up for notification of the release of the financial report were also sent details of its sustainability report, symbolising the importance the company placed on this information.

Regulations, standards and guidelines

In addition to regularity disclosures, which vary by jurisdiction, there are many standards and guidelines that organisations can adopt voluntarily in determining what to include in their CS reports. Table 12.1 gives some examples.

Table 12.1 **Some of the standards and templates in common use for sustainability reporting**

AccountAbility AA1000 series Covering: framework; assurance; engagement and accountability principles	Principles-based standards that provide the basis for improving the sustainability performance of organisations in all sectors. They relate to processes rather than performance, and centre on stakeholder engagement and issue salience, as opposed to purely the company's own senior management perspective
Global Reporting Initiative (GRI)* Currently in its third iteration, known as G3.1	Comprehensive framework to encourage comparability in CS reporting. Principles relate to: materiality, stakeholder inclusiveness, sustainability context, completeness, balance, clarity, accuracy, timeliness, comparability, reliability. A company can choose from six levels of application, and there are over 80 potential disclosures that could be made
Accounting for Sustainability (A4S)*	The Accounting for Sustainability Project works with businesses, investors, the public sector, accounting bodies, NGOs and academics to develop practical guidance and tools for embedding sustainability into decision-making and reporting processes

* Organisation is represented on the IIRC.

The method and content of CS reporting is constantly evolving, and regulations and standards are being developed all the time.

Ligteringen and Zadek[279] report over 300 standards, tools and guidelines for corporate sustainability and reporting covering a range of sectors and industries.

There are different advantages and disadvantages to each standard, and it can be difficult to determine which standard is most appropriate. Consultants or networking events can be useful to a company in learning from the experience of others. Some organisations might choose to 'shadow' a standard, developing familiarity and assessing its pros and cons before formal adoption. For example, ISO system standards and GRI reporting guidelines have the advantage in that they can be applied broadly over the company in different geographical and cultural locations. On the downside, the systems-based compliance and level of detail can be onerous and expensive to implement, and full compliance can lead to long and somewhat tedious reports.

Conclusion

Sustainability reporting is becoming more mainstream. Nonetheless, there is no harmonisation and there are many conflicting and overlapping sources of advice on content and structure. The following considerations may be useful to guide decisions for organisations wishing to introduce or to improve their reporting:

- **Clarify your reasons.** Once you define why you are reporting and who your audience is, this will help inform the nature and content of the report

- **Start relatively small and focused.** Choose the strategically important issues for the company first, and check that robust data exists. Do not underestimate the time needed to develop and refine reporting systems for new data

- **Use your stakeholders.** Stakeholder review can help assess the perceptions around your existing sustainability reporting and can also be useful in identifying how your reporting could be improved

- **Review your peers and reporting leaders.** Review the standards and approaches adopted by your peers and those that have gained reporting award recognition. Be sure to assess their adoption critically: do not mimic unless there is a clear case for doing so

- **Shadow report.** Develop the report (or new measures) internally to ensure robustness and comprehensibility before going public

- **Consider data-assurance centralisation.** Ideally, your data for sustainability reporting would be as robust as data for your financial reporting. Although CSR departments or teams may be involved in the sustainability strategy and development, it is useful to consider harnessing your performance-reporting experts to manage the data gathering and data-assurance rigour

- **Look at web reporting.** Not only a cheaper alternative than hard copy for external, public reporting, but also able to be adapted in the future to address ESG reporting to investors, local communities and environmental NGOs in a language-specific and targeted manner

- **Consider external assurance.** Having produced a few reports, and ironed out initial problems, consider the worth of improving the credibility of your reports via external, independent assessments from a qualified provider

Useful websites

www.theiirc.org

The International Integrated Reporting Committee (IIRC) has many resources on integrated reporting

www.globalreporting.org

The Global Reporting Initiative (GRI) website sets out all of the regulations and recommendations surrounding GRI and explains how it operates

www.accountability.org

AccountAbility produces the AA1000 Framework, providing guidance on sustainability reporting as well as assurance standards for those verifying sustainability reports

database.globalreporting.org

In 2011, GRI introduced this Sustainability Disclosure Database, which enables searches on report characteristics

www.corporateregister.com

The Corporate Register is a global corporate responsibility resources website and hosts a comprehensive directory of corporate non-financial reporting. It is searchable by company, country and year, and also by how well the report complies with GRI and its level of certification. It includes company reports certified under AA1000

www.accountingforsustainability.org

The Accounting for Sustainability project established by the Prince of Wales in 2004

Appendix

Corporate sustainability at Cranfield School of Management

Cranfield School of Management is a founding member of EABIS, The Academy for Business in Society, one of the earliest signatories of the UN Principles of Responsible Management Education, a member of the European Foundation for Management Development (EFMD) Sustainability Network, and part of the Pears Foundation Business School Partnership. Embedding responsibility and sustainability in our work is one of the School's strategic objectives.

Research

Many of the School of Management's faculty have researched and written on various aspects of sustainability and responsibility in recent years. The School's Corporate Responsibility and Sustainability

Management Theme pages on our website contain details of faculty specifically interested in these topics. Ongoing research topics at the School include board diversity, the governance of responsibility and sustainability, ethical leadership, engaging employees for sustainability, nudging consumer behaviour towards sustainable consumption, and sustainability in the supply chain.

In 2012, the School is supporting the development of a multidisciplinary set of teaching cases on the Dutch company Desso, a leading exponent of cradle-to-cradle manufacturing. Through Cranfield's participation in the Pears Foundation Business School Partnership and other initiatives, we are producing teaching cases about corporate responsibility and sustainability around the world. Half of the latest cohort of Doctor of Business Administration students is researching questions related in some way to responsibility and sustainability.

We welcome enquiries from companies wishing to explore co-funding of a Cranfield Research Club investigating some aspects of responsibility and sustainability.

Teaching

One of the School's strategic priorities is to improve the practice of responsible management. This is reflected in our teaching on executive and graduate programmes.

The School's main general management, open executive programmes—the Cranfield Business Leaders Programme and the Advanced Development Programme—include sessions on responsibility and sustainability as an integral part of equipping business leaders with the skills to thrive in a resource-constrained, globally connected economy of the 21st century.

The Non-Executive Director programme prepares would-be non-executives of for-profit, not-for-profit and public-sector boards as part of improving the practice of governance.

Cranfield's Centre for Customised Executive Development works with more than 60 corporate clients around the globe; and can design customised interventions on responsibility and sustainability.

The Doughty Centre for Corporate Responsibility also offers in-company facilitation for company boards and senior management teams to explore these issues and the material questions for them.

Ethics, personal and organisational responsibility, and sustainable development are addressed across the Cranfield MBA in different core and elective courses, and through a range of extra-curricular opportunities for students including independent projects, travel bursaries and regular external speakers.

In 2012, responsibility and sustainability modules will be included in several of the Cranfield MScs including Finance, International HR Management, and Purchasing and Supply.

Practice

The latest insights from research and comment on topical issues affecting corporate responsibility and sustainability can be found on the School of Management's website and particularly through the corporate responsibility and sustainability management theme pages and the home page of the Doughty Centre.

Faculty advise a range of organisations where corporate responsibility and sustainability feature.

The Cranfield CR Network hosts a regular programme of internal and external speakers; and Cranfield faculty are frequent speakers and facilitators at academic and practitioner conferences about corporate responsibility and sustainability. Short films about responsibility and sustainability are posted on the Cranfield YouTube channel, and Twitterati can follow the Doughty Centre on Twitter at: twitter.com/doughtycentre

School as a responsible organisation

The School and University are significant organisations in their own right as employers, customers, suppliers and neighbours. The School's sustainability strategy is overseen by the School executive and implemented by the Finance Director with individual senior faculty and staff championing specific impact pillars (marketplace, workplace, environment and community). The School is part of an ambitious university-wide project to measure the Carbon Brainprint of Cranfield University: the positive impact on helping other organisations to reduce their carbon emissions.

Recognising that corporate sustainability enables organisations to incorporate the creation of social and environmental, as well as economic, value into core strategy and operations, the School has signed the UN Principles of Responsible Management Education (PRME). As a management school, Cranfield supports the growing responsible business education movement by teaching the next generation of business leaders, by researching and sharing tactics, as well as leading by example. The work of the School's PRME Taskforce brings together faculty and staff from across the institution including the directors of the MBA and other graduate programmes.

We welcome dialogue and the opportunity to exchange lessons and experiences with others on a similar journey, through our membership of EFMD and EABIS and through engagement with initiatives such as the Aspen Institute Center for Business Education and the Global Network for Corporate Citizenship.

Notes

Introduction

1 F.M. Horwitz, 'Transforming the Business School', *BizEd*, May/June 2010: 34-39; F.M. Horwitz, 'Putting PRME into Practice in a Business School,' *Global Focus* 4.2 (2010): 26-29.

2 For example, see A. Dahlsrud, 'How Corporate Social Responsibility is Defined: An Analysis of 37 Definitions', *Corporate Social Responsibility and Environmental Management* 15.1 (2008) 1–13; onlinelibrary. wiley.com/doi/10.1002/csr.132/abstract, accessed 24 April 2012.

3 Dahlsrud, 'How Corporate Social Responsibility is Defined': ii.

4 www2.goldmansachs.com/ideas/environment-and-energy/goldman-sachs/gs-sustain/index.html, accessed 24 April 2012.

5 J. Porritt, *Capitalism as if the World Matters* (London: Earthscan, rev. edn, 2007).

6 R. Ackerman, *The Four Legs of the Table* (Cape Town: David Philip Publishers, 2005).

7 M.E. Porter and M.R. Kramer, 'The Big Idea: Creating Shared Value', *Harvard Business Review* (Jan/Feb 2011); hbr.org/2011/01/the-big-idea-creating-shared-value/ar/1, accessed 24 April 2012.

Chapter 1

8 Accenture, *A New Era of Sustainability: UN Global Compact–Accenture CEO Survey 2010* (Accenture, 2010).

9 For an accessible summary see by WBCSD (World Business Council for Sustainable Development), 'Vision 2050'; www.wbcsd.org/vision2050.aspx (2010), accessed 24 April 2012; or Business in the Community, 'Visioning the Future: The Forces for Change'; www.bitc.org.uk/visioning_the_future (2010), accessed 24 April 2010.

10 Based on purchasing power parity, Goldman Sachs, quoted in WBCSD, 'Vision 2050', estimates c. 100 million p.a.; and Accenture, 'New Paths to Growth: The Age of Aggregation', *Outlook* 3 (2011), suggests c.150 million p.a. extra to 2030.

11 J. Beddington, 'The Perfect Storm', lectures at Thailand Science Park, Bangkok, and the National University of Science, Vietnam, 30 September 2009; www.bis.gov.uk/go-science/news/speeches/the-perfect-storm, accessed 24 April 2012.

12 KPMG, *Corporate Sustainability: A Progress Report* (KPMG, 2011).

13 Accenture, *A New Era of Sustainability: UN Global Compact–Accenture CEO Survey 2010*.

14 Board oversight; embedded in strategy and operations of subsidiaries; embedded in global supply chains; participation in collaborations and multi-stakeholder partnerships; and engagement with stakeholders such as investors.

15 Deloitte CFO Survey, quoted in *The Economist*, 8 April 2011.

16 A. Witty, The Pears Business School Partnership Lecture, Cranfield University, 18 January 2012.

17 Knowledge management for corporate sustainability explored in: M. McLaren and J.C. Spender, *Supporting Corporate Responsibility Through Effective Knowledge Management* (A Doughty Centre for Corporate Responsibility How-to Guide, 5; Doughty Centre, Cranfield School of Management, 2011).

18 A. Macqueen, *The King Of Sunlight: How William Lever Cleaned Up The World* (London: Corgi, 2005, paperback edn).

19 This heritage is captured in a short Unilever film: *Unilever Sustainability Story*; www.youtube.com/watch?v=kcrePlUKH1Q&feature=player_embedded, accessed 24 April 2012.

20 Personal communication from André van Heemstra to author, 2011.

21 M. Cormack and N. Fitzgerald, *The Role of Business in Society: An Agenda for Action* (Conference Board, Harvard University and International Business Leaders Forum, 2006; www.hks.harvard.edu/m-rcbg/CSRI/publications/report_12_CGI Role of Business in Society Report FINAL 10-03-06.pdf, accessed 24 April 2012).

22 www.sustainable-living.unilever.com.

23 'USLP One Year On', Progress Report Briefing, London, 24 April 2012.

24 www.sustainable-living.unilever.com.

25 M. Barnett, 'The New CSR: This Time It's Profitable', *Marketing Week*, 14 April 2011; www.marketingweek.co.uk/analysis/cover-stories/the-new-csr-this-time-its-profitable/3025435.article, accessed 24 April 2012.

26 I. Gupta and S. Srivastava 'A Person of the Year: Paul Polman', *Forbes*, 1 June 2011; www.forbes.com/2011/01/06/forbes-india-person-of-the-year-paul-polman-unilever_2.html, accessed 24 April 2012; and see A. Saunders, 'The MT Interview: Paul Polman of Unilever', *Management Today*, 1 March 2011; www.managementtoday.co.uk/features/1055793/the-mt-interview-paul-polman-unilever, accessed 24 April 2012.

27 S. Smith, 'Is Unilever's Sustainability Drive a Hostage to Fortune?', *Marketing Week*, 9 December 2010; www.marketingweek.co.uk/opinion/is-unilever's-sustainability-drive-a-hostage-to-fortune?/3021399.article, accessed 24 April 2012.

28 See T. Jackson *Prosperity Without Growth: Economics for a Finite Planet* (London: Earthscan 2009) and specifically Chapter 4, 'The Dilemma of Growth'.

29 www.sustainable-living.unilever.com/the-plan, accessed 24 April 2012.

30 www.unilever.com/sustainability/economic/impact-studies, accessed 24 April 2012.

31 WBCSD (World Business Council for Sustainable Development) 'Unilever Brand Imprint: Engaging Brand Strategy Teams On Sustainable Consumption' (People Matter Engage Case Study; WBCSD, 2010).

32 In 2005, for example, Action Aid produced a report, *Tea Break*, targeted at Hindustan Lever, one of the Unilever companies, which it described as profiting from worsening conditions for workers on plantations; mallenbaker.net/csr/page.php?Story_ID=1428, accessed 24 April 2012.

33 www.sustainable-living.unilever.com/wp-content/uploads/2010/10/Unilever_Value_Chain_External_Low_Res_Windows_Media.mp4, accessed 24 April 2012.

34 Quoted in S. Stern, 'Outsider in a Hurry to Shake Up Unilever', *Financial Times*, 4 April 2010.

35 A number of academics and practitioners have proposed models of stages of maturity. For example, D. Dunphy, A. Griffiths and S. Benn, *Organizational Change for Corporate Sustainability* (London: Routledge, 2003); C. Tuppen and J. Porritt, *Just Values* (London: British Telecommunications plc, 2003); Jean-François Rischard *The Five Stage*

Classification of Business Engagement, 2003; S. Zadek, 'The Path to Corporate Responsibility', *Harvard Business Review* (December 2004); P. Mirvis and B. Googins, *Stages of Corporate Citizenship* (Boston, MA: Boston College Center for Corporate Citizenship, 2006); F. Maon, A. Lindgreen and V. Swaen, 'Organizational Stages and Cultural Phases: A Critical Review and a Consolidative Model of Corporate Social Responsibility Development', *International Journal of Management Reviews* 12.1 (2010): 20-38. A forthcoming Doughty Centre Occasional Paper by Ron Ainsbury and David Grayson examines these.

36 H. Dodgson quoted in D. Grayson and A. Hodges, *Everybody's Business: Managing Risks and Opportunities in Today's Global Society* (London: Financial Times/Dorling Kindersley 2011).

37 P. Gilding, *The Great Disruption: How the Climate Crisis Will Transform the Global Economy* (London: Bloomsbury, 2011).

38 Boston Consulting Group and World Economic Forum, *Redefining the Future of Growth: The New Sustainability Champions* (Geneva: World Economic Forum, 2011).

Chapter 2

39 R. D'Aveni, *Commodity Trap* (Boston, MA: Harvard Business School Press, 2010).

40 G.B. Sprinkle and L.A. Maines 'The Benefits and Costs of Corporate Social Responsibility', *Business Horizons* 53.5 (September–October 2010): 445-53; M.E. Porter and M.R. Kramer, 'Strategy and Society: The Link between Competitive Advantage and Corporate Social Responsibility', *Harvard Business Review*, December 2006: 78-92; S. Waddock and N. Smith, 'Corporate Responsibility Audits: Doing Well by Doing Good', *MIT Sloan Management Review*, Winter 2000: 75-83.

41 Grant Thornton, *Corporate Social Responsibility: A Necessity not a Choice* (International Business Report; London: Grant Thornton International, 2008).

42 M. Winston, 'NGO Strategies for Promoting Corporate Social Responsibility', *Ethics and International Affairs* 16.1 (2002): 71-87.

43 A.G. Scherer and G. Palazzo, 'Toward a Political Conception of Corporate Responsibility: Business and Society Seen from a Habermasian Perspective', *Academy of Management Review* 32.4 (2007): 1,096-1,120; M. Haigh and M.T. Jones, 'The Drivers of Corporate Social Responsibility: A Critical Review', *Business Review* 5.2 (2006): 245-51.

44 I. Davis, 'The Biggest Contract', *The Economist* (26 May 2005).

45 T. Morgan and G.C. Avery, 'Corporate Social Responsibility Practices in the Australian Consumer Goods Industry: Preliminary Findings', *Journal of Diversity Management* 3.2 (2008): 9-17; A. Pendleton *et al.*, *Behind The Mask: The Real Face of CSR* (London: Christian Aid UK, 2004).

46 H. Volberda, R. Morgan, P. Reinmoeller, M.A. Hitt, R.D. Ireland and R. Hoskisson, *Strategic Management: Competition and Globalization* (Andover, UK: Cengage, 2011).

47 J. Balogun and M. Jenkins, 'Re-conceiving Change Management: A Knowledge-Based Perspective', *European Management Journal* 21.2 (2003): 247-57; I. Nonaka and H. Takeuchi, *The Knowledge Creating Company* (Oxford: Oxford University Press, 1995).

48 The Sarbanes-Oxley Act was enacted in July 2002 after the high-profile corporate scandals involving companies such as Enron and World-Com. United States Securities and Exchange Commission, *Study of the Sarbanes-Oxley Act of 2002 Section 404 Internal Control over Financial Reporting Requirements* (Office of Economic Analysis, United States Securities and Exchange Commission, 2009; www.sec.gov/news/studies/2009/sox-404_study.pdf, accessed 24 April 2012).

49 E.H. Schein, *Organizational Culture and Leadership* (San Francisco, CA: Wiley & Sons, 4th edn, 2010): 265.

50 M. Sleeboom, 'Stem Cell Research in China: An Intertwinement of International Finances, Ambition, and Bioethics', *IIAS Newsletter* 29 (November 2002; www.iias.nl/iiasn/29/IIASNL29_49.pdf, accessed 24 April 2012).

51 *BBC News*, 'Reporter Takes Fake Bomb on Plane', *BBC News* (24 August 2004; news.bbc.co.uk/2/hi/uk_news/3593376.stm, accessed 24 April 2012); *Sun*, 'Sun Man Reveals Runway "Bomb"', *The Sun* (9 February 2008; www.thesun.co.uk/sol/homepage/news/article782095.ece, accessed 24 April 2012).

52 Y. Zhang, H. Li, M.A. Hitt and G. Cui, 'R&D Intensity and International Joint Venture Performance in an Emerging Market: Moderating Effects of Market Focus and Ownership Structure', *Journal of International Business Studies* 38 (2007).

53 Adapted from Volberda *et al.*, *Strategic Management*.

54 C.K. Prahalad and V. Ramaswamy, *The Future of Competition* (Boston, MA: Harvard Business School Press, 2004).

55 C.K. Cox, (2005); 'Organic leadership: The Co-creation of Good Business, Global Prosperity, and a Greener Future', PhD thesis, Ben-

edictine University, 2005; AAT 3180735; J. Auriac, 'Corporate Social Innovation', *OECD Observer* 279 (May 2010): 32.

56 Source: E. Cohen, 'Reporting: How Hasbro Does It', *Sustainable Business Forum*, 22 December 2011 (sustainablebusinessforum.com/node/55544, accessed 24 April 2012); A. Leach, 'Hasbro Publishes List of Core Suppliers', *Supply Management: The Purchasing and Supply Website* (10 December 2011; www.supplymanagement.com/news/2011/hasbro-publishes-list-of-core-suppliers, accessed 24 April 2012); Hasbro, 'CSR Industry Collaboration'; csr.hasbro.com/das02-products.php, accessed 24 April 2012.

57 I. Nonaka and H. Takeuchi, *The Knowledge Creating Company* (Oxford: Oxford University Press, 1995).

58 G. Groves, R. Lee, L. Frater and G. Harper, *CSR in the UK Nanotechnology Industry: Attitudes and Prospects* (BRASS Working Paper 57; Cardiff: Centre for Business Relationships, Accountability, Sustainability and Society, 2010).

59 Source: *The Economist, New York Times, Forbes*.

60 M. Morsing and M. Schultz, 'Corporate Social Responsibility Communication: Stakeholder Information, Response and Involvement Strategies', *Business Ethics: A European Review* 15.4 (2006): 323-38.

61 M. Salanova, S. Agut and J.M. Peiro, 'Linking Organizational Resources and Work Engagement to Employee Performance and Customer Loyalty: The Mediation of Service Climate', *Journal of Applied Psychology* 90.6 (2005): 1,217-27.

62 N. Taleb, *The Black Swan* (London: Penguin Books, 2008).

63 B.S. Bissey, 'Understanding the Rules When It Comes to Vendors and Inducements', *Journal of Health Care Compliance* 6.5 (2004).

64 Adapted from Volberda *et al.*, *Strategic Management*.

65 D.G. Ancona and C. Chong, 'Entrainment: Pace, Cycle, and Rhythm in Organizational Behavior', *Research in Organizational Behavior* 18 (1996): 251-84.

66 D.A. Leonard-Barton, 'Core Capabilities and Core Rigidities: A Paradox in Managing New Product Development', *Strategic Management Journal* 13 (Summer 1992): 111-25.

67 J.P. Kotter, *Leading Change* (Boston, MA: Harvard Business School Press, 1996).

68 C. Duhigg and D. Barboza, 'In China, Human Costs are Built Into an iPad', *New York Times* (25 January 2012; www.nytimes.com/2012/01/26/business/ieconomy-apples-ipad-and-the-human-costs-for-workers-in-china.html?pagewanted=all, accessed 24 April 2012).

69 M. Higgs and D. Rowland, 'Emperors With Clothes On: The Role of Self-awareness in Developing Effective Change Leadership', *Journal of Change Management* 10.4 (2010).

70 Siemens Corporate Compliance Office, *Business Conduct Guidelines* (Munich: Siemens, January 2009; www.siemens.com or www.siemens.ca/web/portal/en/AboutUs/Documents/BusinessConductGuidelines.pdf, accessed 24 April 2012): 2.

71 Adapted from Siemens.com, Siemens Business Conduct Guidelines, 2009; E. Wyatt, 'Former Siemens Executives Are Charged with Bribery', *New York Times*, 13 December 2011.

72 *BBC News*, 'US Plans Overhaul of Toy Safety' *BBC News* (February 2008; news.bbc.co.uk/2/hi/business/7252130.stm, accessed 24 April 2012).

73 S. Kumar and V. Putman, 'Cradle to Cradle: Reverse Logistics Strategies and Opportunities across Three Industry Sectors', *International Journal of Production Economics*, 2008: 115.

74 United Nations Environmental Programme, *Social Impact Assessment: Impact Analysis Training Resource Manual* (Nairobi: UNEP, 2nd edn, 2002; www.unep.ch/etu/publications/EIA_2ed/EIA_E_top13_body.PDF, accessed 24 April 2012).

75 R.E. Freeman, *Strategic Management: A Stakeholder Approach* (Cambridge, UK: Cambridge University Press, 2010).

76 E.R. Pederson, 'Making Corporate Social Responsibility (CSR) Operable: How Companies Translate Stakeholder Dialogue into Practice', *Business and Society Review* 111.2 (2006).

77 O. Salzmann, 'Corporate Sustainability Management in the Energy Sector: An Empirical Contingency Approach' Dissertation, Technische Universität Berlin, 2006.

78 F. Schultz and S. Wehmeier, 'Institutionalization of Corporate Social Responsibility Within Corporate Communications: Combining Institutional, Sensemaking and Communication Perspectives', *Corporate Communications: An International Journal* 15.1 (2010).

79 J.J. Lucey, 'Why is the failure rate for organisation change so high?', *Management Services* 52.4 (2008).

80 T.R. Hargett and M.F. Williams, 'Wilh. Wilhelmsen Shipping Company: Moving from CSR Tradition to CSR Leadership', *Corporate Governance* 9.1 (2009).

81 M. Bourne, A. Neely, K. Platts and J. Mills, 'The Success and Failure of Performance Measurement Initiatives', *International Journal of Operations and Production Management* 22.11 (2002).

Chapter 3

82   Economist Intelligence Unit, *Doing Good: Business and the Sustainability Challenge* (London: Economist Intelligence Unit, 2008): 5.

83   B. Russell, *History of Western Philosophy* (London: George Unwin Press, 1946/1996): 2.

84   K. Grint, *The Arts of Leadership* (Oxford: Oxford University Press, 2001).

85   G. Eweje, 'Multinational oil companies' CSR Initiatives in Nigeria: The Scepticism of Stakeholders in Host Communities', *Managerial Law* 49.5/6 (2007): 218-35.

86   J. Elkington, *Cannibals with Forks: The Triple Bottom Line of 21st Century Business* (Oxford: Capstone, 1997).

87   S. Heaney, 'Crediting Poetry', Nobel Laureate Speech, 1995.

88   'Dust', © 2005 by Wendell Berry from *Given*. Reprinted by permission of Counterpoint.

89   J. McVea and R.E. Freeman, 'A Names and Faces Approach to Stakeholder Management: How Focusing on Stakeholders as Individuals Can Bring Ethics and Entrepreneurial Strategy Together', *Journal of Management Inquiry* 14.1 (2005): 51-69.

90   P. Radin, *The Trickster: A Study in American Indian Mythology* (New York: Schocken Books, 1972).

91   R.E. Quinn, *Change the World: How Ordinary People Can Accomplish Extraordinary Results* (San Francisco: Jossey Bass, 2000).

92   D. Barry and S. Meisiek, 'The Art of Leadership and Its Fine Art Shadow', *Leadership* 6.3 (2010).

Chapter 4

93   Quoted in Business for Social Responsibility (BSR) and UN Global Compact LEAD, *Board Adoption and Oversight of Corporate Sustainability* (Discussion Paper; BSR and UN Global Compact LEAD, 2011).

94   SDA Bocconi School of Management, Doughty Centre for Corporate Responsibility at Cranfield School of Management and Vlerick Leuven Gent Management School, *Sustainable Value* (report on behalf of the Academy for Business in Society [EABIS], 2009).

95   A. White, *The Stakeholder Fiduciary: CSR, Governance and the Future of Boards* (San Francisco: Business for Social Responsibility, 2006), quoted in UN Global Compact LEAD, *Moving Upwards: The Involvement of Boards of Directors in the UN Global Compact* (UN Global Compact, 2010).

96 P. Kielstra, *Doing Good: Business and the Sustainability Challenge* (London: Economist Intelligence Unit, 2008), quoted in UN Global Compact LEAD, *Moving Upwards: The Involvement of Boards of Directors in the UN Global Compact* (UN Global Compact, 2010).

97 E.G. Hansen and H. Spitzeck, *Stakeholder Governance: An Analysis of BITC Corporate Responsibility Index Data on Stakeholder Engagement and Governance* (Doughty Centre for Corporate Responsibility Occasional Paper; Bedford, UK: Cranfield School of Management, September 2010).

98 Business for Social Responsibility (BSR) and UN Global Compact LEAD, *Board Adoption and Oversight of Corporate Sustainability* (2011).

99 'Retooling the Boardroom for the 21st Century', panel discussion at US Network Symposium, San Francisco, 19 October 2009, quoted in UN Global Compact LEAD, *Moving Upwards: The Involvement of Boards of Directors in the UN Global Compact* (UN Global Compact, 2010).

100 A. Cramer, 'Giving Sustainability a Seat In the Boardroom', *GreenBiz. com*, 20 April 2011.

101 H. Spitzeck, *The Governance of Corporate Responsibility* (Doughty Centre 'How to' Guide, 'How to Do Corporate Responsibility Series, 4; Cranfield: Doughty Centre, Cranfield University School of Management, 2010; www.doughtycentre.info).

102 H. Spitzeck, E.G. Hansen and D. Grayson, 'Joint Management–Stakeholder Committees: A New Path To Stakeholder Governance?', *Corporate Governance* 11.5, JMSC Special Issue (2011): 560-68.

103 Business for Social Responsibility (BSR) and UN Global Compact LEAD, *Board Adoption and Oversight of Corporate Sustainability* (Discussion Paper; BSR and UN Global Compact LEAD, 2011).

104 www.cauxroundtable.org/index.cfm?&menuid=17&parentid=16, accessed 24 April 2012.

105 US Network Symposium, 'Summary of Key Points', 18 October 2009, quoted in UN Global Compact LEAD, *Moving Upwards: The Involvement of Boards of Directors in the UN Global Compact* (UN Global Compact, 2010).

106 A. Kakabadse and N. Kakabadse, *Leading the Board: The Six Disciplines of World Class Chairmen* (Basingstoke, UK: Palgrave Macmillan, 2008).

107 A. Kakabadse, N. Kakabadse and A. Myers, *Chairman of the Board: A Study of Role, Contribution and Performance of UK Board Directors*

(Cranfield School of Management and Manchester Square Partners, 2008).

108 D. Barton, 'Capitalism for the Long Term', *Harvard Business Review*, March 2011.

Chapter 5

109 D.P. Keegan, T.G. Eiler and C.R. Jones, 'Are Your Performance Measures Obsolete?', *Management Accounting*, June 1989; A.M. Ghalayini and J.A. Noble, 'The Changing Basis of Performance Measurement', *International Journal of Operations & Production Management* 18.8 (1996).

110 A. Neely, M. Gregory and J. Platts, 'Performance Measurement System Design: A Literature Review and Research Agenda', *International Journal of Operations & Production Management* 15.4 (1995); R.S. Kaplan and D.P. Norton, 'The Balanced Scorecard: Measures That Drive Performance', *Harvard Business Review* 71.5 (1992).

111 R.S. Kaplan and D.P. Norton, 'Using the Balanced Scorecard as a Strategic Management System', *Harvard Business Review*, February 1996; R.S. Kaplan and D.P. Norton, 'Transforming Balanced Scorecard from Performance Measurement to Strategic Management: Part II', *Accounting Horizons* 15.2 (2001).

112 IBM, *Driving Performance through Sustainability: Strategy, Synergy And Significance*, IBM Institute for Business Value, Global Services Report 2011; public.dhe.ibm.com/common/ssi/ecm/en/gbe03414usen/GBE03414USEN.PDF, accessed 22 April 2012; Pricewaterhouse-Coopers, *The Sustainability Agenda: Industry Perspectives*, PricewaterhouseCoopers, 2008; www.pwc.com/en_GX/gx/sustainability/sustainability_agenda.pdf, accessed 22 April 2012.

113 A. Hillman and G. Keim, 'Shareholder Value, Stakeholder Management, and Social Issues: What's The Bottom Line?', *Strategic Management Journal* 22 (2001); S.A. Waddock and S.B. Graves, 'Assessing the Link between Corporate Governance and Social/Financial Performance', for *Proceedings of the International Association for Business and Society Conference*, Paris, June 1999.

114 The Doughty Centre for Corporate Responsibility and Business in the Community (BITC), *The Business Case for Being a Responsible Business* (Cranfield, UK: Cranfield School of Management, 2011; www.bitc.org.uk/resources/publications/the_business_case.html, accessed 24 April 2012).

115   C.E. Hull and S. Rothenberg, 'Firm Performance: The Interactions of Corporate Social Performance with Innovation and Industry Differentiation', *Strategic Management Journal*, 2008: 29.

116   H. de Castres, Chief Executive Summary, AXA, quoted at the *Colloquium on Climate Change: What Risks for Business?* 28 October 2005, cited in J. Llewellyn and C. Chaix, *The Business of Climate Change II: Policy is Accelerating, with Major Implications for Companies and Investors* (New York: Lehman Brothers, 2007).

117   *McKinsey Quarterly Survey* 2007; www.mckinseyquarterly.com/ How_companies_think_about_climate_change_A_McKinsey_Global_ Survey_2099, accessed 24 April 2012.

118   T. Leahy, 'Tesco, Carbon and the Consumer', speech at Forum for the Future/TESCO event 18 January 2007; www.tesco.com/climatechange/ speech.asp, accessed 24 April 2012.

119   *BBC News*, 'Food Labelling Campaign Launched', *BBC News*, 4 January 2007; news.bbc.co.uk/1/hi/uk/6228469.stm, accessed 24 April 2012.

120   M. Munasinghe, P. Dasgupta, D. Southerton, A. Bows and A. McMeeking, *Consumers, Business and Climate Change* (ed. G. Walker; Manchester: Sustainable Consumption Institute, University of Manchester, 2009).

121   Business in the Community and the Doughty Centre for Corporate Responsibility, *The Business Case for Being a Responsible Business* (Cranfield, UK: Doughty Centre; London: Business in the Community, 2011).

122   G. Pohle and J. Hittner, *Attaining Sustainable Growth through Corporate Social Responsibility* (IBM Institute for Business Value, 2008).

123   D.L. Ferguson, 'Corporate Social Performance in the Utility Sector', Masters of Research Thesis, Cranfield School of Management 2007 (citation of Little [2002]; KPMG [2005]; ACCA [2004]; Willard [2002]).

124   G. Johnson and K. Scholes, *Exploring Corporate Strategy* (London: Financial Times/Prentice Hall, 6th edn, 2002).

125   J.E. Ebert, D.T. Gilbert and T.D. Wilson, 'Forecasting and Backcasting: Predicting the Impact of Events on the Future', *Journal of Consumer Research* 36 (2009); www.naturalstep.org/backcasting.

126   D. Ferguson, *Measuring Business Value and Sustainability Performance: A Practitioner's Guide* (Cranfield, UK: EABIS/Doughty Centre, May 2009; https://dspace.lib.cranfield.ac.uk/handle/1826/3795, accessed 24 April 2012).

127   Based on author's abbreviated summary of A. Neely, R. Huw, J. Mills, K. Platts and M. Bourne, 'Designing Performance Measures: A Structured Approach', *International Journal of Operations and Production Management* 17.11 (1997).
128   Based on author's adaptation and development of Neely *et al.*, 'Designing Performance Measures'.
129   E. Mitchell, 'Selecting Key Performance Indicators at Thames Water', *Corporate Responsibility Management* 2.1 (2005).

Chapter 6

130   R. Nidumolu, C.K. Prahalad and M.R. Rangaswami, 'Why Sustainability is Now the Key Driver of Innovation', *Harvard Business Review* 83.9 (2009): 56-64.
131   S.L. Hart, 'Beyond Greening', *Harvard Business Review* 75.1 (January–February 1997): 66-76.
132   Nidumolu *et al.*, 'Why Sustainability is Now the Key Driver of Innovation'.
133   S.L. Hart, 'Beyond Greening'.
134   L. Berchicci and W. Bodewes, 'Bridging Environmental Issues with New Product Development', *Business Strategy and the Environment* 14.5 (2005): 272-85.
135   S. Paramanathan, C. Farrukh, R. Phaal and R. Probert, 'Implementing Industrial Sustainability: The Research Issues in Technology Management', *R&D Management* 34.5 (2004): 527-37.
136   P. Desrochers, 'Victorian Pioneers of Corporate Sustainability', *Business History Review* 83.4 (Winter 2009): 703-29.
137   S.L. Hart, 'Innovation, Creative Destruction and Sustainability', *Research-Technology Management* 48.5 (September–October 2005): 21-27.
138   Nidumolu *et al.*, 'Why Sustainability is Now the Key Driver of Innovation'.
139   Nidumolu *et al.*, 'Why Sustainability is Now the Key Driver of Innovation'.
140   M. Weber, 'The Business Case for Corporate Social Responsibility (CSR): A Company-Level Measurement Approach to CSR', *European Management Journal* 26.4 (2008): 247-61.
141   C.K. Prahalad, *The Fortune at the Bottom of the Pyramid* (Harlow, UK: Pearson Education 2005).

142 *The Economist*, 'A Snip at the Price', *The Economist*, 30 May 2009: 74.

143 Hart, 'Innovation, Creative Destruction and Sustainability'.

144 L. Blyth, 'Micro-solar Technologies: Testing the Market', *Appropriate Technology* 31.4 (December 2004): 62-63.

145 R. Gruener, S. Lux, K. Reiche and T. Schmitz-Guenther, 'Solar Lanterns Test: Shades of Light', *Appropriate Technology* 36.2 (June 2009): 26-29.

146 R. Rao, 'A Firm Footing!', *Appropriate Technology* 35.4 (December 2008): 61-63.

147 E. Petala, R. Wever, C. Dutilh and H. Brezet, 'The Role of New Product Development Briefs in Implementing Sustainability: A Case Study', *Journal of Engineering Technology Management*, 2010.

148 Nidumolu *et al.*, 'Why Sustainability is Now the Key Driver of Innovation': 57.

149 D. Pujari, G. Wright and K. Peattie, 'Green and Competitive Influences on Environmental New Product Development Performance', *Journal of Business Research* 56.8 (2003): 657-71.

150 K. Goffin, F. Lemke and U. Koners, *Identifying Hidden Needs: Creating Breakthrough Products* (Basingstoke, UK: Palgrave Macmillan, 2010).

151 J. Hall and H. Vredenburg, 'The Challenges of Innovating for Sustainable Development', *MIT Sloan Management Review* 45.1 (Fall 2003): 61-68.

152 Petala *et al.*, 'The Role of New Product Development Briefs in Implementing Sustainability': 11.

153 Pujari *et al.*, 'Green and Competitive Influences on Environmental New Product Development Performance'.

154 S.A. Waage, 'Re-considering Product Design: A Practical "Road-map" for Integration of Sustainability Issues', *Journal of Cleaner Production* 15.7 (2007): 638-49.

155 Paramanathan *et al.*, 'Implementing Industrial Sustainability'.

156 R.G. Cooper and E.J. Kleinschmidt, 'Determinants of Timeliness in Product Development', *Journal of Product Innovation Management* 11.5 (1994): 381-96.

157 Based on inputs from a number of companies including Unilever (thanks to Dr Helen David) plus ideas from the literature including key points (in bold) from Waage, 'Re-considering Product Design'.

158 Paramanathan *et al.*, 'Implementing Industrial Sustainability'.

159 Case based on Unilever, *Sustainable Development: An Overview* (Unilever, 2008) and interviews with Dr Helen David and Dr Henry King (both of Unilever, UK) in September 2010.

Chapter 7

160 Y.K. van Dam and P.A.C. Apeldoorn, 'Sustainable Marketing', *Journal of Macromarketing* 16 (1996): 45-56.

161 K. Peattie, 'Towards Sustainability: The Third Age of Green Marketing', *Marketing Review* 2 (2001): 129-46.

162 A. Crane, 'Facing the Backlash: Green Marketing and Strategic Reorientation in the 1990s', *Journal of Strategic Marketing* 8 (2000): 277-96.

163 Peattie 'Towards Sustainability'; C.M. Bridges and W.B. Wilhelm, 'Going Beyond Green: The "Why" and "How" of Integrating Sustainability into the Marketing Curriculum', *Journal of Marketing Education* 30.1 (2008): 33-46.

164 P. de Pelsmacker, L. Driesen and G. Rayp, 'Do Consumers Care about Ethics? Willingness to Pay for Fair-Trade Coffee', *Journal of Consumer Affairs* 39.2 (2005): 363-85.

165 People Science and Policy, 'Exploring Public Attitudes to Climate Change and the Barriers and Motivators to Travel Behaviour Change', Department for Transport report prepared by People Science and Policy (22 Jan 2009; www.peoplescienceandpolicy.com/projects/climate_change.php, accessed 24 April 2012).

166 I. Ajzen, 'From Intentions to Actions: A Theory of Planned Behavior', in J. Kuhl and J. Beckman (eds.), *Action-Control: From Cognition to Behavior* (Heidelberg, Germany: Springer, 1985): 11-39.

167 E.ON, 'Knowledge is power: E.ON joins forces with its customers to get the nation "Energy Fit" ', media release 14 May 2010; pressreleases.eon-uk.com/blogs/eonukpressreleases/archive/2010/05/14/1536.aspx, accessed 24 April 2012.

168 C.R. Sunstein and R.H. Thaler, 'Exploiting the Shame Meter', *Scientific American* 18.5 (2008).

169 R.P. Bagozzi and U. Dholakia, 'Goal Setting and Goal Striving in Consumer Behavior', *Journal of Marketing* 63 (1999): 19-32.

170 P.C. Stern, 'Information, Incentives, and Pro-environmental Consumer Behavior', *Journal of Consumer Policy* 22.4 (1999): 461-78.

171 Choice architecture is presenting choices in a way that influences the decision.

172 R.H. Thaler and C.R. Sunstein, *Nudge* (New Haven, CT: Yale University Press, 2008).

173 Thaler and Sunstein, *Nudge*.

174 G. Armstrong, P. Kotler, M. Harker and R. Brennan, *Marketing: An Introduction* (Harlow, UK: FT Pearson, 2009).

175 'Just concentrate'; www.unilever.com/brands/hygieneandwelbeing/aroundthehouse/articles/greenandgrowing.aspx, accessed 24 April 2012.

176 www.lickglobalwarming.org.

177 www.vivavi.com.

178 www.oxfam.org.uk/get_involved/campaign/impact/starbucks.html.

179 www.howies.co.uk/?utm_source=google&utm_medium=cpc&utm_term=howies&utm_campaign=howies&utm_content=1, accessed 24 April 2012.

180 B. Groom, 'Jobs Optimism Drives Green Agenda', *Financial Times*, 10 February 2010: 4.

Chapter 8

181 'Iceland Pays the Price of Rose's Organic Neglect', *The Independent*, 23 January 2001.

182 Adapted from various sources including M. McDonald and H. Wilson, *Marketing Plans* (Chichester, UK: Wiley, 7th edn, 2011).

183 H. Mintzberg, 'Patterns in Strategy Formation', *Management Science* 24.9 (1978): 934-48.

184 A. Khan, 'Market Orientation, Customer Selectivity and Firm Performance', PhD thesis, Cranfield School of Management, 2009.

185 H. Wilson, R. Street and L. Bruce, *The Multichannel Challenge* (Oxford: Butterworth-Heinemann, 2008).

186 Adapted from Wilson *et al.*, *The Multichannel Challenge*.

187 D. Grayson, 'What's good for the planet is good for business', The Sustainable Business Blog, 13 June 2011; www.guardian.co.uk/sustainable-business/blog/business-case-sustainability-shared-value, accessed 24 April 2012.

188 L.J. Ryals, *Managing Customers Profitably* (Chichester, UK: Wiley, 2008).

Chapter 9

189 J.T. Mentzer, W. DeWitt, J.S. Keebler, S. Min, N.W. Nix, C.D. Smith and Z.G. Zacharia, 'Defining Supply Chain Management', *Journal of Business Logistics* 22.2 (2001).

190 Marks & Spencer, 'M&S Reports on Plan A Progress in 2010/11', press release, 9 June 2011; corporate.marksandspencer.com/page.aspx?point erid=ec1319321f3040aca17d8bd341211872, accessed 24 April 2012.

191 Supply Chain Council, 'SCOR 10', 2011; supply-chain.org/scor/10.0, accessed 10 December 2011.

192 W. McDonough and M. Braungart, *Cradle to Cradle: Remaking the Way We Make Things* (New York: North Point Press, 2002).

193 A. Kriwet, E. Zussman and G. Seliger, 'Systematic Integration of Design-for-recycling into Product Design', *International Journal of Production Economics* 38 (1995): 15-22.

194 P. Dewhurst, *Design for Disassembly: The Basis for Efficient Service and Recycling* (Report no. 63, Kingston, RI: Department of Industrial Engineering and Manufacturing Engineering, University of Rhode Island, 1992).

195 D. Mangun and D.L. Thurston, 'Incorporating Component Reuse, Remanufacture and Recycle into Product Portfolio Design', *IEEE Transactions on Engineering Management* 49.4 (2002): 479-90.

196 News, *Industrial Engineer* 35.5 (2003): 10.

197 H. Skipworth. and A. Harrison, 'Implications of Form Postponement to Manufacturing a Customized Product', *International Journal of Production Research* 44.8 (2006): 1,627-52.

198 www.consulting.xerox.com.

199 Business in the Community, 'Marks & Spencer: Engaging Suppliers to Reduce Emissions'; www.bitc.org.uk/resources/case_studies/marks_spencer_.html, 2008, accessed 24 April 2012; 'Tesco: Product Carbon Footprinting in Practice'; ukintaiwan.fco.gov.uk/en/about-us/working-with-taiwan/climate-change/uk-company-success/tesco, 17 May 2011, accessed 24 April 2012.

200 www.ethicaltrade.org.

201 L. Whitney, 'Wal-Mart to Label Products with Eco Ratings', *CNet* (16 July 2009; news.cnet.com/8301-11128_3-10288186-54.html, accessed 24 April 2012).

202 O. Bruel, O. Menuet and P.-F. Thaler, *Sustainable Procurement: A Crucial Lever to End the Crisis?* (Jouy-en-Josas, France: HEC; Paris: Eco-Vadis, 2009).

203 G. Alvarez, C. Pilbeam and R. Wilding, 'Nestlé Nespresso AAA Sustainable Quality Program: An Investigation into the Governance Dynamics in a Multi-Stakeholder Supply Chain Network', *Supply Chain Management* 15.2 (2010).

204 P.A. Argenti, 'Collaborating with Activists: How Starbucks Works with NGOs', *California Management Review* 47.1 (2004); C. Gresser and S. Tickell, *Mugged: Poverty in Your Coffee Cup* (Oxford: Oxfam International, 2002; www.maketradefair.com/assets/english/mugged.pdf, accessed 24 April 2012).

205 Alvarez *et al.*, 'Nestlé Nespresso AAA Sustainable Quality Program'.

206 UNEP, *Assessing the Environmental Impacts of Consumption and Production: Priority Products and Materials* (Report of the Working Group on the Environmental Impacts of Products and Materials to the International Panel for Sustainable Resource Management; Paris: UNEP, 2010; www.unep.org/resourcepanel/Publications/PriorityProducts/tabid/56053/Default.aspx, accessed 24 April 2012).

207 R.S. McLeod, 'Ordinary Portland Cement', *Building for a Future* (Autumn 2005; www.buildingforafuture.co.uk/autumn05/ordinary_portland_cement.pdf, accessed 24 April 2012).

208 D. O'Rourke, 'Market Movements: Nongovernmental Organization Strategies to Influence Global Production and Consumption', *Journal of Industrial Ecology* 9 (2005): 115–28.

209 Greenpeace, 'Guide to Greener Electronics', May 2012, 15th edn; www.greenpeace.org/international/Global/international/publications/toxics/2010/ranking%20tables%20may%202010-all.pdf, accessed 24 April 2012.

210 Hewlett Packard, 'HP's Compliance with Restriction of Hazardous Substances (RoHS) Directives', August 2010; www.hp.com/hpinfo/globalcitizenship/environment/pdf/leadposition.pdf, accessed 24 April 2012.

211 Coca-Cola Company, 'Product Water Footprint Assessment: Practical Application in Corporate Water Stewardship', press release, September 2010; www.thecoca-colacompany.com/presscenter/nr_20100908_water_footprint_report.html.

212 www.thecoca-colacompany.com/ourcompany/index.html, accessed 24 April 2012.

213 A.K Chapagain, A.Y. Hoekstra, H.H.G. Savenije and R. Gautam, 'The Water Footprint of Cotton Consumption: An Assessment of the Impact of Worldwide Consumption of Cotton Products on the Water Resources in the Cotton Producing Countries', *Ecological Economics* 60.1 (2006).

214 F. Caro, J. Gallien, D. Miguel and J. García, 'Zara Uses Operations Research to Reengineer its Global Distribution Process', *Interfaces* 40.1 (2010).

215 IGD, 'The Road to Success', IGD announcement, 22 February 2010; www.igd.com/index.asp?id=1&fid=1&sid=3&tid=41&cid=1440, accessed 24 April 2012.

216 J. Birchall and E. Rigby, 'Oil Costs Force P&G to Rethink Supply Network', *FT.com*/Retail & Consumer, 26 June 2008; www.ft.com/cms/s/314b9b86-439e-11dd-842e-0000779fd2ac.html, accessed 24 April 2012.

217 D. Simchi-Levi, D. Nelson, N. Mulani and J. Wright, 'Crude Calculations; Why High Oil Prices are Upending the Way Companies Should Manage Their Supply Chains', *Wall Street Journal*, 22 September 2008.

218 Defra, *Comparative Life-Cycle Assessment of Food Commodities Procured for UK Consumption Through a Diversity of Supply Chains* (FO0103; London: Department of Environment, Food and Rural Affairs, 2008; randd.defra.gov.uk/Default.aspx?Menu=Menu&Module=More&Location=None&Completed=0&ProjectID=15001, accessed 24 April 2012).

219 S. Robson, D. Fisher, A. Palmer and A. McKinnon, *Reducing the External Costs of the Domestic Transportation of Food by the Food Industry* (London: Department of Environment, Food and Rural Affairs, 2007; archive.defra.gov.uk/evidence/economics/foodfarm/reports/Costfoodtransport/Defra-17May2007.pdf, accessed 24 April 2012).

220 Freight Best Practice Scotland, *Fuel Saving in a Scottish Haulage Fleet*; (London: Department for Transport/Scottish Government, July 2009; www.transportscotland.gov.uk/road/freight/best-practice, accessed 24 April 2012).

221 Marks & Spencer, 'Marks & Spencer: Teardrop Trailers Transport Products Sustainably', 25 Jan 2010; ukintaiwan.fco.gov.uk/en/about-us/working-with-taiwan/climate-change/uk-company-success/marks-spencer, accessed 24 April 2012.

222 IGD, 'Tesco: Reducing Carbon Emissions in Distribution', IGD, 10 July 2008; www.igd.com/index.asp?id=1&fid=1&sid=5&tid=49&folid=0&cid=387, accessed 24 April 2012.

223 Greenroofs.com, 'US Postal Service, Morgan Processing and Distribution Center'; www.greenroofs.com/projects/pview.php?id=1070, accessed 24 April 2012.

224 WWF, *The Climate Savers Programme: How Corporations Can Save the Planet* (WWF, March 2007; www.worldwildlife.org/climate/ WWFBinaryitem8752.pdf, accessed April 2012).

225 D. Blanchard, 'Supply Chains Also Work in Reverse', *IndustryWeek* 256.5 (2007): 48-49.

226 Hewlett Packard, 'HP's Compliance with Restriction of Hazardous Substances (RoHS) Directives', August 2010; www.hp.com/hpinfo/ globalcitizenship/environment/pdf/leadposition.pdf, accessed 24 April 2012.

227 Defra, *Waste Strategy for England, 2007* (Cmnd 7086; London: Department for Environment, Food and Rural Affairs, 2007; archive.defra. gov.uk/environment/waste/strategy/strategy07/documents/waste07-strategy.pdf, accessed 24 April 2012).

228 C. Mena, A. Humphries and R. Wilding, 'A Comparison of Inter- and Intra-organizational Relationships: Two Case Studies from UK Food and Drink Industry', *International Journal of Physical Distribution & Logistics Management* 39.9 (2009).

229 H.L. Lee, V. Padmanabhan and S. Whang, 'Information Distortion in a Supply Chain: The Bullwhip Effect', *Management Science* 43.4 (April 1997): 546-58; H.L. Lee, V. Padmanabhan and S. Whang, 'The Bullwhip Effect in Supply Chains', *MIT Sloan Management Review* 38.3 (Spring 1997): 93-102.

230 A.B. Lovins, L.H. Lovins and P. Hawkins, 'A Road Map for Natural Capitalism', *Harvard Business Review*, May–June 1999.

Chapter 10

231 www.baxter.com/press_room/press_releases/2010/06_24_10_ sustainability.html, accessed 24 April 2012.

232 Confederation for British Industry, *Getting Involved: A Guide to Switching on Your Employees to Sustainability* (CBI on Climate Change; CBI, 2009; www.cbi.org.uk/business-issues/energy-and-climate-change/ climate-change-and-business/switching-on-your-employees, accessed 24 April 2012).

233 M. Lindorff and J. Peck, 'Exploring Australian Financial Leaders' Views of Corporate Social Responsibility', *Journal of Management & Organization*, 2010: 16.

234 W.H. Macey and B. Schneider, 'The Meaning of Employee Engagement', *Industrial and Organizational Psychology* 1.1 (2008).

235   M. Bourne, M. Franco-Santos, A. Pavlov, L. Lucianetti, V. Martinez and
      M. Mura, *The Impact of Investors in People on People Management
      Practices and Firm Performance* (Cranfield, UK: Cranfield School of
      Management, 2008; www.investorsinpeople.co.uk/Documents Hidden/
      Research/Cranfield Impact of IIP on people management.pdf, accessed
      24 April 2012).

236   C.B. Bhattacharya, S. Sen and D. Korschun, 'Using Corporate Social
      Responsibility to Win the War for Talent', *MIT Sloan Management
      Review* 49.2 (Winter 2008).

237   Brighter Planet, *Employment Engagement Survey 2009: An Analysis of
      the Extent and Nature of Employee Sustainability Programs* (Middle-
      bury, VT: Brighter Planet, February 2010; attachments.brighterplanet.
      com/press_items/local_copies/55/original/employee_engagement_2009.
      pdf?1265816076, accessed 24 April 2012).

238   J.K. Harter, F.L. Schmidt and C.L.M. Keyes, 'Well-being in the Work-
      place and Its Relationships to Business Outcomes: A Review of Gallup
      Studies', White Paper 2002; media.gallup.com/documents/whitePaper--
      Well-BeingInTheWorkplace.pdf, accessed 24 April 2012.

239   A.M. Konrad, 'Engaging Employees through High-Involvement Work
      Practices', *Ivey Business Journey Online* 1 (2006).

240   C. Bones, 'Aligning and Understanding Engagement within the Organi-
      sation', *CritcalEYE.net* 14.6 (2006).

241   R. Wellins and J. Concelman, 'Creating a Culture for Engagement',
      Workforce Performance Solutions 2005; www.ddiworld.com/pdf/wps_
      engagement_ar.pdf; accessed 22 July 2010.

242   TowersPerrin, *Working Today: Understanding What Drives Employee
      Engagement: The 2003 TowersPerrin Talent Report* (Stamford, CT:
      TowersPerrin   2003;   www.keepem.com/doc_files/Towers_Perrin_
      Talent_2003%28TheFinal%29.pdf, accessed 24 April 2012.

243   Gallup, *Employee Engagement: What's Your Ratio?* (Washing-
      ton,   DC: Gallup   2010;   www.gallup.com/consulting/121535/
      Employee-Engagement-Overview-Brochure.aspx, accessed 24 April
      2012).

244   Bones, 'Aligning and Understanding Engagement within the Organisa-
      tion'.

245   R.J. Pech, 'Delegating and Devolving Power: A Case Study of Engaged
      Employees', *Journal of Business Strategy* 30.1 (2009).

246   J. Storey, P. Wright and D. Ulrich (eds.), *The Routledge Companion to
      Strategic Human Resource Management* (London: Routledge, 2008).

247   Bhattacharya *et al.*, 'Using Corporate Social Responsibility to Win the War for Talent'.

248   T.M. Welbourne, 'Employee Engagement: Beyond the Fad and into the Executive Suite', *Leader to Leader* 44 (Spring 2007): 45-51.

249   U. Steger (ed.), *The Business of Sustainability: Building Industry Cases for Corporate Sustainability* (New York: Palgrave Macmillan, 2004).

250   M. Clarke and M. Meldrum, 'Creating Change From Below: Early Lessons for Agents of Change', *Leadership & Organization Development Journal* 20.2 (1999).

251   The term 'greenfield approach' comes from the preferred approach by real estate and commercial property developers to use new undeveloped land, i.e. an untouched 'green field'. This avoids any historical construction developments that could interfere with smooth property developments. Used here, it therefore refers to a situation whereby a new management initiative or process is being developed and implemented with no prior legacy or initiation attempts that could interfere with its acceptance and success within the company.

252   D. Butcher and M. Clarke, *Smart Management: Using Politics in Organisations* (New York: Palgrave Macmillan, 2nd edn, 2008).

253   Butcher and Clarke, *Smart Management*.

254   Clarke and Meldrum, 'Creating Change from Below'.

255   The benefits or returns are so clear and obvious that it does not require any serious management debate, deliberation or thought, or use of the brain—thus the 'no brainer' term.

256   K. Moss 'Police or Release: How to Foster Employee Engagement in a Sustainable Culture', *CSR Perspective* (blog), 7 October 2011; csrperspective.com/category/employee-engagement-2, accessed 24 April 2012.

Chapter 11

257   K.E. Weick, *Sensemaking in Organizations* (Thousand Oaks, CA: Sage, 1995); J. Balogun and G. Johnson, 'Organizational Restructuring and Middle Manager Sensemaking', *Academy of Management Journal* 47.4 (2004): 523-49.

258   Weick, *Sensemaking in Organizations*.

259   J. Balogun and G. Johnson, 'Organizational Restructuring and Middle Manager Sensemaking', *Academy of Management Journal* 47.4 (2004): 523-49.

260 Balogun and Johnson, 'Organizational Restructuring and Middle Manager Sensemaking'.

261 D. Grayson, 'The CR Management Black-Hole', *Management Focus*, Autumn 2008: 6-9.

262 S.M. Jackson, 'Exploration into the Relationship between Managers' Sensemaking and CSR Outcomes', unpublished MSc thesis, Cranfield University, 2009.

263 S.M. Jackson, *Mind the Gap* (Doughty Centre Occasional Paper; Cranfield, UK: Cranfield School of Management, 2010).

264 Weick, *Sensemaking in Organizations*.

265 Grayson, 'The CR Management Black-Hole'.

266 C. Gribben and I. Woudstra-Van-Grondelle, *A Snapshot of Executive Development for Corporate Responsibility Professionals in the UK* (Ashridge, UK: Ashridge and Corporate Responsibility Group, 2007).

267 Balogun and Johnson, 'Organizational Restructuring and Middle Manager Sensemaking'.

Chapter 12

268 C. Spence and R. Gray, *Social and Environmental Reporting and the Business Case* (Research Report 98; London: Certified Accountants Educational Trust for Association of Certified Chartered Accountants, 2007): 5.

269 P.J. DiMaggio and W.W. Powell, 'The Iron Cage Revisited: Institutional Isomorphism and Collective Rationality in Organizational Fields', *American Sociological Review* 48 (1983): 147-60.

270 www.unpri.org/principles, accessed 24 April 2012.

271 CFA Institute, *Environmental, Social, and Governance Factors at Listed Companies: A Manual for Investors* (CFA, 2008; www.cfapubs.org/toc/ccb/2008/2008/2, accessed 24 April 2012).

272 Institute of Directors in Southern Africa, *The King Report on Governance for South Africa* ('King III'; Parklands, South Africa: Institute of Directors in Southern Africa, 2009).

273 European Commission Internal Market and Services DG, 'Summary Report of the Responses Received to the Public Consultation on Disclosure of Non-financial Information by Companies', April 2011; ec.europa.eu/internal_market/consultations/docs/2010/non-financial_reporting/summary_report_en.pdf, accessed 24 April 2012.

274 In 2011 UK regulators issued a consultation paper on narrative reporting that is likely to extend such disclosures: Department for Business

Innovation and Skills, 'The Future of Narrative Reporting: A Further Consultation',2011;www.bis.gov.uk/Consultations/future-of-narrative-reporting-further-consultation, accessed 24 April 2012.

275 *Federal Register* 75.25, 8 February 2010 / Rules and Regulations; www.sec.gov/rules/interp/2010/33-9106fr.pdf, accessed 24 April 2012.

276 www.puma.com.

277 www.solarcentury.co.uk.

278 Institute of Directors in Southern Africa, *The King Report*: 54.

279 E. Ligteringen and S. Zadek, 'The Future of Corporate Responsibility Codes, Standards and Frameworks', Global Reporting Initiative and AccountAbility, 2005; available at www.greenbiz.com/research/report/2005/04/21/future-corporate-responsibility-codes-standards-and-frameworks, accessed 24 April 2012.

About the authors

Unless otherwise stated, all authors are affiliated to the Cranfield School of Management.

Shahpar Abdollahi is Senior Research Fellow and Lecturer in Marketing and Sales. Shahpar joined the School in 2009 as a Senior Research Fellow and Lecturer in Marketing and Sales. Her doctoral thesis explored the role of social capital in knowledge acquisition from internal and external sources in the process of new product development. Expanding on those themes she now conducts research in the fields of business strategy, organisational behaviour, team learning and the management of key customer relationships. Her research interests combine strategic and organisational learning in the context of knowledge-intensive teams.

Paul Baines is Reader in Marketing and Director MSc Strategic Marketing. He is Managing Editor, Europe, *Journal of Political Marketing*, and author/co-author of more than a hundred published articles, book chapters and books on marketing issues. His research has particularly focused on political marketing, public opinion and propaganda (for governments, special interest groups, companies and political parties); and market segmentation and positioning (for political parties, governments, special interest groups and companies). Paul's consultancy experience includes marketing research and marketing/PR strategy development.

Peter Baker is Visiting Fellow, Centre for Logistics and Supply Chain Management. He has conducted over 70 supply-chain projects across a wide range of industries and public-sector organisations around the world. These projects have included supply-chain strategy, procurement, international logistics, distribution centre design, inventory control, transport operations and supporting computer systems. He is currently an independent consultant and as a Visiting Fellow at Cranfield lectures in such areas as warehousing and distribution centre design. Peter is co-author of *The Handbook of Logistics and Distribution Management* and *UK Warehouse Benchmarking Report*, and editor of *The Principles of Warehouse Design*.

Ruth Bender is Reader in Corporate Financial Strategy. She joined the Cranfield faculty in 1994, having completed her MBA there. Prior to this she was a partner in Grant Thornton, where latterly she specialised in corporate finance. Her main teaching areas include financial strategy (she is co-author of *Corporate Financial Strategy*, Butterworth-Heinemann), working capital management, corporate responsibility and corporate governance. Her research interest is in the practical implications of corporate governance. In particular, she has worked with remuneration committees and audit committees of larger companies. Ruth's PhD focused on executive remuneration.

Mike Bernon is Senior Lecturer in Supply Chain Management, teaching on the Cranfield Executive Business Leaders and Advanced Executive Development programmes. He also works with companies to design, develop and deliver innovative customised executive development programmes for global clients. He is also involved with the Executive and full-time MBA programme and Masters in Logistics and Supply Chain Management. Mike continues to be a visiting lecturer to universities and academic institutions across Europe and the Far East. His current research interests are in supply-chain sustainability, carbon-footprint measurement and reverse logistics. He has been the principal investigator for a number of major research programmes including for the EPSRC, World Bank, Department for Transport and Knowledge Transfer Partnerships. He chairs the Cranfield Sustainable Supply Chain Forum and the CILT(UK) Reverse Logistics Forum.

Mike Bourne is Professor of Business Performance and Director of the Centre for Business Performance at Cranfield. He has spent the last 15 years working with companies supporting senior management teams through the process of designing, implementing and using their balanced scorecards and related performance-management techniques. His current research activities are in the arena of corporate performance measurement and management, including the interface with the planning and budgeting process and performance-related pay. He has authored over 100 publications, and is co-author of several books including *Balanced Scorecard*, *Getting the Measure of your Business* and *Change Management in a Week*.

Pippa Bourne is Regional Director, Institute of Chartered Accountants in England and Wales (ICAEW). Her role involves implementing ICAEW's strategy in the East of England, raising the profile of chartered accountants and helping provide local services. She is the author of several books on the theme of managing and measuring performance including *Balanced Scorecard in a Week* and *Managing Change* (both Hodder & Stoughton); *Achieving High Performance* and *Motivating People* (both DK); and, with Mike Bourne, *The Handbook of Corporate Performance Management*, (Wiley). Her specialties are performance measurement and management and linking action to strategy. She is currently studying for a certificate in coaching at the University of Cambridge Institute of Continuing Education.

Martin Clarke is Programmes and Business Director, Centre for General Management Development and Co-Director for the Cranfield General Management Programme and Advanced Development Programme. Martin works as a leadership and organisation development consultant to a broad range of international companies. His experience lies chiefly in the area of organisation and strategic development, working with executive teams and business leaders. He is frequently asked to comment in the press and is the author of numerous books/chapters and articles on the subject of leadership, organisation design and the role of organisation politics in business.

Radu Dimitriu is Lecturer in Strategic Marketing. His doctoral work focused on how consumers evaluate brand extensions depending on their perception of the market where the brand is extending. His broader research interests are in the areas of branding and brand extensions, strategic marketing, consumer behaviour and psychology, and marketing sustainability. Radu has presented his research both at international conferences and to companies. He has industry experience as marketing and statistical analysis, and his most recent appointment consisted of a senior analyst position in a marketing consultancy dealing with customer database analysis and strategy.

With over a decade of experience in marketing, stakeholder engagement, and communications, **Nadine Exter** is a manager in and Lead Advisor for the Doughty Centre for Corporate Responsibility, an action-research centre within the Cranfield School of Management. Previous to this, Nadine co-founded a successful SME, advised on change management in the public sector, and ran learning networks between public and private sectors. In 2008 she completed her MBA at Cranfield, where she focused on how to enable organisations to be responsible. Her research includes the various roles employees can take for developing sustainable organisations, engaging the employee base and building a culture for engagement in sustainability, and building the business case for being a responsible business. Publications include 'How to Develop a Champions Network'; 'Engaging Employees for Corporate Responsibility'; 'The Business Case for Corporate Responsibility' (with BITC); 'Sending the Right Message' (chapter in an ebook with Ogilvy); 'Engaging Employees with Sustainable Business: How to Change the World whilst Keeping your Day Job' (book in progress, due Q2 2013); 'The Sustainability Profession: The How, What and Why' (occasional paper in progress, due Q4 2012). Nadine also shares advice via various webinars and online presentations with partners such as BITC, 2Degrees, Guardian Sustainability Pages and Clarity Communications.

David Ferguson is Visiting Fellow at the Doughty Centre for Corporate responsibility. He has 20 years' experience working on developing and delivering projects with the private, public and voluntary sector. He completed his PhD within the Doughty Centre as an industry-sponsored company case study investigating the operationalisation of corporate sustainability performance. David's academic interest relates to the emerging area of corporate sustainability performance-management systems. David's first authored publication was for the National Healthcare Council for Scotland in 1999 on management training quality standards. Recent publications on corporate sustainability relate to Ashridge/ACCA publication (international MBA competition) in 2004, corporate governance in 2007 and through EABIS (European Academy of Business and Society) in 2008.

Keith Goffin is Professor of Innovation and New Product Development. His research interests are innovation culture, project-to-project learning and enhanced methods of market research, so-called 'hidden needs analysis'. He has published many articles in journals and newspapers such as the *Journal of Product Innovation Management, Research-Technology Management* and the *Financial Times*. The second edition of his book *Innovation Management: Strategy and Implementation Using the Pentathlon Framework* (with Prof. Rick Mitchell) and his latest book *Identifying Customers' Hidden Needs: Creating Breakthrough Products* (with Fred Lemke and Ursula Koners) were published in 2010. In May 2011 Keith was selected as the *Financial Times* Professor of the Week for his work on hidden needs.

David Grayson CBE is Professor of Corporate Responsibility and Director of the Doughty Centre for Corporate Responsibility. He joined Cranfield as director of the new Doughty Centre in April 2007, after a 30-year career as a social entrepreneur and campaigner for responsible business, diversity and small business development. His books include: *Corporate Social Opportunity: Seven Steps to Make Corporate Social Responsibility Work*

For Your Business and *Everybody's Business* (2001)—both co-authored with Adrian Hodges. He has also contributed to several other books including *The Accountable Corporation* and *What If?* His research interests focus on how companies profitably embed sustainability. He is a member of the editorial advisory group of *Ethical Corporation*.

Frank M. Horwitz is Director of Cranfield School of Management. He has an international reputation in the field of international HRM, especially in emerging markets. His research interests include: human capital strategies, workplace flexibility, high performance work practices, leading and managing knowledge workers, organisational redesign, performance incentives, mergers and acquisitions, cross-cultural and international HRM, employment discrimination and diversity. He is on the editorial boards of the *International Journal of Human Resource Management*, *International Journal of Cross-Cultural Management*, *Journal of Chinese HRM*, *Corporate Governance* and other leading international journals. He has co-authored a number of books including: *Employment Equity and Affirmative Action: an International Comparison*; *Managing Human Resources in Africa*; *Managing Resourceful People*; and *On the Edge: How South African Companies Cope with Change*.

Sharon Jackson is a Doughty Centre Research Associate and associate of the Cranfield Centre for Customised Executive Development. She has had a 15-year career within global commerce in the electronic component sector, operating in both distribution and manufacturing. Sharon has held senior executive roles across small and medium-sized enterprises and global transnational corporations. Her business skills include international business development and the implementation of global trading agreements. Sharon is currently completing her PhD in the School of Management.

Andrew Kakabadse is Professor of International Management Development and a Visiting Professor at Australian, US and Irish universities. He is a Fellow of the International Academy of Management, the British Psychology Society and the British Academy of Management. Andrew has consulted and lectured around the world. Current areas of interest focus on improving the performance of top executives and top executive teams, excellence in consultancy practice, leadership, corporate governance, conflict resolution and international relations. He is currently embarked on a major world study of boardroom effectiveness and governance practice. Andrew has published 38 books, over 210 journal articles and 18 monographs. He is co-editor of the *Journal of Management Development* and *Corporate Governance: The International Journal of Business in Society*.

Simon Knox is Emeritus Professor of Marketing and former Professor of Brand Marketing, He is a consultant to a number of multinational companies in both consumer and business markets. He is a regular speaker at international conferences and is currently leading research looking at best practices in strategic marketing and the impact of sustainability on the corporate brand. His recent books include *Competing on Value* (FT Pitman), *Creating a Company for Customers* (FT Prentice Hall) and *Customer Relationship Management* (Butterworth-Heinemann) and he has published in the *Journal of Business Research*, *Long Range Planning* and *MIT Sloan Management Review*.

Donna Ladkin is Professor in Leadership and Ethics. Originally from the USA, Donna gained experience in arts management in the States and management within higher education in the UK before pursuing her MBA and PhD at Cranfield. Her research focuses on bringing to light the aesthetic and ethical dimensions of leading and leadership. She is the author of numerous articles published in journals such as *Leadership Quarterly*, *Leadership*, *Academy of Management Learning and Education* and the *Journal of Business Ethics*, and the book *Rethinking Leadership: A New Look at Old Leadership Questions* published in 2010 by Edward Elgar.

Emma K. Macdonald is Senior Research Fellow, Deputy Director of the MSc in Strategic Marketing and Research Director of the Cranfield Customer Management Forum. She has published in *Industrial Marketing Management*, *Journal of Business Research* and *Journal of Marketing Management* and in professional publications and reports. Recognition for her work includes a 2009 'Cube d'Or' (gold prize) from the French direct marketing association for her PhD thesis, and four academic best-paper conference awards. Most recent of these was a 'Best in Conference' award at the 18th International Colloquium in Relationship Marketing (2010) for her work (with Prof. Hugh Wilson) on measuring brand engagement.

Stan Maklan is Senior Lecturer in Strategic Marketing. He is an experienced academic, marketer and management consultant with senior, international line management experience in blue-chip consumer and business marketing companies. Stan lectures on Cranfield's full-time MBA, MSc in Marketing and PhD research programmes in addition to executive courses. He directs the Marketing Leaders' Programme, is on the Editorial Advisory Board of the *International Journal of Market Research* and a member of the Academic Liaison Committee at the Chief Marketing Officers Council. He has co-authored *Competing on Value* about corporate brand development, and a case-history-based book about customer-relationship management.

Javier Marcos-Cuevas is Lecturer in Sales Performance, Centre for Strategic Marketing and Sales. An independent consultant, his main areas of expertise are selling and sales management, organisational learning and organisational development. He combines leading-edge research with innovative training methodologies in the delivery of his programmes and the design of consulting assignments. His research interests focus on the development of sales and key account capabilities, addressing personal and team performance, and sales organisations' effectiveness. He also researches organisational knowledge and learning processes within and across organisations. An evidence-based approach enables him to combine research evidence and practical expertise to provide specific guidelines for managers and long-lasting organisational development solutions.

Carlos Mena is Director of the Centre for Strategic Procurement and Supply Management and head of the Executive Procurement Network (EPN). Carlos has been responsible for more than ten research projects in supply chain related fields such as global sourcing, sustainable supply chains and collaboration. In these projects he has collaborated with world leading organisations such as ASDA (Wal-Mart), British Airways, Coca-Cola, Ford, M&S, Tata, Tesco and P&G. He regularly presents at international conferences and lectures in a variety of subjects including Procurement, Supply Chain Management, Lean Manufacturing, Operations Strategy and Sustainability.

Andrew Palmer is a Visiting Fellow. He is a renowned expert in strategic logistics network design and related quantitative modelling techniques. He is the original author of the CAST supply chain network planning software, used by more than 300 major companies worldwide. For over 30 years Andrew has been involved in a wide range of commercial, UK government and European Commission sponsored projects. His research interest focuses on the sustainability of freight transport and collaboration to improve vehicle capacity utilisation and reduce empty running. He is a visiting lecturer at a number of universities in Europe and is an honorary research fellow at Heriot Watt University.

Patrick Reinmoeller is Professor of Strategic Management. He is the Director of the programmes Directors as Strategic Leaders and Breakthrough Strategic Thinking. He is Associate Editor of the *International Journal of Business Environment* and a member of the editorial board of several international journals. Reviewing for leading journals, he has won Academy of Management reviewer awards. His research interests include strategic management, organisation theory, knowledge and innovation, and international strategy and currently his research focus is on organisational resilience, knowledge creation and social innovation. Patrick has published on strategy, innovation and knowledge creation in leading US, European and Asian journals. He is Core Member of the China Business Research Centre at Erasmus University, the Netherlands and Visiting Professor at the University of Pretoria and the NUCB in Japan.

Lynette Ryals is Professor of Strategic Sales and Account Management and Director of the Demand Chain Management Community. She specialises in key account management and marketing portfolio management, particularly relating to B2B customer management. Her professional background is in financial services (she is a Registered Representative of the London Stock Exchange and a Fellow of the Society of Investment Professionals). Before joining Cranfield she worked for a major management consultancy. At Cranfield she is involved in research and executive development programmes for clients in professional services and manufacturing. She is the Director of Cranfield's Key Account Management Best Practice Research Club and a member of the School of Management's Executive Board. She is the Pro Vice Chancellor of Cranfield University.

Heather Skipworth is a Senior Research Fellow. She joined the Cranfield faculty in 2004 on completion of her doctorate there, addressing the application of the form postponement strategy in manufacturing industry. She manages the Agile Supply Chain Research Club and works on a variety of projects in the Supply Chain Research Centre. Typically her research is in collaboration with companies including O2, British American Tobacco, BAE Systems, Siemens Magnet Technology, Applied Materials and Kongsberg Automotive. Particular areas of interest include form postponement, mass customisation and customer-responsive supply-chain strategy and the outsourcing of logistics and procurement in the NHS. Heather also lectures on the MSc Programme.

Alan Smart is a Senior Lecturer. He has worked in the UK, Europe and the Middle East in marketing, operations, purchasing and general management roles. He has been involved in business start-ups, product launches in overseas markets, and the establishment of foreign joint ventures. He has taught on Masters programmes within the School. In 2003–8 he set up and directed management courses for Maersk Logistics and has taught on and managed numerous similar programmes for executive clients in the School. Alan's research has focused on the role of e-commerce and automation in purchasing management, publishing on this topic in several academic journals. In 2010 he completed his PhD in the role of e-procurement in purchasing management.

Simon Templar is a Lecturer at the Centre for Logistics and Supply Chain Management. A qualified accountant, he has over 20 years' experience in industry, ranging from 'bananas to telecommunications' in a range of management roles, including finance, sales and marketing, physical distribution management and human resource management. Simon currently lectures on management accounting and supply-chain costing on MSc courses and on in-company and external programmes delivered by Cranfield for which he has designed a range of distance/blended learning products. His current PhD research explores the impact of transfer pricing on supply-chain management decisions.

Hugh Wilson is Professor of Strategic Marketing and Director, Cranfield Customer Management Forum, a syndicate of leading firms such as IBM, HSBC and BP exploring best practice in the development of profitable relationships in a multi-channel world. Hugh's research interests include customer experience and engagement, marketing and sustainability, and multi-channel customer management. Hugh writes extensively for both academics and executives. His most recent books are *The Multichannel Challenge* (2008) and *Marketing Plans* (7th edn, 2011, with Malcolm McDonald). Other practitioner publications include a recent blog and a forthcoming article on customer experience for *Harvard Business Review* (with Emma Macdonald). Recent media coverage includes an interview on 'Persuasion' for BBC Radio Four programme *Fry's English Delight*.

Index

NOTE: Page numbers in *italic figures* refer to figures, tables and boxes; n following a page number refers to Notes.